London's Night Buses

Volume One 1913-1983

Philip Wallis

Capital Transport

ISBN 978-185414-348-8

First published 2011

Published by Capital Transport Publishing
www.capitaltransport.com

Printed by 1010 Printing International Ltd

Ah, London! London! our delight
Great flower that opens but at night
Great city of the Midnight Sun
Whose day begins when day is done.
Anon

Extract from T.O.T. number 5 which announced the
introduction of the London General Omnibus
Company's first all-night motor bus route 94
between Cricklewood and Liverpool Street station
from 14/15 July 1913.

Title page Barking garage's RT 690 is seen
at the Mansion House station bus stop in
Queen Victoria Street during July 1977.
This stop was remote from the N98's line
of route and was uniquely used by just the
Sunday to Friday nights 00.16 N98 journey
from Mansion House Station to Romford
Station. *David Bowker*

CONTENTS

ACKNOWLEDGEMENTS

A good number of people have contributed towards elements of the research for this book and without their endeavours and involvement the published work would have been a much less complete product.

The assiduous researches of the late Derek Giles at both the British Library and the National Newspaper Library yielded much useful material, particularly concerning the earliest years of London's all-night horse-tram and horse-bus services, which would have remained largely unknown but for his efforts. E. R. Oakley kindly gave me permission to extract information from his 'Notes and Diary of Events', which he prepared in connection with his seminal two volume work on London County Council Tramways. The contributions of these two gentlemen facilitated the preparation of a reasonably confident and comprehensive account of the early years of London's public all-night road passenger transport services.

The late Ken Glazier afforded me access to London Transport's Allocation Books and, characteristically for one who was always ready to share his knowledge with others, gave me much advice based upon his deep knowledge of London Transport's operations. Respected London commentator Dennis Cox helped my research considerably, not only with the loan of timetables but also as a source of advice who has usually been able to answer even the most obscure query on route-related matters. Dennis Cox is also very knowledgeable of fare and ticket-related matters and Appendix 1 Fare Policies was developed around original Notes supplied by him. Appendix 2 Christmas All-Night Services is essentially based upon comprehensive Notes supplied by John Bull and I am most grateful to him for allowing the benefit of his extensive research into the matter, as well for his help with other aspects of research for this book.

The staff at both the London Transport Museum's Library and the London Metropolitan Archive have afforded me every assistance with access to material held therein. John Hart and Martin Kingsnorth of The Omnibus Society's London Collection at Acton, as well as Alan Mills and Ted Gadsby of the Omnibus Society's Library at Walsall, have sought out research material on my behalf. Members of the London Historical Research Group of the Omnibus Society have kindly responded to questions posed by me in that Group's Bulletins. Laurie Akehurst of that Group kindly provided me with much background information on the operations of Fleet Coaches and Upminster Services and the fate of their all-night services following acquisition by the London Passenger Transport Board.

I am most grateful to the London Omnibus Traction Society for permission to extract information from its publications including The London Bus and London Bus Magazine. David Stewart, Editor of The London Bus, kindly extended to me further personal help in resolving specific queries as well as by introducing me to certain of the photographic contributors. The PSV Circle kindly gave me permission to extract information from its comprehensive range of publications on vehicle-related matters but which in former years also included an element of route-related coverage. Other help or information has been provided by David Bowker, the late John Gillham, Chris Holland, Peter Larking, Peter Nichols, Malcolm Papes, Derek Persson, Derek Roy, David Ruddom, David Seddon, Rosie Thacker from the Tramway Museum Society, John Wylde and the late Reg Westgate, to all of whom I am most grateful. Draft manuscripts were reviewed by Dennis Cox and David Ruddom, Chairman of the Omnibus Society's London Historical Research Group, as well as by Ken Glazier whilst he was able to do so. Their informed criticisms have further honed the accuracy of the book's content and I am most appreciative of their significant contributions.

All-night bus photography is an arduous, demanding and occasionally dangerous pastime. I am very grateful to all the photographers who have afforded me access to their collections and such contributions are credited in appropriate caption copies. It is my hope that the book's photographic content will adequately convey the ambience of all-night service operations. One of the key photographic contributors, Mike Harris, has prepared the specially drawn maps. I would also like to thank my erstwhile neighbour Barbara Fairbrother who typed the early chapters.

Finally, but crucially, this work would not have reached publication without the help and full support of my wife Rosalind. Not only has she tolerated my nocturnal wanderings around London with camera and tripod but she has also employed her computer expertise and keyboard skills to transform my original manuscript into an acceptable form for the publisher.

Bus Garage codes used in the text

AC	Willesden
AD	Palmers Green
AE	Hendon
AH	Nunhead
AK	Streatham
AL	Merton
AP	Seven Kings
AR	Tottenham
BK	Barking
CF	Chalk Farm
D	Dalston
G	Forest Gate
J	Holloway
H	Hackney
M	Mortlake
P	Old Kent Road
R	Hammersmith
T	Leyton
V	Turnham Green
W	Cricklewood
WG	West Green

NOTES ON THE TEXT AND ABBREVIATIONS

NIGHTS OF OPERATION

Operational times of all-night bus routes often overlap either side of midnight over two successive days, with services starting in the late evening of one day and finishing during the early morning hours of the next day. Generally speaking dates quoted in the text span both days of operation, but sometimes, for brevity, the text may refer to operation as being, for example, on 'Friday night' and in such instances it is implicit that an overnight service running into the next day is involved.

VEHICLE TYPES

The author has assumed that readers of this book will have some understanding of the vehicle-type codes used by successive operators since the London General Omnibus Company Ltd. Those readers wishing to refresh or expand their knowledge of London bus-type codes, models, specifications and manufacturers are recommended to consult the many fleet-books and vehicle-type histories that have been published over very many years.

VEHICLE ALLOCATIONS TO ROUTES

The primary reference sources for this book have been London General, London Passenger Transport Board, London Transport (Executive and Board) and London Regional Transport *Traffic Notices, Traffic Circulars* and *Allocations of Scheduled Buses* as appropriate published since 20 June 1915. These sources have been supplemented by reference to listings of *Allocations to Routes* published between 1967 and 1976 by The PSV Circle and since 30 January 1971 by the London Omnibus Traction Society as well as by photographic evidence. Readers should bear in mind that vehicle-type changes to particular routes were sometimes progressively introduced over a period of time and also that operational exigencies sometimes led to the substitution of buses other than the allocated type.

GYRATORY (ONE-WAY) TRAFFIC SYSTEMS

In view of the scale, complexity and sometimes-changeable nature of gyratory traffic flow systems across Greater London no attempt has been made to detail every variation. However gyratory systems, or alterations to such systems, which had a profound effect on all-night bus routes are chronicled.

TEMPORARY ROUTE DIVERSIONS OR CURTAILMENTS

Temporary diversions or curtailments to all-night bus routes due to road and utility works, construction projects, accidents, police or security incidents, weather, natural disasters and war are not chronicled.

CLOCK SYSTEMS

This book adheres to the 12-hour clock system until 30 June 1964 when London Transport's public all-night bus timetable adopted use of the 24-hour clock system which is used thereafter in the text.

ABBREVIATIONS

Su – Sunday night / Monday morning
M – Monday night / Tuesday morning
Tu – Tuesday night / Wednesday morning
W – Wednesday night / Thursday morning
Th – Thursday night / Friday morning
Fr – Friday night / Saturday morning
Sa – Saturday night/Sunday morning

LCC – London County Council (Tramways)
LGOC – London General Omnibus Company
LPTB – London Passenger Transport Board
LT – London Transport (Executive and Board)
MET – Metropolitan Electric Tramways
Northmet – North Metropolitan Tramways Company
TfL – Transport for London
UERL – Underground Electric Railway Company

am – *ante meridiem*, before noon
Av – Avenue
BR – British Railways
Cr – Crescent
Emb – Embankment
Gar – Garage
GB – Griffith-Bell (electric power stud contact system)
GLC – Greater London Council
I-S – Inter-Station Route
Jct – Junction
Jny/Jnys – Journey/Journeys
Min – Minutes
Opo – One-person operated
pm – *post meridiem*, after noon
Pvr – Peak vehicle requirement
RLST – Round London Sightseeing Tour
Rd – Road
SLTC – South London Tram Conversion
SNJ – Special Night Journeys
St – Street
Stn – Station
TGWU – Transport and General Workers Union
TSU – Transport Studies Unit (of Oxford University)
UXB – Unexploded Bomb
V&A – Victoria & Albert (Docks)
Weekdays – Monday to Saturday inclusive.

PREFACE

I first became aware of London's All-Night Buses when, as a 1950s schoolboy, I started writing off periodically to London Transport at 55 Broadway, SW1 requesting bus maps. Its replies, invariably sent by return of post, included Central Area Red Bus and Trolleybus maps. It was whilst poring over those maps, thus gaining my first rudimentary knowledge of London's geography, that I noticed listings of all-night services printed in blue type on their reverse sides. At that tender age I did not fully comprehend the significance of the qualification 'Saturday night and Sunday morning excepted'.

My awareness of London's all-night services progressed to contact with the capital's all-night buses when, as a young Army officer in the late 1960s, I was based at Chattenden Barracks, near Strood in Kent. Occasional forays to London in search of entertainment gave me my first sightings of London Transport's Nighters in service – provided that such a trip had been made on a Friday night. More usually I went up to Town on Saturday nights. Although that period has since been dubbed 'The Swinging Sixties', much of the old order still prevailed. Strict licensing laws, which had originated during the First World War, continued to be applied so that most licensed premises, entertainment establishments and pretty well everything else too closed at 11 o'clock in the evening. By midnight the resultant exodus of humanity had dissipated with only the odd straggler left to be encountered, or drunk to be avoided, on London's near deserted streets. The qualification 'Saturday night and Sunday morning excepted' came vividly back to mind as I walked along London's bus-less streets in the early hours of a Sunday morning, partly exploring and partly just hoping to find somewhere – anywhere – to buy a coffee. Both coffee and buses eluded me until I reached Victoria station with plenty of time in hand before catching the 04.25 newspaper train back to the Medway Towns.

Wandsworth to Farringdon Street route N88's allocation was converted from RM-type Routemaster to DM-type Fleetline from 19/20 September 1975. Wandsworth garage substituted RT 2318 to make one return journey over the route on Thursday night/Friday morning 18/19 September 1975, its last night of official Routemaster operation, during which the RT was photographed at Wandsworth Plain. An RT-type had previously formed the N88's allocation until 16/17 April 1970.

Back in civilian life, I renewed my acquaintance with London's Nighters in 1979. The nation was on the cusp of a profound change in governmental attitude towards traditional industrial structures following the election of Margaret Thatcher's Conservative government. State-owned industries, such as coal and steel, and 'lame duck' industrial conglomerates would be decimated or dismantled, according to one's political persuasion, as the government slashed state subsidies and encouraged privatisation. By this date the London Transport Executive was in serious difficulty both operationally and financially and split by political factions within. I realise now that the Executive's troubles were echoed by the buses working the Nighters which I saw and travelled on in 1979 and the early 1980s. 1970s-built Daimler/Leyland Fleetlines then predominated in allocations across the Nighters but Scania Metropolitans bought 'off the peg' as a hurried measure to replace already failing Fleetlines were to be found on routes N85 and N86. The fact that those Metropolitans worked as 'one-person operated' buses whilst most Fleetlines on routes such as the N68 or N88 worked as crew-buses, with driver and conductor, was symptomatic of the Executive's uncertainty of purpose. The N90 retained Routemaster operation throughout the 1970s and beyond whilst operation of that venerable vehicle-type was restored to some other Nighters in late 1980. I recall a journey on the Routemaster-operated N90 one coldish night in December 1980. Express coach services had just become deregulated and I had been watching coach departures from the ill-fated British Coachways terminus at Euston Road coach park. I saw the late night departures set off, which included a coach bound for Scotland run by an embryonic operator, Stagecoach, before I headed back on to the Euston Road. Eventually, at about 01.10, a Pimlico-bound N90 appeared which I hailed and boarded. The handful of other passengers and the conductor were huddled on the foremost seats of the lower deck, for warmth, so I joined them and, as I did so, a couple of passengers glanced at me and nodded a sort of greeting as I took a seat. I felt a sense of comradeship with my unknown fellow passengers and the crew as the Routemaster sped along London's empty streets, rarely stopping and then only if requested. On that journey we were part of a small but exclusive band, united by night-time travel, and I felt something of a wrench when I left the bus at Victoria. *Viatores Nocte*.

Career demands, domestic commitments and a newly-found but compulsive involvement with the sport of water-skiing combined to make me lose track of London's Nighters for nearly 20 years until I revisited London one Saturday night around Midsummer 1999. I was astounded by the transformation of London's nightlife that had taken place over the intervening years. The deserted streets that I recalled from my visits in earlier years now thronged with people patronising a plethora of cinemas and theatres, pubs and restaurants as well as clubs and discotheques that remained open until well into the early hours.

A vastly increased number of all-night buses struggled through heavily congested West End traffic that did not ease up until about three o'clock in the morning and then only slightly. I remember standing in Trafalgar Square and looking on with amazement at the banked up lines of all-night buses loading outside Canada House and the National Gallery – and walking up a near-gridlocked Charing Cross Road, past Leicester Square and on to Tottenham Court Road station to watch heavily-laden northbound departures on routes such as the N5, N29, N73 and N279 and marvel at the sheer scale of London's all-night bus route operation.

That visit in June 1999 so re-stimulated my interest in London's Nighters that I determined to delve into their origins and the subsequent research process has culminated in the publication of this book and work on a second volume. I had held a vague knowledge that some of London's all-night bus routes had tramway origins but my research surprised me by both the scale and age of such tramway antecedents. Full details of all-night tramway operations, as well as all-night trolleybus routes, have been included within the text in order to give a comprehensive account of the development of London's public all-night road passenger transport services. Since 1999 I have made numerous night-time visits to the capital in order to observe, photograph and travel on London's all-night buses.

I consider myself to have been twice fortunate in having known both the London Transport all-night route network, with its infrequent and mostly irregularly-timed services, and in having renewed my acquaintance with London's Nighters late on in the London Regional Transport era when all routes displayed 'N'-prefixed route numbers and before Transport for London's expansion of the 24-hour service concept eliminated the 'N' prefix from many route numbers.

I hope that this book has succeeded in capturing, in words and pictures, the essence of what the late Ken Glazier, that eminent authority on London's buses and their operations, once described to me as 'The Romance of London's Nighters'.

Philip Wallis
Bramley, Hampshire
July 2011

The rapid growth of London during the last decades of the Victorian era increased demand for public passenger transport services outside daytime and evening hours. Early morning Workmen's Cars on the tramways had developed from the 1880s, whilst the Great Eastern Railway had introduced an all-night train service on its Liverpool Street – Walthamstow branch on 1 June 1897. The capital's first all-night horse-tram and horse-bus services were introduced in the final year of the nineteenth century.

NORTH METROPOLITAN TRAMWAYS

The distinction of inaugurating London's all-night public road passenger transport services fell to The North Metropolitan Tramways Company with the introduction of a 30-minute frequency all-night horse-tram service over the Stratford – Aldgate route from Sunday night/Monday morning 1/2 January 1899. Northmet introduced two other 30-minute frequency all-night horse-tram services from Holborn to Hampstead (by 13/14 January 1899) and Holborn to Stamford Hill (at an unknown date in January 1899). A contemporary issue of *Street Railway Journal* reported that, 'The North Metropolitan company has found the venture a success in every way and is extending its night service'. This predicted expansion of Northmet's all-night services manifested itself with the introduction of a 30-minute frequency all-night horse-tram service between Poplar and Aldgate on Sunday night/Monday morning 19/20 February 1899.

The euphoria surrounding Northmet's early all-night services, as reported in *Street Railway Journal*, seems to have dissipated rapidly since Mr Richardson, the Chairman of Northmet, was reported in *Light Railway and Tramway Journal* issue of September 1899 as having said, 'The all-night service was an experiment . . . it showed no profit, so far . . . County Council gets 12½% on it and that was what killed it. The experiment . . . would not continue much longer'. The 12½% referred to by Northmet's Chairman was the payment by the company of that proportion of the gross receipts from the routes it operated to London County Council under the terms of its lease on the tramway. An attempt by Northmet to increase its revenue from all-night services was noted in issue 1 of *The Tram and Bus Gazette*, the official organ of the General Tram and Bus Workers Union, published on 28 September 1899, which reported, 'A new timetable for four lines (from 1/2 October 1899) seems to rule out night workers in Fleet Street and elsewhere from enjoying cheap fares'. This commentary referred to the retardation to 4am as the start time for Workmen's fares which had previously been available on all departures after midnight. At an unknown date in 1899, but implicitly after 1/2 October, Northmet introduced a further all-night horse-tram service between Highgate, Archway Tavern and Holborn via Caledonian Road.

The Light Railway and Tramway Journal issue of November 1900 commented upon 'The discontinuance of the all-night cars on the North Metropolitan Co's lines in the northern portion of London'. The Hampstead, Poplar and Stamford Hill services are referred to in the commentary whilst the Highgate and Stratford services are implicitly included. That same journal's issue of 2 August 1901 reported, 'A memorial, signed by over 250 men engaged in London newspaper offices, was addressed at the end of May to the North Metropolitan Tramways Co. appealing for the re-establishment of the early morning tramway service from Holborn to Highgate and Hampstead between 1 and 3 o'clock A.M. The signatories pointed out that a service of trams to return home was urgently needed; that the men came to the City by the company's vehicles, and therefore aided in swelling the day traffic; that there was an increasing population coming to the City each morning for market work; and that there were always casual passengers, who substantially augmented the regular traffic. Mr R. C. Adamson, the Managing Director, in expressing the regret of the directors that they were unable to re-establish the early morning service, states in a letter to the memorialists that the loss sustained by the company in running these services in 1899 and part of 1900 was aggravated by the London County Council's claiming 12½% of the gross receipts. Not one of the cars, Mr Adamson continues, run between 1 and 3 earned anything like the working expenses, and the company is further reluctantly compelled to withdraw for want of patronage several early morning cars between Stratford and Aldgate'.

This was not the end of Northmet's operation of all-night horse-tram services. Following representations made to it by the Institute of Journalists and 'several other parties interested', the London County Council wrote to The North Metropolitan Tramways Company on 26 February 1902 asking if 'In the interest of the night workers of the newspapers, at the markets and at the Post Office it will facilitate the resumption of all-night car services . . . between Holborn and Hampstead and Holborn and Highgate'. In order to facilitate the restoration of these services London County Council agreed to forgo its entitlement to payment of 12½% of the gross receipts on those two all-night services if the company 'Will give an undertaking to continue the services until the expiration or determination of the lease'. The company's solicitor was instructed to reply that the Directors, while prepared to recommence the services, would not undertake to continue them until the expiration or determination of the lease.

Northmet's Holborn to Hampstead and Holborn to Highgate all-night routes – but no others – were reinstated circa 29 March 1902. However problems persisted, for Northmet's Board Minutes of 8 October 1902 recorded, that 'the Hampstead and Holborn and Highgate and Holborn

Left B 185 is seen posed on the wrong side of the road outside the Criterion Theatre entrance to Piccadilly Circus Underground Station in 1913 possibly on, or close to, 14/15 July of that year which was the inaugural night of operation for route 94. Not all passengers appear to be workmen – a soldier is seated on the lower deck whilst on the upper deck a gentleman doffs his hat. Another gentleman in top hat and tail-coat approaches the bus's platform. *TfL/London Transport Museum*

all-night services from 29 March to 4 October (1902) showed a loss of £385' and went on to recommend the withdrawal of the Highgate all-night service. Nothing further has been established about the precise fate of Northmet's Hampstead and Highgate all-night services beyond the knowledge that they were withdrawn at some date before London County Council Tramways took over operation of Northmet's network from 1 April 1906 upon the early determination of the company's lease. All-night services did not feature in a listing of Northmet tram routes of which London County Council Tramways assumed operation from 1 April 1906, whilst it is recorded that London County Council Tramways re-introduced all-night services to tramways north of the River Thames in January/February 1907.

LONDON UNITED TRAMWAYS

Railway World, issue of 9 February 1899, reported that at the beginning of the year London United Tramways had introduced two 30-minute frequency all-night horse-tram operated services between Uxbridge Road (Shepherds Bush) and Acton and between Hammersmith and Kew Bridge. The feature continued by promising that when electrification of these two tram lines was completed, all-night services would be run more frequently and at lower fares. The tramways concerned were all electrified from 4 April 1901 to provide the first public service of electrically-powered tramcars in London, but nothing further has been traced concerning London United Tramways all-night services.

LONDON COUNTY COUNCIL HORSE-TRAMS

London County Council Tramways introduced its first two all-night horse-tram operated services on Sunday night/ Monday morning 12/13 February 1899. Both routes, each with a 23-minute frequency, shared common termini at New Cross Gate and at Blackfriars Road, where the services terminated south of Blackfriars Bridge. One service travelled via Old Kent Road whilst the other was routed via Peckham and Camberwell. One week later, on 19/20 February 1899, LCC Tramways introduced its third all-night horse-tram service between Clapham, Plough and Westminster Bridge Road (south side of Westminster Bridge) via Kennington Gate, which operated every 25 minutes. At an unknown date in 1900, LCC Tramways introduced a 25-minute frequency all-night service between Brixton, Water Lane and Blackfriars Road via Kennington Gate and Elephant & Castle. From 25/26 June 1901, LCC Tramways made available a transfer facility at Kennington Gate which allowed passengers to interchange between Blackfriars Road and Westminster Bridge Road tramcars.

An impression of the ambience surrounding London's all-night horse-tram services at the turn of the twentieth century is conveyed by this short extract from a contemporary book *Living London*, published in 1902:

'In Blackfriars Road the change from the brilliant light of the bridge to the gloom of the streets is striking. But here there is still life. The tramcars run the long night through and at 2am the belated wayfarer may for the modest sum of a halfpenny be borne drowsily to the Elephant & Castle and go far beyond if he wishes it.'

ALL-NIGHT HORSE-BUS SERVICES

At the time of the introduction of LCC Tramways' all-night horse-tram services no tramway lines crossed any of the central London bridges which spanned the River Thames. Horse-bus services already provided onward connecting services across the Thames into the City and Westminster for daytime travellers and this principle was extended to the new all-night services when, from the night of 12/13 February 1899, LCC Tramways inaugurated London's first all-night bus route with a horse-bus service across Blackfriars Bridge which linked the Blackfriars Road tram terminus with Farringdon Street Station. On 19/20 February 1899, LCC Tramways put on a second all-night horse bus service between Westminster Bridge Road and Charing Cross.

A move by LCC Tramways on 12 June 1899, when it combined the operation of its daytime Westminster Bridge Road and Waterloo Road horse-bus services to form one route, was perceived as a threat to their businesses by certain Associations of horse-bus proprietors who initiated legal action against LCC Tramways. LCC Tramways asserted that it had an implied power to run horse-buses, ancillary to its right to operate tramways under the London County Tramways Act 1896, when the case came to trial. The Council's contention was rejected by the trial judge, whose verdict was subsequently upheld by the Court of Appeal and finally by six judges in the House of Lords. Thus London County Council Tramways was compelled to cease operation of its horse-bus services including the all-night routes which operated for the last time on Wednesday night/Thursday morning 5/6 March 1902. The King's Cross and Barnsbury Association assumed operation of horse-bus services crossing Blackfriars Bridge from 7 March 1902 and the Atlas and Waterloo Association assumed operation of horse-bus services across Westminster Bridge from the same date. An appendix to the 1905 Report of the Royal Commission on London Traffic recorded that, in 1903 between the hours of 11.15pm and 5.30am, the Blackfriars Road to Farringdon Street route operated every 15 minutes whilst the Westminster Bridge Road to Charing Cross route ran at 30-minute intervals between midnight and 1.35am, after which the service was suspended until 5.30am. The journey time on both routes was nine minutes with each route having a through fare of ½d.

Claude Sisley, a historian of horse-drawn transport, recorded in his Archive 'When the Star Omnibus Company quarrelled with the Associations in autumn 1905 they (Star) put more buses on the road and ran them all night . . . Tillings put on buses by night to be equal with them'. The Archive does not mention the routes involved.

The extension of LCC Tramways' daytime and all-night tram services across Westminster Bridge in December 1906 and across Blackfriars Bridge in September 1909 must have adversely impacted the revenues of horse-bus services across those bridges. The Sisley Archive records that a horse-bus service between Blackfriars and Farringdon Street (not detailed whether or not with an all-night element) was still extant in September 1912 'because it was a short road and served as a link between tram services north and south of London . . . I have no record of the road coming to an end but I do not think it can have lasted much longer'.

London's Known All-Night Horse Bus and Horse Tram Routes

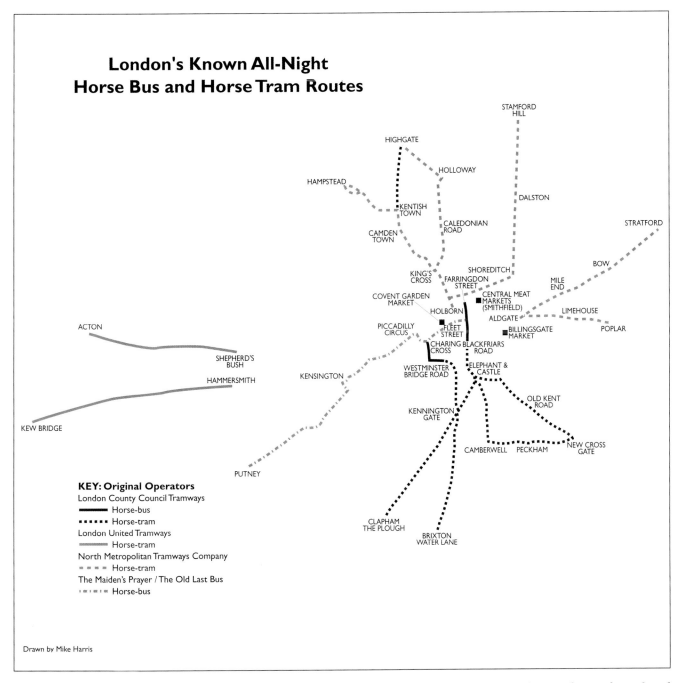

KEY: Original Operators
London County Council Tramways
▬▬▬ Horse-bus
▪▪▪▪▪ Horse-tram
London United Tramways
▬▬▬ Horse-tram
North Metropolitan Tramways Company
▬ ▬ ▬ Horse-tram
The Maiden's Prayer / The Old Last Bus
▪—▪—▪ Horse-bus

Drawn by Mike Harris

THE MAIDEN'S PRAYER AND THE OLD LAST BUS

The Sisley Archive recorded 'There was a pirate horse-bus that ran every night from Piccadilly Circus to Putney about 1.15 in the morning. As it was largely patronised by Piccadilly tarts it was called *The Maiden's Prayer*. The fare was one shilling all the way and the bus was always crowded out with passengers. There was a stampede when it came up, people would stand on the roof.' Sisley presumed that this bus was owned by some private cabmaster in the Putney district and was sure it was not a London General or Road Car Company bus.

It is not clear whether this is the same bus as that referred to by a columnist in *The Daily Chronicle* of 13 July 1913 whose recollections were prompted by, 'The all-night bus service which is about to be started (LGOC route 94 on 14/15 July 1913) brings back to memory *The Old Last Bus* which used to run regularly up to six or seven years ago. It used to rumble up Fleet Street about 1.30am, pull up by St Martin's Church and go down Piccadilly to South Kensington and Putney an hour after all the other buses had ceased running. Passengers were mostly regular customers and were invariably waited for.'

ELECTRIFICATIONS AND EXTENSIONS
SOUTH OF THE THAMES

Thus far motive power for all-night tram and bus services had been provided by horses. As early as 1898 London County Council had recognised that the future for its tramway operation lay with the adoption of electric power. Following trials carried out within the confines of Camberwell depot in 1901 the decision to electrify its tramways, using the conduit system, was taken. The conduit system provided electrical power from a conduit sunk below the road surface between the tram tracks. Electrical power was picked up by the tramcar using a trailing "plough" which followed along the conduit slot. The conduit system appealed to LCC because it avoided the use of overhead power cables and supporting poles, which the Council considered to be aesthetically unsuited to the capital's streets.

LCC Tramways opened its first sections of conduit equipped electric tramways to traffic on 15 May 1903. E. R. Oakley's Notes record that the Council's first electrically powered all-night tram service was introduced on the night of 15/16 May 1903, when a route was introduced between Clapham (The Plough) and Blackfriars Road via Kennington Gate and Elephant & Castle. This new night route actually formed a composite from the existing Clapham – Kennington Gate section of the Westminster Bridge Road route and the Kennington Gate – Blackfriars Road section of the route from Brixton (Water Lane). These two latter routes continued to be operated in their own right, but still using horse-powered tramcars, although the full length of the tramway between Clapham and Westminster Bridge Road had been converted to electrical power from 15 May 1903. The reason for the introduction of this composite electrically-powered night tram route may have been as a form of insurance against the unreliability of early electrical power supplies, coupled with lack of experience in its operational use. In the event of power failure at night the roads concerned would still have had a service provided by the two respective night horse-tram routes, assuming that the horse trams could get past any immobilised electric cars. Thereafter, conversion of night tram routes from horse power to electrical power was delayed for several weeks after the daytime equivalent routes had been so converted. Thus the next conversion to electrical power, that of the two New Cross Gate – Blackfriars Road night routes on 27/28 March 1904, followed about two months after the daytime routes over the same tracks had been so converted, on 17 January 1904 (via Old Kent Road) and 24 January 1904 (via Camberwell Green and Peckham). The final conversion from horse power to electrical power of South London LCC night tram routes occurred on Sunday night/Monday morning of 26/27 June 1904, when both the Clapham – Westminster Bridge Road and Brixton – Blackfriars Road were so treated. The latter route had had its service suspended for about three months, from 3 April 1904, in connection with the conversion to the conduit system of the cable-car line between Kennington and Streatham, over which night horse trams shared the same track. Despite the conversion of these latter two routes to electric power, the 'composite' Clapham – Blackfriars Road night service continued to operate. On 17/18 October 1904 a modest extension was made to the New

Cross Gate – Blackfriars Road via Old Kent Road night tram route, when the service was projected beyond New Cross Gate to reach a new terminus at New Cross (Marquis of Granby). Frequencies then applicable to these all-night tram routes, which operated from Sunday nights to Friday nights, ranged from 23 to 28 minutes.

A significant development in London's tramway history occurred on 15 December 1906. On that day an electrified extension to the tramway across Westminster Bridge and on to Victoria Embankment, as far as Blackfriars (John Carpenter Street), opened to traffic. By this date LCC Tramways had gained considerable experience with the operation of electric tramways at night. There was no delay in extending the night tram route from Clapham (The Plough) to Westminster Bridge Road across Westminster Bridge to reach a new terminus at Victoria Embankment (Charing Cross – District Railway Station). LCC Highways Committee's Minutes dated 21 December 1906 implied that the extension was certainly in operation by the night of Thursday/Friday 20/21 December 1906, possibly having first operated on the night of 18/19 December. The Highways Committee's Minutes dated one week later, 28 December 1906, revealed the intriguing information that LCC Tramways had arranged for two night tramcars to depart Clapham (The Plough) at 1.45am and 2.05am bound for Balham and Tooting. These departures were timed to connect at Clapham (The Plough) with night trams arriving from Blackfriars Bridge (1.25am departure) and Victoria Embankment (1.39am departure) respectively. The Minutes added, 'The trial cars will run for one month'. It has not been possible to establish whether this first-ever night tram service to Tooting continued beyond its one month trial period.

A listing of all-night tram routes published in *The Light Railway and Tramway Journal* of 1 March 1907 details a service operating between Brixton and Victoria Embankment (Charing Cross District Railway Station). It is unclear whether this related to a service of through tramcars or was a recognition of the interchange facility provided at Kennington Gate between Brixton – Blackfriars Road and Clapham – Victoria Embankment all-night tram services.

LCC Tramways' increasing reliance on electrical power for its system might well have been the reason for the withdrawal of the 'composite' night tram route between Clapham (The Plough) and Blackfriars Road after operation on 1/2 March 1908. As already noted, this route was covered in its entirety at night by appropriate sections of the Clapham – Charing Cross Station and Brixton – Blackfriars Road routes, whose lines met at Kennington Gate. A significant extension was made to the Clapham night tram route from Sunday night/Monday morning 20/21 December 1908. On that date the route was projected beyond Clapham (The Plough) via Balham to reach a new terminus at Tooting Broadway. The revised route between Tooting Broadway and Charing Cross Station maintained its former 28-minute frequency so necessitating an increase in allocation from two to three tramcars on the route. At an unestablished date in 1909 the last four outbound journeys on this route started further east along Victoria Embankment, at Waterloo Bridge. By 1912 all journeys on the Tooting night route ended at Waterloo Bridge.

A landmark in the history of London's tramways was reached on 14 September 1909. On that day Blackfriars Bridge, which had been widened over the previous two years in order to accommodate a pair of conduit-equipped tramway tracks, was reopened to traffic. On the north side of Blackfriars Bridge the tramway tracks met up at John Carpenter Street with the extant tracks, which ran along Victoria Embankment from Westminster Bridge, so completing a tramway loop along the Embankment accessible via both Blackfriars Bridge and Westminster Bridge. This loop was to become very significant in later developments on the all-night tram network. It seems highly probable that the three night tram routes from Brixton, New Cross (Marquis of Granby) via Old Kent Road and New Cross Gate via Peckham, which had terminated in Blackfriars Road, were extended across Blackfriars Bridge to reach a new terminus at Victoria Embankment (John Carpenter Street) from the night of 14/15 September 1909.

On Sunday night/Monday morning, 7/8 November 1909 a further night tram route was introduced by LCC Tramways. This lengthy, hourly-frequency route operated from Earlsfield via Wandsworth, Battersea and Vauxhall, before crossing Westminster Bridge to reach Victoria Embankment. Unlike the existing Tooting night tram route, this new route traversed the full length of Victoria Embankment to reach its terminus at Victoria Embankment (John Carpenter Street), which it shared with the night trams arriving over Blackfriars Bridge. Thus all-night tram routes reaching Victoria Embankment from both Blackfriars Bridge and from Westminster Bridge directions met for the very first time. Fourteen months later, after operation on the night of 1/2 January 1911, that section of the Earlsfield route between Earlsfield and Battersea (Prince's Head) was withdrawn. The contracted route thereafter operated between Battersea (Prince's Head) and Blackfriars (John Carpenter Street), still maintaining an hourly frequency.

FRESH START FOR NORTHERN ROUTES
Northmet's lease was determined early on 1 April 1906 when LCC Tramways assumed responsibility for the Company's operations, which at that time remained entirely operated by horse-trams. LCC Tramways set about electrifying its new Northern network, a process which would take several years to complete. The contrast between the modernity of London County Council Tramways' system south of the Thames, upon which many tramways had been progressively converted to electrical power from 15 May 1903 onwards, and its recently acquired, still horse-tram operated, northern counterpart, was most marked. *The Daily News* of 10 January 1907 referred to the trams in north London as 'expensive, obsolete cars, cheerless, ill-lit'.

London County Council Tramways reinstated all-night services over its northern network in the early months of 1907 using both horse trams and electric trams, according to the route. As on its southern network, services operated six days of the week from Sunday night/Monday morning to Friday night/Saturday morning. The first northern route to have a night service restored was noteworthy since it incorporated a substantial route extension, as well as conversion

to electrically-powered tramcar operation. This took place on Sunday night/Monday morning 27/28 January 1907, when the former Northmet Poplar – Aldgate route was diverted at Aldgate (Gardiner's Corner) to operate via Commercial Street, Great Eastern Street, Old Street, Clerkenwell Road and Theobalds Road to reach a new terminus at Bloomsbury (Southampton Row). This first all-night service north of the River Thames to be reinstated by London County Council Tramways operated to a 30-minute frequency, offering a total of ten return journeys. Three days later, on 30/31 January 1907, a new electrically-powered night tram route was introduced between Highbury station and Bloomsbury via The Angel and Rosebery Avenue. It will be recalled that one of Northmet's original night tram routes had operated between Stamford Hill and Holborn. On the night of 10/11 February 1907 an electrically-powered night tram service was reinstated over the Stamford Hill – Shoreditch Church section of that route. The Shoreditch terminus was but a temporary expedient, since this route was restored to its full former working between Stamford Hill and Holborn after the tramway along Old Street, between Shoreditch and Great Eastern Street, had been converted to electrical power. The probable date for this latter extension was 29/30 March 1907, when the 25-minute frequency route required the allocation of three tramcars.

The night of Sunday/Monday 10/11 February 1907 also saw a night service restored to two other northern routes but in both instances horse trams, as opposed to electric trams, were used. A 30-minute frequency service was restored to the night tram route between Highgate (Archway Tavern) and Holborn via Caledonian Road and King's Cross. The other route to gain a night service of horse trams was that between Bow Bridge and Aldgate. It will be recalled that Northmet's very first night tram route from Aldgate had extended beyond Bow Bridge to Stratford. That section of Northmet's tramway between Bow Bridge and Stratford had subsequently passed into the ownership of West Ham Corporation Tramways so that the revived LCC Tramways night route terminated at Bow Bridge, which was at the boundary of the London County Council area. Later in 1907 the Bow Bridge service was probably subject to disruption when the line was converted to electrical power using the Griffith-Bell stud contact system. The line re-opened on 25 June 1908 using a mixture of GB stud contact electric trams and horse trams. It would seem that a full night service was not restored at this juncture, the contemporary timetable simply referring to three early morning journeys starting at 4.05am ex Bow Bridge. The GB stud contact system quickly proved to be unsafe in operation and the cars so equipped were withdrawn on 17 July 1908, after which this section of the tramway reverted to full horse-tram operation. Further disruption occurred between May and July 1909 whilst the line was converted to overhead electric power between Bow Bridge and Mile End, and to conduit power over the remaining section between Mile End and Aldgate. Sunday night/Monday morning 1/2 August 1909 is a possible date for the resumption of a full night service between Bow Bridge and Aldgate. Tramcars would have had to use a change pit at Mile End to pick up a 'plough' for power over the conduit section thence to Aldgate.

Mention has already been made of a new, electrically-powered night tram service introduced on the night of 30/31 January 1907 between Highbury station and Bloomsbury via The Angel and Rosebery Avenue. On the night of Sunday/Monday 16/17 February 1908, this route was projected beyond Highbury station via Holloway to reach a revised terminus at Highgate (Archway Tavern). Between termini, this new route more or less displaced the original night tram route between Highgate (Archway Tavern) and Holborn via Caledonian Road and King's Cross, operation of which had continued to be maintained by horse trams. It is probable that this Caledonian Road route was withdrawn after operation on the night of Friday/Saturday 14/15 February 1908, which thereafter left Caledonian Road without a night tram service. Later in 1908, on 1/2 November, LCC Tramways introduced a night tram service between Finsbury Park and King's Cross, which restored a service to Caledonian Road. This new night service used electrically-powered tramcars since the section of tramway along Caledonian Road had been converted for such use by 15 August 1908. However, electric trams could not operate beyond King's Cross via Gray's Inn Road to reach Holborn, which would certainly have been a more useful destination for night passengers. The reason lay in the fact that the tramway link between Caledonian Road and Gray's Inn Road had not been converted to electrical power. The inability of this new night service to reach Holborn may well have accounted for its early demise in January 1909, after only a few weeks' operation. E. R. Oakley's Notes also contained reference to the withdrawal of a London County Council Tramways night horse-tramway service between Highgate (Archway Tavern) and Kentish Town via Junction Road, on 14/15 February 1908, but it has not been possible to establish an introduction date for such workings. In a similar vein, it has not been possible to establish with certainty, the date for the reintroduction of LCC Tramways' night service over the Hampstead Heath – Holborn tramway. London County Council's Highway Committee's Minutes of 29 January 1907 stated the Council's intention to re-introduce, inter alia, an all-night service over the Hampstead Heath – Holborn tramway, although LCC Tramways' first Official Guide, published on 1 July 1908, contained no reference to an all-night service, or even 'Workmen's Service' over that section of tramway. It is not in dispute that the all-night service was restored, at an unknown date, since E. R. Oakley's Notes indicate that the all-night horse-tram operated service between Hampstead Heath and Holborn was withdrawn after operation on the night of 21/22 April 1909. This brought an end to regular horse-tram operation of all-night services. The reason for withdrawal of the service was the closure of the tramway from Great College Street to Hampstead Heath, via Kentish Town and Malden Road, for conversion to electrical power supply. The line re-opened as an electric tramway from 10 September 1909 and, since the section of tramway beyond Great College Street via Pancras Road to King's Cross and Holborn had already been converted to electrical operation, it is likely that an all-night service of electrically-powered tramcars was restored between Hampstead Heath and Holborn at, or shortly after, that date. Certainly an all-night service was in operation by December 1912, since a

timetable attributable to that date indicates that a 30-minute frequency then prevailed between Sunday nights/Monday mornings and Friday nights/Saturday mornings, requiring an allocation of two trams from Hampstead (Cressy Road) depot.

The practice of supplementing London's all-night public road passenger transport services at times of national celebration may be traced back to at least 1911. *The Light Railway and Tramway Journal* issue of 7 July 1911 reported, 'As regards meeting the requirements of the public on Coronation Day (of His Majesty King George V on Wednesday 21 June 1911), and in the Metropolitan area the next day also, the tramways may fairly claim to have risen to the situation in a most thorough and enterprising manner. During the period they ran what was practically an all-night service . . . so that the enthusiastic crowds who remained to view the illuminations were enabled to get home without having to indulge in unwanted pedestrianism.'

Disruption to the all-night tram routes may well have occurred towards the end of March 1912. At the end of the first decade of the 20th century industrial unrest, exacerbated by politically-inspired agitation, became quite widespread as workers in a variety of key industries went on strike. On 1 March 1912 a coalminers' strike started. This action threatened to deplete coal stocks held at power stations, thereby making LCC Tramways' system vulnerable to the threat of power supply disruption. The Council reduced the general level of service across its electric tramway network from 11 March, with further economies being applied from 25 March. *The Light Railway and Tramway* issue of 29 March 1912 reported, 'In order to save the electric current the London County Council are to use old horse-drawn trams on some all-night services this week.' It has not been possible to establish which routes reverted to horse-drawn operation, but as the coalminers' strike ended on 6 April 1912, it is probable that such temporary use of horse-drawn tramcars on all-night services was shortlived.

During the autumn of 1912 London County Council started to introduce a system of route numbers for its tram services, the first listing of all such routes appearing in the Tramway Map and Guide for December 1912. All-night tram services were specifically excluded from the numbering scheme and so continued to operate as unnumbered routes.

Only two other changes affected London's all-night tram services prior to the outbreak of the First World War in August 1914. The first such alteration occurred on the night of Wednesday/Thursday 8/9 October 1913, when the night tram routes from New Cross (Marquis of Granby) via Old Kent Road and from New Cross Gate via Peckham were extended from Blackfriars Road (John Carpenter Street) further west along Victoria Embankment to a revised terminus at Waterloo Bridge. On the night of Friday/Saturday 17/18 April 1914, the New Cross (Marquis of Granby) route was extended a considerable distance beyond its outer terminus to travel via Lewisham to reach a revised terminus at Catford (Rushey Green). Since the previously prevailing 25-minute frequency was maintained, an increase in allocation from three to four trams from New Cross depot was necessary to maintain the new schedule.

LONDON'S FIRST ALL-NIGHT MOTOR BUS ROUTES

London's first all-night bus route to be operated by motor buses was London General's route 94, which operated between Cricklewood (Crown) and Liverpool Street Station via Kilburn, Marble Arch, Oxford Street, Regent Street, Charing Cross, Fleet Street, Ludgate Hill, Cannon Street and Bank. There exists a degree of confusion within official LGOC sources as to the exact date of this route's introduction. The official Route Record Card records the Cricklewood garage worked service as having been inaugurated on Wednesday night/Thursday morning 16/17 July 1913. This is at variance with the announcement of the route's introduction contained within the London Traffic Combine's contemporary bulletin *T.O.T (Train. Omnibus. Tram)* No. 5 dated 12 July 1913, which stated that route 94 would commence 'the night of 14th July, between the 14th and 15th days of the month,' that is to say Monday night/Tuesday morning of that week with a 20-minute frequency. Transport historian Charles Lee's Archive concurs with the date given in *T. O. T* No. 5, recording that route 94 commenced on 15 July 1913 and that '24 passengers were carried on the first trip.' *T.O.T* No. 5 makes very clear the rationale which led to route 94's introduction. 'Almost alone of the districts of London, the North West quarter is cut off from communication with the centre during the hours of night. Attention has been called to this omission by persons working on the press getting out the morning newspapers, by postmen getting ready the morning's mail, by musicians, servants and other people who have to attend on the termination of the pleasure of those who seek it until late hours before they can clear up and get away home. Even during the night there are casual people of all kinds and on sundry errands wanting to travel, and in the early morning are those who deal in perishable commodities who have to get to market early to see to the replenishing of their stores for daily purchase. Such service is conveniently near to the Central Meat Markets at Ludgate Circus, Billingsgate at the Bank corner, Covent Garden at Southampton Street in the Strand, the GPO at St Paul's Churchyard, and all the newspaper offices.' At that time the north-west quarter of London was certainly disadvantaged compared with most other districts in respect of night-time – as well as daytime – public transport facilities heading towards central London, both by road and by rail. As previously detailed in this chapter, northern, eastern, south-eastern and south-western districts of London already benefited from night tram services. Comparable night tram services had not developed in the north-western quarter due to the absence of tramway infrastructure. The Metropolitan Electric Tramways' Harrow Road tracks ended at Paddington, quite some distance from Central London, whilst there was no tramway at all along Edgware Road. Even the Underground was relatively late going to the north-west quarter, with the Bakerloo Line paralleling Edgware Road via Maida Vale and then to Willesden Junction not opening until 1915.

According to *T. O. T* No. 5, route 94 was introduced 'somewhat in the fashion of an experiment . . . upon its reception will turn the further development of services of this kind.' In 1912 London General had been taken over by the Underground

Electric Railway Company. Further tube line acquisitions in 1913 had given UERL a dominant, but not monopolistic, position in the provision of London's passenger transport which led to the group becoming known as the London Traffic Combine. New initiatives, aimed at both reducing competition between the Combine's road and rail operations and increasing passenger usage, abounded at this time. The introduction of night bus route 94 would seem to have fitted in well with the Combine's innovative spirit of the day. The reliability and speed of the B-type motor bus, with which London General had re-equipped its fleet in 1910/1911, would certainly have added confidence to its decision to proceed with this new night-time initiative.

Four months after the introduction of London's first night motor bus route 94, London General introduced a second night motor bus route. Starting on Wednesday night/Thursday morning 12/13 November 1913, a new 54-minute journey time route 94A linked Willesden (Pound Lane) with Liverpool Street Station, providing a night service facility for the first time along Harrow Road. New route 94A and existing route 94 met at Edgware Road, whence both routes shared a lengthy common section through the West End and the City to their Liverpool Street terminus. By the time of issue of LGOC's June 1914 Map and Guide, which was the first to quote service frequencies, 94 and 94A each operated every 30 minutes, each route requiring an allocation of four buses from Cricklewood and Willesden garages respectively. Scheduling of the two routes gave a combined 15-minute frequency over the common section of routes 94 and 94A between Edgware Road (junction Chapel Street) and Liverpool Street Station. It is most likely that this coordination dated from route 94A's introduction on 12/13 November 1913, from which date it is probable that route 94 adopted a 30-minute frequency, rather than the '20-minute' frequency referred to in *T. O. T* No. 5.

Considerable uncertainty surrounds the next recorded development on routes 94 and 94A. LGOC's official Route Record Card details the introduction, on 21/22 December 1913, of a service on both routes between 'West Kilburn and Oxford Circus.' However, contemporary and later issued London General Maps and Guides carry no timing details for, nor indeed bear any reference at all, to this 'additional service'. The earliest dated London General Traffic Notice seen by the author, which was also the first to give a comprehensive listing of routes, No. 17 of 20 June 1915, carried no reference to such 'additional service'. Whilst doubts may exist as to whether or not the West Kilburn 'additional service' ever operated, no such uncertainty surrounds the next development which affected route 94A. In the early morning of Monday 8 June 1914, a supplementary service was introduced on the 94A, operating between Liverpool Street Station and Elephant & Castle via Bank, London Bridge and Borough High Street. A 30-minute service, initially comprising six return journeys on weekday mornings, operated between 4.23am and 6.53am ex Liverpool Street, and between 4.40am and 7.10am ex Elephant & Castle. Supplementary route 94A's allocation was achieved by utilising Willesden garage-based buses on layover at Liverpool Street from the main 94A route. The additional running time needed to complete the return trip between Liverpool Street and Elephant & Castle necessitated an increase in allocation from four to five buses on route 94A. The main purpose of the supplementary service on 94A was to offer a connection into the City for passengers reaching Elephant & Castle on early morning London County Council trams. It would also have offered a facility for passengers arriving at London Bridge station by train.

Table A: Vehicle Allocations 29/30 June 1914 – Sunday to Friday nights		
Route	*Allocation*	*Depot/Garage*
Tram routes north of Thames		
Stamford Hill – Holborn	3 trams	Stamford Hill
Bow Bridge – Aldgate	2 trams	Bow
Poplar – Bloomsbury	3 trams	Poplar
Highgate – Bloomsbury	2 trams	Holloway
Hampstead Heath – Holborn	2 trams	Hampstead
Sub Total	**12 trams**	
Tram routes south of Thames		
Catford – Victoria Embankment	4 trams	New Cross
New Cross – Victoria Embankment	3 trams	New Cross
Brixton – Victoria Embankment	2 trams	Streatham
Tooting Broadway – Victoria Embankment	3 trams	Clapham
Battersea – Victoria Embankment	1 tram	Wandsworth
Sub Total	**13 trams**	
Total	**25 trams**	
Motor Bus routes		
94 Cricklewood – Liverpool Street Station	4 buses	Cricklewood
94A {Willesden – Liverpool Street Station	5 buses	Willesden
{Liverpool Street Station – Elephant & Castle		
Sub Total	**9 buses**	
GRAND TOTAL	**34 trams and buses**	

By the summer of 1914 London's all-night public road passenger transport services had achieved stability and showed every prospect of further growth. The all-night tram services, provided by London County Council Tramways, had recently seen a substantial extension of the New Cross route to Catford from 17/18 April 1914. The London Traffic Combine, in the form of London General, had inaugurated all-night motor bus services in 1913 and, as witnessed by the supplementary service on route 94A to Elephant & Castle, introduced on 7/8 June 1914, seemed to be seeking further opportunities to develop services. On 30 June 1914, 25 tramcars and 9 motor buses were allocated to all-night services, giving an impressive total of 34 vehicles out on such work over six nights of the week.

Sadly, the prospect of further growth for the budding all-night road passenger service network was about to be stunted by the privations which were caused as a consequence of the outbreak of the First World War – although, ironically, the cataclysmic turn of events on the world stage was destined to spawn two further, albeit short-lived, all-night bus routes.

ALL-NIGHT TRAM CUTBACKS
The outbreak of the First World War was officially declared on 4 August 1914. The first 'casualty' of that conflict, as far as all-night road passenger transport services were concerned, was the extension of the Old Kent Road night tram service beyond New Cross to Catford (Rushey Green), which was withdrawn after operation on the night of Friday/Saturday 16/17 October 1914, a bare six months following its introduction. This route reverted to its previous pattern of operation, between New Cross and Waterloo Bridge on Victoria Embankment, thereby effecting a reduction of one, from four to three, in New Cross depot's allocation of trams to the route.

By February 1916 the national situation had become extremely serious. The country was ruled by a Coalition Government, with Herbert Asquith as Prime Minister, which had at its disposal Emergency Powers under the 1915 Defence of the Realm Act. Since the summer of 1915 London had been subjected to German bombing raids from Zeppelin airships, which caused destruction to property as well as death and injury to unfortunate victims, amongst whose numbers, sadly, were included London General Omnibus Company and London County Council Tramways staff on duty. Recruiting campaigns seeking men to join up with the armed forces were unremitting – although the voluntary element of such campaigns disappeared in February 1916 with the introduction of conscription of all single men between the ages of 18 and 41 years. All industries were depleted by male employees leaving for service with the Crown, and the transport industry was no exception. In many cases women helped to fill gaps as, for instance, when on 20 October 1915 women started to be taken on, for the first time, as bus and tram conductresses.

The economic consequences of the war were serious too with shortages of commodities, fuel and raw materials. London County Council was forced to make stringent economies whenever it could which affected, *inter alia*, its all-night tram routes. The February 1916 issue of *Railway and Travel Monthly* reported that London County Council Tramways had just '16 cars in service' on its night tram route network, which compared with 25 cars on night service duties at 30 June 1914. The economies to the night tram route network were achieved by frequency reductions: from 25 to 30 minutes on both the New Cross via Old Kent Road and New Cross Gate via Peckham routes (to two trams on each route), from

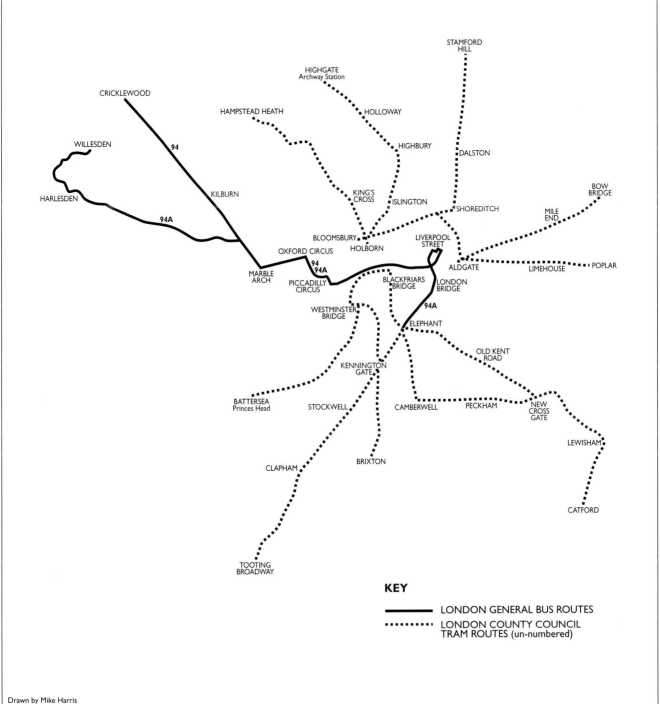

ALL-NIGHT BUS & TRAM ROUTES
at 29/30 June 1914

CRICKLEWOOD

WILLESDEN

HARLESDEN

94

KILBURN

94A

HAMPSTEAD HEATH

HIGHGATE
Archway Station

HOLLOWAY

STAMFORD
HILL

HIGHBURY

DALSTON

KING'S
CROSS

ISLINGTON

SHOREDITCH

BOW
BRIDGE

MILE
END

BLOOMSBURY

LIVERPOOL
STREET

HOLBORN

OXFORD CIRCUS

94

94A

MARBLE
ARCH

PICCADILLY
CIRCUS

BLACKFRIARS
BRIDGE

LONDON
BRIDGE

ALDGATE

LIMEHOUSE

POPLAR

94A

WESTMINSTER
BRIDGE

ELEPHANT

OLD KENT
ROAD

KENNINGTON
GATE

BATTERSEA
Princes Head

STOCKWELL

CAMBERWELL

PECKHAM

NEW
CROSS
GATE

LEWISHAM

CLAPHAM

BRIXTON

CATFORD

TOOTING
BROADWAY

KEY

——————— LONDON GENERAL BUS ROUTES

··········· LONDON COUNTY COUNCIL
TRAM ROUTES (un-numbered)

Drawn by Mike Harris

25 minutes to alternate 25/50 minutes on the Stamford Hill route (to two trams), from 30 minutes to alternate 30/60 minutes on the Poplar route (to two trams) and from 30 minutes to 60 minutes on both the Hampstead Heath and Highgate routes (to one tram on each route). Frequencies on the all-night routes to Battersea (60 minutes), Brixton (28 minutes) and Tooting Broadway (28 minutes), with allocations of one, two and three trams respectively, remained unchanged. Additionally, the entire night service over the Bow Bridge – Aldgate route had been withdrawn by October 1915, which also saved the need for night-time plough-shifter attendant at the Mile End change-pit. Those routes operating north of the River Thames suffered the most drastic pruning, seemingly following their disadvantaged pattern of earlier years when The North Metropolitan Tramways Company's tenure had led to disruption in their operation and the much later conversion of these routes from horse to electrical power. Their counterparts south of the Thames escaped relatively unscathed.

THE FIRST INTER-STATION NIGHT MOTOR BUS ROUTES

On the night of Wednesday/Thursday 25/26 August 1915, London General introduced a new night motor bus route, numbered 95, which operated between Victoria Station and King's Cross Station on Sunday to Friday nights, with four return journeys. The 95's headway was uneven, with the first two closely timed departures ex Victoria at 3.10am and 3.15am, followed by two later, closely timed departures at 4.10am and 4.15am. Effectively the second and fourth departures were duplicate journeys to the first and third departures. Route 95 was allocated two buses from Battersea garage, which operated 'When Working' journeys in service from Battersea (Wellington Road) to Victoria Station prior to taking up the main service. Initially, the 95 was routed via Park Lane, Edgware Road, Marylebone Road and Euston Road. The route's passenger objective was made quite clear in Traffic Notice 28, which instructed that 'Top Boards' should display 'Victoria Station and King's Cross Station', whilst 'window boards' should display 'Praed Street (for Paddington Station), Marylebone, Euston, St Pancras and King's Cross' – all these points being main line railway stations.

Shortly afterwards, on the night of Thursday/Friday 2/3 September 1915 a second night motor bus route, numbered 93, was introduced between Victoria Station and Liverpool Street Station. The 93, which featured two return journeys leaving Victoria at 2.15am and 3.10am, operated as a panhandled unidirectional service with only the section of route along Victoria Street, between Victoria Station and Parliament Square, being served by journeys operated in both directions. From Parliament Square the 93 crossed Westminster Bridge to travel via York Road, serving Waterloo Station. Thence the 93 was routed via Stamford Street and across Blackfriars Bridge, serving Blackfriars Station and passing near to Cannon Street Station, before proceeding via Bank to the route's Liverpool Street station terminus. The 93's return journey was routed via Ludgate Circus, Fleet Street and Strand, where the route served Charing Cross

Station. Thence buses on the 93 travelled via Whitehall, Parliament Square and back to Victoria Station. Route 93, which operated on Sunday-Friday nights, was allocated one bus, from Battersea garage, which vehicle, like those on sister route 95, operated 'When Working' journeys in service from Battersea (Wellington Road) to Victoria Station via Chelsea, before taking up the main service. On the same date that route 93 was introduced, existing route 95 was subject to a substantial re-routeing, transforming it into a unidirectional circular service. Outward buses from Victoria Station continued to follow the 95's original routeing to King's Cross. Return journeys from King's Cross were diverted off Euston Road to travel via Woburn Place, Kingsway, Aldwych, Strand, Whitehall, Parliament Square and Victoria Street to reach the route's Victoria Station terminus. The 95's schedule remained substantially unaltered, continuing to operate four return journeys between Victoria Station and King's Cross Station.

The primary traffic objective of both routes 93 and 95 was the conveyance of soldiers between London's main line railway termini serving the northern, eastern and western areas of the country and Victoria Station, the principal railhead for troop trains bound for south coast ports, although intermediate fare stages, such as Liverpool Street to Chancery Lane on the 93 and Victoria to Marble Arch on the 95, were applied to these routes. The final destination, sometimes in the most literal sense, for many of the passengers on routes 93 and 95 would have been the battlefields of northern Europe.

The introduction of routes 93 and 95, in August and September 1915, increased the night bus requirement to 12 buses, four on route 94, five on route 94A, one on route 93 and two on route 95. With 24 tramcars then required to maintain LCC's all-night tram network, a combined total of 36 buses and trams was needed to maintain London's night road passenger transport services. This represented the highest vehicle requirement since the inception of all-night services in London in 1899. This vehicle requirement was destined to be short-lived, however, since, following the withdrawal of the night service on the Bow Bridge tram route and the reductions in frequency which affected many of the remaining tram routes by February 1916, the night tram requirement reduced to 16 cars, thereby giving a combined bus and tram requirement of 28 vehicles.

There must have been a lull in troop movements a couple of months after the introduction of routes 93 and 95 since both routes were suspended after operation on Wednesday morning, 3 November 1915. This suspension was only temporary, however, as both the 93 and 95 were reinstated from the night of 15/16 December 1915, according to LGOC's official Route Cards. Traffic Notice 46, dated 25 December 1915, noted that the two routes' re-instatement was to be 'at the discretion of the General Superintendent (LGOC) and be worked on such occasions as the exigencies of Military Traffic may demand'.

In early 1916 uncertainty arises as to the official conditions, as well as nights, on which routes 93 and 95 operated. LGOC's official Route Cards indicated that, from the night of Sunday/Monday 9/10 January 1916, routes 93 and 95 were relieved of the constraint of operation 'at the discretion of the General Superintendent' and thereafter ran a normal schedule on weekday early mornings. This assumption is apparently contradicted by Traffic Notice 55, which, from 18/19 February 1916, qualified the operation of both routes as being 'subject to receipt of instructions from the Controller's Office, Leicester Square'. That same Traffic Notice also detailed a Sunday morning schedule for both routes 93 and 95 – thereby identifying London's first night bus services to have operated on all seven nights of the week. It should be borne in mind that in 1916 Allied troop numbers were being increased in France for that summer's Somme offensive, so that troop movements across London would have been at a high level, thereby creating demand for routes 93 and 95. In Traffic Notice 55 route 93 remained as a two-journey service between Victoria Station and Liverpool Street Station. Route 95, however, was shown as having a revised frequency of '15 and 25 minutes', with the first departure from Victoria at 2.15am and the last journey leaving at 3.40am. With an outward journey time of 21 minutes from Victoria Station to King's Cross Station and a return journey time of 26 minutes, a quick calculation indicates that either four buses would have been needed to maintain the schedule, or that the frequency quoted is erroneous, since the service intervals quoted would not coincide with a 3.40am last departure ex Victoria. The author is inclined to think that the service intervals should have read '15 and 55 minutes', which would be coincident with the timing of the last journey, as well as maintaining the original allocation of two buses to route 95.

WITHDRAWAL OF ALL-NIGHT MOTOR BUS ROUTES

Due to the effects of the war, by mid 1916 the national situation had become extremely grave, with manpower and materials shortages adversely affecting the performance of all industries. The concept of putting clocks forward one hour, under a 'Daylight Saving Scheme', in order to conserve coal and fuel stocks, was first introduced on 21 May 1916. Allied Forces launched a major offensive against the German army on the Somme on 1 July 1916. The High Command's expectation of a decisive breakthrough quickly faded as near stalemate developed between the opposing armies in their trenches on the Western Front. London's original all-night motor bus routes, 94 (Cricklewood – Liverpool Street Station) and 94A (Willesden – Liverpool Street Station, with supplementary service between Liverpool Street Station and Elephant & Castle) were withdrawn in their entirety after operation on the night of Friday/Saturday 14/15 July 1916. A notice, placed in *Municipal Journal* of 21 July 1916 by LGOC, attributed the need to 'temporarily' withdraw routes 94 and 94A, as well as a number of daytime bus routes, as being due 'to the restrictions in the supply of petrol'. Inter-station routes 93 and 95 were recorded on both official LGOC Route Cards, as well as in Traffic Notice 85, as having been withdrawn after operation on Wednesday morning 23 August 1916, thereby eliminating all-night bus operation from the streets of London.

Electric Railway and Tramway Journal of 6 August 1915 reported that Metropolitan Electric Tramways had made special arrangements with the government in respect of the Enfield small arms factory 'to run special cars all day and all night to convey workers to and from those shops.' In support of the war effort a number of LGOC daytime routes were boosted during 1916 by the addition of 'munitions service' journeys, which mostly ran in the early hours of the morning, to convey workers to sites such as at Colindale, Park Royal and, principally, Woolwich Arsenal.

Following the demise of London's all-night bus routes, the only all-night road passenger transport services to operate in the capital, apart from munitions services, were provided by 16 London County Council tramcars. Six cars continued to provide all-night services over parts of the network in north and east London, whilst ten cars covered sections of the tramway south of the River Thames. These cars continued to operate to the reduced schedules introduced by February 1916.

The debilitating effects of the War intensified privations and increased the strain upon resources, such that speculation arose concerning the withdrawal of LCC Tramways all-night tram services. *The Electric Railway and Tramway Journal* issue of 19 April 1918 reported that Sir Albert Stanley, President of the Board of Trade, had said, 'So far as I know it is not seriously proposed to curtail (London's) night services.'

The Electric Railway and Tramway Journal issue of 9 August 1918 reported, 'Metropolitan Electric Tramways are trying the experiment for one month of running cars at 1.00am and 1.30am from Finsbury Park to Wood Green for the convenience of printers and other newspaper workers'. At the time Finsbury Park was the northern terminus of the Underground's Piccadilly Line.

An Armistice, which ended the First World War, was signed on 11 November 1918.

CHAPTER 2
ALL-NIGHT BUS ROUTE REVIVAL

K 76 has been stopped outside the Punch Tavern at 99 Fleet Street, just west of Ludgate Circus, by two LGOC officials to allow the photographer to take this view in late 1923. The top and bottom 'via boards' as displayed on this route 94A bus have transposed the correct sequence of routeing.
TfL/London Transport Museum

The transition from war to peace did little to improve the fortunes of an exhausted, war-weary nation, further subjected to the effects of the Spanish 'Flu outbreak in late 1918 and early 1919, which pandemic caused more deaths around the world than those of the First World War. Shortages of manpower and materials persisted long after the cessation of hostilities. At the beginning of 1920 just 16 tramcars, still operating to the reduced wartime schedules introduced by February 1916, provided, on Sunday to Friday nights, the sole night-time public road passenger transport services in London. The *Electric Railway and Tramway Journal* issue of 8 July 1919 recorded that London County Council Tramways all-night trams ran a weekly car mileage of 1,470 which yielded average receipts of 6.19d per car mile against which operating costs calculated at 14.27d a car mile had to be offset with resultant loss of 8.08d per car mile. That journal commented, 'The all-night services have always been run at a loss, but in view of the public convenience afforded, the services have been continued. As the Council is no doubt aware no similar services are provided by the omnibus companies of any other Metropolitan street passenger authority.'

SOME ALL-NIGHT TRAM ROUTE EXTENSIONS . . .
AND A RETRACTION

The night of Sunday/Monday 16/17 May 1920 saw the introduction of a 1½ mile long extension of the Brixton night tram route, beyond its Water Lane terminus, to travel via Brixton Hill and Streatham Hill to reach a new terminal point outside St. Leonard's Church in Streatham High Road. The extended route maintained its former 28-minute frequency, thereby necessitating an increase in allocation from two to three trams from Streatham (Telford Avenue) depot, now passed *en route*, to cover the extended Streatham to Blackfriars (John Carpenter Street) route. Having been introduced as an experiment, at the request of night workers living in Streatham, this first post-First World War extension to the night tram network did not prove remunerative since the extension to Streatham was withdrawn after operation on the night of Friday/Saturday 11/12 March 1921. Thereafter the route reverted to its former operation, between Brixton (Water Lane) and Blackfriars, with a related reduction in allocation back to two tramcars.

The practice of enhancing London's all-night road passenger transport services to handle hordes of New Year's Eve revellers is long established. *Electric Railway and Tramway Journal* issue of 7 January 1921 reported that, 'On New Year's Eve (Friday night / Saturday morning 31 December 1920 / 1 January 1921) the all-night service of the London County Council Tramways was considerably enhanced and, in addition, special late services ran on other routes.'

From Tuesday night/Wednesday morning 31 January/ 1 February 1922, both the Brixton and Tooting night tram routes underwent a significant alteration to terminal working arrangements at their London end. Prior to that date, the Brixton route had reached the Embankment by way of Blackfriars Bridge, terminating at John Carpenter Street, whilst the Tooting route had crossed Westminster Bridge to reach its terminus along the Embankment at Waterloo

Bridge. From the night of 31 January/1 February 1922, both routes were revised to form an extremely long loop-shaped terminal working which utilised the full length of Victoria Embankment. At Kennington Gate, night tramcars from Brixton were re-routed via Kennington Road to reach Victoria Embankment via Westminster Bridge and to depart Victoria Embankment via Blackfriars Bridge, thence travelling via Elephant & Castle and Kennington Park Road to complete a traverse of the loop at Kennington Gate. Night tramcars from Tooting performed exactly the opposite manoeuvre, that is to say, from Kennington Gate they travelled via Kennington Park Road and Elephant & Castle to reach Victoria Embankment via Blackfriars Bridge. The full length of Victoria Embankment was then traversed before Tooting-bound tramcars crossed Westminster Bridge and travelled via Kennington Road to complete their journey over the loop at Kennington Gate. A full circuit of the loop working, from Kennington Gate and back to Kennington Gate, was the considerable distance of 5½ miles. The long-standing transfer facility at Kennington Gate for night tram passengers, first introduced by London County Council Tramways on the night of 25/26 January 1901, was maintained under the revised routeing arrangements. Thus, for example, a passenger from Tooting bound for the Westminster end of Victoria Embankment could transfer at Kennington Gate on to a Westminster Bridge bound tramcar from Brixton, thereby avoiding the need to travel 'the long way' round the loop via Blackfriars Bridge. The revised routeing required an allocation of three tramcars on each route from Sunday nights to Friday nights – Clapham depot provided three tramcars for the Tooting route whilst Streatham depot allocated three for the Brixton night route, which included some positioning journeys in service to and from Streatham (Telford Avenue) depot.

It will be recalled that the Embankment (Waterloo Bridge) – New Cross (Marquis of Granby) via Old Kent Road night tram route had been extended, on 17/18 April 1914, to Catford (Rushey Green), only to have this extension withdrawn barely six months later, after operation on 16/17 October 1914, due to wartime exigencies. Happily, this 2½-mile long extension to Catford was reinstated from Sunday night/Monday morning 19/20 November 1922. The previously prevailing 30-minute frequency was maintained on this route, so necessitating an increase in allocation from two to three tramcars from New Cross depot.

By the night of 31 December 1922/1 January 1923, the frequency of the Stamford Hill – Holborn route was altered to give an even 30-minute headway, as opposed to the alternate 25- and 50-minute frequency imposed by February 1916, during the First World War. However, extremely tight scheduling – a characteristic of all-night tram routes – which allowed just one minute layover/recovery time at termini after each 29-minute long journey, meant that Stamford Hill depot's allocation for the route remained constant at just two tramcars. Also established by November 1923 but with origins probably dating back to 25/26 October 1908 were two Monday – Saturday early morning journeys on tram route 21 which departed from Finsbury Park at 3.22am and 4.16am to travel via Holloway, Caledonian Road and King's Cross to

Holborn, Gray's Inn Road whence the return journeys to Finsbury Park left at 3.56am and 4.48am. These journeys were the precursors for North Finchley – Holborn early morning trolleybus journeys on routes 521/621 and which subsequently became Special Night Journeys over motor bus route 221.

REINSTATEMENT OF ALL-NIGHT BUS ROUTES

On the night of Tuesday/Wednesday 17/18 August 1920, London General reinstated all-night bus routes 94 (Cricklewood – Liverpool Street station) and 94A (Willesden – Liverpool Street Station). As reintroduced routes 94 and 94A were but a shadow of their former selves in respect of service frequency. Each route, which operated six nights of the week from Sunday through to Friday, was scheduled to work just three return journeys respectively, with an allocation of one bus from Cricklewood garage (94) and one bus from Willesden garage (94A). Prior to their wartime suspension over four years earlier, after operation on 14/15 July 1916, each route had a 30-minute frequency, which had necessitated an allocation of four buses from Cricklewood garage for route 94 and five buses from Willesden garage for route 94A – the greater allocation from Willesden having been necessary to cover the 94A's supplementary early morning service between Liverpool Street Station and Elephant & Castle, which spur working was not reinstated in 1920. Some minor alterations to outer terminal arrangements were also made. On reintroduction, the Cricklewood terminus of route 94 became the LGOC Garage, rather than 'The Crown' as formerly used. The Willesden terminus of route 94A remained at Pound Lane on reinstatement, but from the night of 6/7 October 1920 was moved into LGOC's Willesden garage, situated off Pound Lane. Both routes subsequently underwent detailed timing adjustments to provide better connections with trains at Liverpool Street station. From Monday night/Tuesday morning 17/18 April 1922, route 94 had an additional bus allocated to work an earlier return journey which left Cricklewood at 11.42pm and returned from Liverpool Street Station at 12.30am. That additional journey was also introduced on Sunday nights from 7/8 May 1922. On Sunday night/Monday morning 18/19 November 1923 an additional early morning short-working between Willesden Garage and Bank, was introduced on route 94A. Routes 94 and 94A were co-ordinated to give an approximately hourly combined headway over their lengthy common section of route between Edgware Road (junction Chapel Street) and Liverpool Street Station.

An insight into how LGOC regarded all-night bus routes 94 and 94A was given by an extract from the London General Bus Map of October 1923. That map informed readers that the LGOC system then comprised 155 motor bus routes, of which total the company claimed that 34 made no contribution to its profits. Included amongst those 34 unprofitable routes were the 94 and 94A which 'run throughout the night between Liverpool Street and Willesden or Cricklewood, for the benefit of night workers'. After stating that the 94 and 94A 'had never paid', London General continued, '(it) would be a hardship to discontinue (the routes), as those who have made their homes in Willesden or Cricklewood might suffer.'

THE LUDGATE CIRCUS SPECIAL NIGHT JOURNEYS

During 1921 London General's vehicle situation began to improve. Significant numbers of 46-seat K-type buses entered service whilst the first production models of the even larger capacity 54-seat S-type entered service from July 1921. A spirit of cautious optimism emanated from London General, leading to the introduction, from 1 June 1921, of later 'last' journeys on a number of daytime routes such as, for example, a later weekday 11.34pm departure from Oxford Circus to Croydon on route 59.

Towards the end of 1921 and continuing into 1922 London General introduced a limited night service over nine bus routes, seven of which terminated at Ludgate Circus – a location also served by existing all-night bus routes 94 and 94A. Ludgate Circus, which forms the crossroads between Fleet Street, Farringdon Street, Ludgate Hill and New Bridge Street, was truly at the very hub of the then-extant newspaper industry, for which industry's workers the new night routes were introduced. The development – and in some cases withdrawal – of these routes between their various dates of introduction in 1921 and the night of 29/30 November 1924, after which all such surviving routes were renumbered under the Bassom scheme, is detailed in Table B opposite.

The Ludgate Circus Special Night Journeys were either night time workings over, or utilised buses allocated to, daytime routes of equivalent number with the exception of route number 88A. It is not clear what route numbers, if any, were displayed by buses working these Special Night Journeys which worked inbound to Ludgate Circus before departing from Ludgate Circus on return journeys between 12.30am and 1am, according to route.

Operation of three of the 'Ludgate Circus' night bus routes – 28, 45 and 63 – was discontinued after only four weeks. Monday-Friday night route 45, and complementary Sunday night route 63 journey, between Ludgate Circus and Chalk Farm covered a common section of route between Holborn and Camden Town with London County Council Tramways' hourly frequency all-night tram route between Holborn and Hampstead. It would seem that the established all-night tram service prevailed in this competitive situation, resulting in the early demise of the two night bus routes. The Sunday night working on route 28 to Golders Green, withdrawn after operation on 27/28 November 1921, was in effect a complementary working on Sunday nights to the Monday-Friday night journeys on route 13 to Hendon, which continued to be operated.

NIGHT SERVICE ON ROUTES 11 AND 29

On Sunday night/Monday morning, 6/7 November 1921, London General introduced a single night-time journey over part of existing daytime route 29 (Victoria Station – Old Southgate). A Palmers Green garage-based bus worked one return journey between Palmers Green and Finsbury Park, departing Palmers Green at 1.09am and returning from Finsbury Park at 1.33am. This journey, which operated on Sunday to Friday nights, provided a connection from Finsbury Park with both the last Piccadilly Line Underground train – at that date the Line's northern terminus – as well as with

Table B: Route Profiles – Ludgate Circus Special Night Journeys
Period – Night 6/7 November 1921 to Night 29/30 November 1924

Route No	Outer Terminal	Date	Commentary	Night(s)	Journey	Garage
88A	Turnham Green	17/18 April 1922	Introduced	M–Fr	1 return	V
		30 Apr/1 May 1922	Sunday night journey introduced	Su–Fr	1 return	
4	Finsbury Park	6/7 Nov 1921	Introduced	Su–Sa	1 return	J
		27/28 Nov 1921	Sun night journey withdrawn	M–Sa	1 return	
		28/29 Oct 1922	Sat night journey withdrawn	M–Fr	1 return	
9	Barnes	6/7 Nov 1921	Introduced	Su–Fr	1 return	M
	(Mortlake Garage)	27/28 Nov 1921	Sun night journey withdrawn	M–Fr	1 return	
28	Golders Green	6/7 Nov 1921	Introduced	Su	2 return	AE
		27/28 Nov 1921	Withdrawn			
63	Chalk Farm	6/7 Nov 1921	Introduced	Su	1 return	CF
		27/28 Nov 1921	Withdrawn			
13	Hendon Garage	7/8 Nov 1921	Introduced	M–Fr	1 return	AE
45	Chalk Farm	7/8 Nov 1921	Introduced	M–Fr	1 return	J *
		25/26 Nov 1921	Withdrawn			

NOTE:
Introduction dates were first night of operation.
Withdrawal dates were last night of operation.
* Allocation of route 45 (Clapham Common – King's Cross) transferred from J (Holloway) to AL (Merton) Garage from 16/17 November 1921.

the night time journey arriving from Ludgate Circus on route 4. It seems that the Special Night Journey on route 29 was withdrawn after operation on 2/3 December 1921 but reinstated from 8/9 March 1922 to operate Monday to Friday nights. Saturday night working was added on 14/15 June 1924.

On the morning of Monday 14 November 1921 two early morning journeys were introduced over a section of route 11 (Shepherds Bush – Liverpool Street Station). From that date two buses from Hammersmith garage worked Monday to Saturday morning journeys which departed Hammersmith bound for Liverpool Street Station at 4.03am and 4.18am and returned from Liverpool Street station at 5.04am and 5.19am. These journeys were retimed, by 4 July 1923, to leave Hammersmith at 3.56am and 4.18am and to return from Liverpool Street Station at 4.56am and 5.18am.

The introduction of the 'Ludgate Circus' Special Night Journeys, along with night journeys on routes 11 and 29, was clearly a speculative move by London General. Not all of these routes proved to be viable, as witnessed by the early withdrawal of the SNJs allied to routes 28, 45 and 63. The surviving routes did prove to be more enduring, none more so than the SNJs on routes 9 and 11 which continued in slightly modified, but still quite recognisable, form up until London Transport's major reorganisation of its All-Night Bus Network on 13/14 April 1984. The SNJs over route 9 survived even that major upheaval, continuing to operate up to 18/19 September 1987, whilst route 11's journeys became incorporated into current route N11.

By 29/30 June 1924, a combined total of 30 trams and buses was needed to maintain London's night-time road passengers transport services on Monday to Friday nights, the combined figure dropping to 26 on Sunday nights. Tram allocations had increased from 16 needed for night services at the beginning of 1920 up to 20. The night bus network, reinstated in 1920, needed a maximum of ten buses to maintain services over the various night routes. When comparing the ratio of trams to buses it must be borne in mind that 18 of the 20 tramcars were in service on routes with a continuous all-night service.

Only two bus routes, 94 and 94A, worked a comparable all-night service, with the bulk of the night bus allocation simply operating a return Special Night Journey over their appropriate route. The tramcar still very much dominated the operation of London's night time road passenger transport services at 29/30 June 1924.

Under the terms of the 1924 London Traffic Act it became necessary for bus operators to obtain the consent of the Commissioner of the Metropolitan Police in respect of routes operated from Monday 1 December 1924. From that same date the Commissioner initiated a re-numbering of London bus routes, which scheme became dubbed the 'Bassom System' after Assistant Chief Constable Bassom, the police officer responsible for devising and implementing details of the scheme. The Bassom System required all shortworkings of a route to be given a suffix letter whilst bifurcations or deviations required a separate route number.

Table C: Bassom System – Sequential Renumbering of Night Bus Routes extant night 30 Nov/1Dec 1924 until night 3 Oct 1934

Original Route Number	Bassom System Route Number	Effective from	Terminals/Notes
4	4B	1/2 Dec 1924	Ludgate Circus-Finsbury Park
9	9C	1/2 Dec 1924	Ludgate Circus-Barnes
11	11D	30 Nov/1 Dec 1924	Hammersmith-Liverpool Street Station
13	13B	1/2 Dec 1924	Ludgate Circus-Hendon
29	29D	1/2 Dec 1924	Finsbury Park-Palmers Green
	129A	8/9 April 1925	Renumbered
	529B	26/27 November 1929	Renumbered
	29C	29/30 March 1934	Renumbered
88A	188	1/2 Dec 1924	Ludgate Circus-Turnham Green
	189	10/11 April 1925	Renumbered
	189	3/4 July 1934	Withdrawn
94	94	30 Nov/1 Dec 1924	Cricklewood-Liverpool Street Station
94A	91	30 Nov/1 Dec 1924	Willesden-Liverpool Street Station
94A	91A	30 Nov/1 Dec 1924	1 return journey shortworking Willesden-Bank
	91A	24/25 Feb 1925	Shortworking absorbed into daytime route 18.

As may be seen from Table C, the only route extant on the night of 30 November/1 December 1924 to retain its original route number was all-night route 94. The only other contemporary all-night bus route 94A became route 91. The latter route's single return short-working between Willesden and Bank became officially numbered route 91A, but on 24/25 February 1925 this journey was rerouted via Southwark Bridge to London Bridge Station and incorporated into the schedule of daytime route 18. All other night bus journeys, with the exception of route 88A, which was renumbered 188 because it bifurcated from the 88 route, received the addition of a suffix letter to their original route numbers.

The Bassom System was complicated and must have created difficulties for LGOC staff in its interpretation and implementation. Confusion certainly crept into official circles concerning route 88A's renumbering. According to Traffic Circular No 524, dated 13 December 1924, the 88A's Sunday to Friday night return journey between Turnham Green and Ludgate Circus had been renumbered as route 188. However, the December 1924 LGOC map referred to this journey as route 88D, whilst by the issue of the next map, in January 1925, it had become route 188D. By the time of issue of the March 1925 map, both mapmaker and Traffic Circular compiler agreed that it was indeed route 188! The Monday-Friday night single bus allocation for route 188 was changed from Turnham Green garage to Hammersmith garage, co-incident with the introduction of the Bassom System on 1 December 1924, although 188's Sunday night allocation remained with Turnham Green garage. As Table C shows, certain routes were renumbered during the period of the Bassom System, principally because the night route number

in use was required for a route elsewhere in London. The Bassom System survived in use for almost ten years until replaced by a revised route-numbering system introduced from 3 October 1934 by the then newly-formed London Passenger Transport Board.

ALL-NIGHT TRAM SERVICES TO CHISWICK AND HAMMERSMITH

London County Council Tramways' timetable of 'All-Night Cars' dated September 1925 detailed timings of an all-night service over the tramway between Chiswick (Young's Corner) and Vauxhall via Hammersmith Broadway, Putney Bridge, Wandsworth, Clapham Junction and Wandsworth Road. This night service covered a significant section of daytime tram route 26 (Kew Bridge – Borough), which route number *may* have been displayed on the single tramcar from Jews Row, Wandsworth depot allocated to work the night service. This operation is of particular interest because a service was provided on all seven nights of the week, unlike the remainder of extant all-night tram services which did not operate on Saturday nights/Sunday mornings. Journeys operated nightly at 1.25am from Chiswick, Young's Corner to Vauxhall, 2.05am from Vauxhall to Hammersmith and 2.38am from Hammersmith to Vauxhall. A 3.14am journey operated from Vauxhall to Chiswick, Young's Corner on Monday to Saturday mornings.

The September 1928 timetable remained essentially as at September 1925 except that the 2.38am Hammersmith to Vauxhall journey no longer operated on Sunday mornings. By November 1932 the journey from Chiswick, Young's Corner to Vauxhall had been truncated to start from Hammersmith at 1.30am on Monday to Saturday mornings (it still ran from Young's Corner on Sunday mornings at 1.22am) whilst the 2.38am departure from Hammersmith had become extended to run to Westminster, County Hall with a return journey from County Hall to Hammersmith at 3.20am.

1926 – THE GENERAL STRIKE AND GYRATORY ROAD SYSTEMS

Deteriorating industrial relations, combined with political unrest, led to the declaration of a General Strike effective from midnight on Monday/Tuesday 3/4 May 1926. It is of interest to note, in the context of night-time road passenger transport services, that the catalyst for the General Strike was the refusal of the Trades Union Congress to repudiate action by printers of the Daily Mirror, who had refused to print an anti-union editorial. Most London County Council Tramways and London General Omnibus Company's employees withdrew their labour, thereby paralysing the capital's road passenger transport networks. Attempts were made to break the strike on the buses through the use of volunteer crews to work emergency circular routes, but any successes achieved by such efforts were small in relation to the scale of disruption to services. Given the difficulty of running emergency daytime services under the prevailing conditions, when a police escort was often essential, it is certain that no all-night bus or tram services ran for the duration of the Strike, which was called off at 12.30pm on Wednesday 12 May 1926. The cumulative effects of the Strike prevented LCC Tramways from restoring a full service across its network until Sunday 16 May 1926, thus making it likely that all-night tram services were restored from Sunday night/Monday morning 16/17 May 1926. LGOC restored a full service from Saturday 15 May 1926, thus the Saturday night/Sunday morning journey on route 129A may have been the first night bus service to be resumed.

Traffic congestion has proved to be an abiding problem in London. In the 1920s, gyratory road systems were hailed as the panacea to such difficulties, with a rash of such one-way traffic flow systems being introduced in central London in 1926. Newly introduced gyratory traffic flows affected both daytime and all-night bus routes, but in the context of this volume their impact on the latter category of routes only is discussed.

TRAFALGAR SQUARE

From Monday 26 April 1926 a clockwise direction gyratory traffic flow was introduced around Trafalgar Square. Prior to that date traffic flows had been bidirectional around all sides of the Square. Eastbound early morning journeys on route 11D, which had previously turned right from Whitehall into Strand, were diverted via the west and north sides of the Square before exiting along Duncannon Street to regain their original line of route along Strand. All-night routes 91 and 94 had previously been routed along the south side of the Square in both directions of travel. Eastbound journeys on routes 91 and 94 were rerouted via Pall Mall East, Trafalgar Square (north side) and Duncannon Street while westbound journeys retained their original line of route via Trafalgar Square (south side) and Cockspur Street. Special Night Journeys on

9C, 13B and 189 remained unaltered as these routes already complied with the traffic flow requirements of the new gyratory scheme. In later years, as the All-Night Bus Network intensified and Trafalgar Square became the focal point for all-night operations, circuitous workings around the Square, to the pattern introduced on 26 April 1926, became a notable characteristic of the all-night bus scene.

Other Central London gyratory systems introduced in 1926 were at Parliament Square on 3/4 January (route 11D), at Hyde Park Corner on 21/22 March (route 9C), and at Marble Arch from 31 October/1 November (routes 91, 94, 189). The most extensive scheme, introduced from 25/26 July 1926, affected traffic flows between Piccadilly Circus and Pall Mall with all eastbound journeys on routes 9C, 13B, 91, 94 and 189 routed via Haymarket and all westbound journeys routed via Waterloo Place. Before this date journeys in both directions on routes 9C and 189 had been routed via Waterloo Place whilst journeys in both directions on routes 13B, 91 and 94 had been routed via Haymarket.

Table D: London General Omnibus Company Ltd Official Allocation of Bus Types to All-Night Bus Routes at 23/24 February 1927				
Route Number	Bus Type			Garage
	M–Fr	Sa	Su	
4B	1 NSo	-	-	J
9C	1 NSc	-	-	M
11D	2 NSc	-	2 NSc	R
13B	1 S	-	-	AE
91	1 NSc	-	1 NSc	AC
94	2 NSc	-	2 NSc	W
129A	1 NSc	1 NSc	-	AD
189	1 S	-	-	R
	-	-	1 NSo	V
GRAND TOTAL	10 buses	1 bus	6 buses	
KEY: NSc - NS type covered-top				
NSo - NS type open-top				
S - S type open-top				

Table D, extracted from LGOC's first published Allocation Book, shows that at the night of Wednesday/Thursday 23/24 February 1927 three night bus routes, 4B, 13B and 189, continued to be worked by open-top buses. At that time covered-top buses were a relatively new phenomenon with the first NS-types so equipped having only entered service in 1925.

From the night of 19/20 October 1927 Turnham Green garage regained from Hammersmith garage the allocation for the Monday-Friday return night journey on route 189. Turnham Green used an open-top NS-type bus for this duty, as it already did with its Sunday night turn on the route.

London General added a new route to the 'Ludgate Circus' group of night bus routes from Tuesday night/Wednesday morning 15/16 November 1927. Numbered 601, and operating between Ludgate Circus and Leyton, Bakers Arms, the route number selected was numerically the first in a new 6xx series of LGOC bus routes. Under the manifold ramifications of the Bassom route-numbering system, the Metropolitan Police had run out of any clear series of route numbers below 600. The new 6xx series of route numbers was progressively extended to embrace both daytime and night-time newly introduced LGOC bus routes. The 601, which operated on Sunday night/Monday mornings to Friday night/Saturday mornings, was initially covered by one covered-top NS-type bus worked out of Leyton garage. In a similar manner to the other 'Ludgate Circus' night bus routes, the 601 comprised one return journey which departed Leyton, Bakers Arms, at 12.03am (12.06am on Sunday night) with return from Ludgate Circus timed at 12.50am. Clearly intended, like the other 'Ludgate Circus' night bus routes, to serve newspaper workers in the Fleet Street area, the 601 ran parallel to night bus routes 91 and 94 as far as Bank, whence it travelled via Bishopsgate to Shoreditch. From here the 601 ran along Kingsland Road, also served by London County Council Tramways' Stamford Hill night tram service, to Dalston, whence the 601 branched off into new territory as far as night bus operations were concerned, travelling via Hackney Downs, Clapton and Lea Bridge Road to the Bakers Arms.

1928 – ALL-NIGHT TRAM ROUTE EXTENSIONS

On Sunday night/Monday morning 29/30 April 1928, London County Council Tramways projected its Victoria Embankment to Catford all-night tram service 1½ miles beyond the route's Catford (St Laurence's Church) terminus to reach a new terminal point at Downham (Bromley Road). The reason for this route extension was because by then London County Council was well advanced with the development of a new housing estate at Downham, located at the outer extremity of LCC's area close to the boundary with Kent. The tramway itself was being projected, in stages, along Downham Way within the new housing estate with the first section, as far as Valeswood Road, getting a service on daytime tram route 54 from 28 September 1926. The intention was to extend the tramway right through the estate to Grove Park, which objective was first served by daytime tram routes on 15 November 1928. That section of tramway along Downham Way was equipped with overhead electrical power supply, being linked up with the conduit-powered tramway, and hence the rest of the LCC network, through the use of a change-pit situated at the west end of Downham Way, just before its junction with Bromley Road. The new Downham extension to the all-night tram network terminated on the conduit-equipped track in Bromley Road, thereby obviating any need to use the change-pit during the night. Such usage would have resulted in increased cost and manpower implications for LCC Tramways but the resultant economies achieved meant that passengers living on the new Downham housing estate had to walk to and from Bromley Road to access the all-night tram service. By tinkering with the route's previous regular 30-minute frequency to give an irregular headway, which varied between

26 and 38 minutes, LCC Tramways contrived to cover the extended route, which now linked Downham with Victoria Embankment (Savoy Street) via Catford, Lewisham, New Cross Gate and Old Kent Road, by still using only three tramcars out of New Cross depot. These tramcars worked eight return journeys over the route as well as three short-workings into, and out of, service between New Cross Gate and Victoria Embankment.

From Tuesday night/Wednesday morning 17/18 July 1928 London County Council Tramways succeeded in combining operations of the Tooting Broadway – Victoria Embankment and Brixton – Victoria Embankment all-night tram routes, which involved a four-mile-long route extension to the Brixton service, whilst avoiding any increase over the previous two routes' allocation of six tramcars. To effect this change the Brixton all-night route was projected beyond its Water Lane terminus via Streatham, Mitcham Lane and Southcroft Road to Tooting Broadway, where it met up with the all-night tram route from Victoria Embankment via Clapham. Effectively operation of the all-night tram routes via Brixton and via Clapham were combined into a figure of eight route working pattern over which tramcars followed cyclical working patterns, as shown in Appendix 3. Through adoption of this cyclical working pattern, as well as by marginally increasing each route's frequency from a previous 28 minutes to 30 minutes, LCC Tramways was able to cover the increased route mileage with three tramcars from Clapham depot and three tramcars from Streatham depot. The long-standing interchange arrangement at Kennington Gate between Blackfriars Bridge and Westminster Bridge routeings was maintained. This newly established figure of eight working for the night services to Tooting Broadway was destined to become an enduring feature of the London all-night tram and, following tramway conversion, all-night bus scene. Although the subsequent replacement bus route workings, by then numbered N87, were re-routed away from the Embankment loop to follow a new bidirectional loop working between Blackfriars Bridge and Westminster Bridge via Strand, Trafalgar Square and Whitehall from 25/26 April 1975, the principle of the cyclical working pattern established on 17/18 July 1928 was maintained for nearly 56 years until final operation on the night of 12/13 April 1984. LCC Tramways' achievement in succeeding to cover an additional 5½ route miles over the Downham and Tooting Broadway all-night tram routes with near 30-minute frequency services, whilst avoiding any increase in tramcar allocation, reflected great credit upon that organisation and, particularly, its scheduling officers.

Patronage of all-night tram routes at this time would seem to have been high. Figures published by LCC Tramways relating to 1928/1929 quoted revenue of 12.6 (old) pence per mile for night cars, which compared well with revenue of 14.6 (old) pence per mile for all tramcar mileage.

Left NS 1147 waits departure time from Liverpool Street bound for Turnham Green on route 614. *C F Klapper / The Omnibus Society, courtesy David Ruddom*

EXPANSION OF THE ALL-NIGHT BUS NETWORK

Until 1928 only two bus routes, 91 and 94, provided a true all-night service. Other night bus routes of that era – 4B, 9C, 11D, 13B, 129A, 189 and 601 – simply comprised single return journey workings (two such in the case of route 11D). From Tuesday night/Wednesday morning 17/18 July 1928 London General introduced a further five night bus routes, three of which were scheduled to give a full all-night service, thereby considerably expanding the night bus network into districts of London previously not served. The three new routes with an all-night service on six nights of the week (Saturday night/ Sunday morning excepted) comprised:

Route 39D: Tottenham (LGOC Garage) – Charing Cross (Trafalgar Square)

Timetable		am	am	am	am	am	am	am	am
Tottenham	dep	12.10	1.10	1.34	2.34	3.20	4.20	4.46	5.46
Charing Cross	dep	12.52	1.52	2.16	3.16	4.02	5.02	5.28	6.28

Running Time: 40 minutes. **Garage:** Tottenham. **Allocation:** 2 NS-type (covered-top).
Note: Under the Bassom system of route numbering, route number 39D was formed as a derivative of daytime route number 39 (Edmonton (Angel) – Southfields Station).

Route 614: Turnham Green (LGOC Garage) – Liverpool Street Station

Timetable		pm	am	am	am	am	am
Turnham Green	dep	11.37	12.57	2.25	3.22	4.23	5.27
Liverpool Street	dep	12.35am	1.55	3.23	4.30	5.26	6.25

Running Time: 55 minutes. **Garage:** Turnham Green. **Allocation:** 2 NS-type(covered-top)

Route 617: Upton Park (Forest Gate LGOC Garage) – Charing Cross (Trafalgar Square)

Timetable		pm	am	am	am	am	am
Forest Gate	dep	11.48	12.38	1.32	2.57	3.48	4.48
Charing Cross	dep	12.40am	1.30	2.18	3.55	4.40	5.40

Running Time: 50 minutes. **Garage:** Forest Gate. **Allocation:** 2 NS-type (covered-top).

NS 2015 was photographed heading southwest down Queen Victoria Street on route 94. *C F Klapper*

Routes 39D and 617 were landmark all-night routes in two important respects. They were the very first LGOC-operated night bus routes to use Charing Cross (Trafalgar Square) as a terminal point. Secondly, these two routes were the first all-night bus routes to serve certain important thoroughfares in the West End. Route 39D plied the length of Charing Cross Road whilst the 617 was routed from Piccadilly Circus along Shaftesbury Avenue before joining Charing Cross Road at Cambridge Circus. These streets were – and indeed still are – at the very heart of London's entertainment industry. Shaftesbury Avenue is renowned for its many theatres, whilst Leicester Square, just off Charing Cross Road, has acted as a magnet for cinemagoers, dancers and diners for very many years. In the now Roaring Twenties, lifestyle for some had become rather frenetic, perhaps in an attempt to expunge from minds still-recent memories of the suffering caused by the First World War. Racy dances, like the Charleston, had arrived from America, whilst in 1927 'talkies' started to supersede silent-screen movies. The relatively closely-timed second and third trips on both routes 39D and 617 perhaps hinted that LGOC saw some potential traffic from those returning home after a night in the West End, either as revellers or, much more likely, as workers in the various entertainment and catering establishments. Indeed the contemporary *Hotel Industry Magazine* started to publish timetables for these services which it described as 'Special Night Service of Omnibuses for Hotel Workers.'

Route 39D crossed the lines of the Hampstead night tram service at Camden Town and those of the Highgate night tram service at Holloway, before traversing the full length of Seven Sisters Road to reach Tottenham. In addition to its routeing through the West End, route 617 also served those working in the newspaper industry around Holborn, leaving the City on the most direct route after Bank via Cornhill to Aldgate. The 617 restored an all-night service to Mile End Road and Bow Road, a major traffic artery that had suffered the loss of its original all-night public service *circa* October 1915 when LCC Tramways had withdrawn its night time Bow Bridge – Aldgate night tram route. The section of route 617 between Bow Bridge and Stratford reintroduced an all-night service over that part of the route once served by London's very first all-night public road passenger transport service, the Stratford – Aldgate all-night tram route introduced by The North Metropolitan Tramways Company on 1/2 January 1899. New route 614 shared a lengthy common section of routeing, between Piccadilly Circus and Liverpool Street Station, with established all-night bus routes 91 and 94. From Piccadilly Circus westwards to its Turnham Green terminus the 614 represented an almost new all-night facility. Between Piccadilly Circus and Knightsbridge the 614 shared common routeing with single return journey route 9C, meeting the 9C again at Hammersmith. The section of route 614 along Brompton Road, through South Kensington and along Fulham Road represented new territory as far as all-night bus operation was concerned. At Walham Green the 614 followed the routeing, via Dawes Road and Fulham Palace Road to Hammersmith, also used by the early morning journeys on route 11D. The section of route 614 between Hammersmith and Chiswick, Young's Corner, was shared

with the tramway used by LCC Tramways' single night-time return journey between Young's Corner and Vauxhall over tram route 26. The 614 shared common routeing with single return journey Ludgate Circus route 189 along Chiswick High Road to the two routes' common terminus at Turnham Green, LGOC garage.

The other two night bus routes introduced on the night of 17/18 July 1928 were correctly described as providing an Early Morning Service in LGOC's Traffic Circular 719, which heralded the introduction of routes 615 and 616. Both these new routes worked between common termini at Liverpool Street Station and Aldwych. The 615, with 3.27am, 3.55am and 5.18am departures from Liverpool Street, was routed via Bank, Cheapside, Holborn Circus, High Holborn and Kingsway. The 616, with 4.38am and 4.58am departures from Liverpool Street, travelled via Houndsditch, Aldgate, Fenchurch Street, Gracechurch Street and King William Street to Bank whence route 616 shared identical routeing with the 615 to their common terminal point on the east side of Aldwych. At this date both Aldwych and Strand carried two directional traffic flows. Returning buses on routes 615 and 616 completed a circuit via Aldwych (east side), Strand and Aldwych (west side) to regain their line of route in Kingsway. The prime purpose of new routes 615 and 616, which operated on Monday to Saturday mornings, was to convey cleaning ladies – colloquially known as 'chars' or 'Mrs Mops' – arriving by train at both Liverpool Street and Fenchurch Street stations to their places of work in City offices. Significant early morning trains at Liverpool Street station included 3.20am and 3.40am arrivals from Brentwood along with a 3.37am arrival from Chingford.

Routes 615 and 616 incorporated 'When Working' garage journeys in service between Dalston garage and Liverpool Street Station via Shoreditch and were operated by covered top NS-type buses from the fleet of the Tramways (MET) Omnibus Company, an LGOC-controlled subsidiary whose buses bore Metropolitan fleet names. Whilst the type of bus first used on routes 615 and 616 is known, uncertainty surrounds the exact number of vehicles allocated. Traffic Circular 719 stated that each route required three buses, implying a combined total of six buses for the two routes. The appropriate Official Allocation Book entry quoted an allocation of two NS-types for route 615 and one NS-type for route 616, giving a combined total of three buses for the two routes. Study of the combined timetables reveals that the 615 and 616 could, in theory, have been worked by just two buses as well as the fact that the two return journeys on route 616 were too closely timed to have been worked by one bus, as quoted in the Allocation Book. It seems likely that routes 615 and 616 shared a combined allocation of three buses. The six buses indicated in Traffic Circular 719 may have represented the LGOC Traffic Department's anticipation of the need for duplication – if so such foresight was vindicated by later developments of route 616.

The advent of pneumatic tyres on buses was innovatory in 1928 to the extent that contemporary LGOC Traffic Circulars highlighted route allocations so converted. The first night bus route to offer its passengers the superior riding qualities of pneumatic-tyred buses was the 9C whose Mortlake garage allocation for daytime route 9, from which the night-time 9C allocation was drawn, was progressively converted from solid-tyred to pneumatic-tyred NS-type buses from 18/19 July 1928 until full conversion had been completed by 17/18 October 1928. On that latter date night bus routes 4B and 189 both suffered a regression, in terms of vehicle age allocation. The 4B's allocation out of Holloway garage was converted from open-top NS-type to older (1920/21) – built open-top K-type whilst Turnham Green garage's allocation for the 189 was switched from open-top NS-type to 1921/23 built open-top S-type.

ALL-NIGHT TRAMS REACH THEIR ZENITH

A press notice released in 1929 by London County Council Tramways stated 'It is more economical to operate late night and early morning cars than to extend the all-night service'. Many daytime tram routes had last outbound departure journeys at around midnight, some even later such as the 1.18am departure from Victoria Embankment (Savoy Street) on route 18 via Westminster Bridge, Kennington and Brixton to Streatham Library. A myriad of weekday early morning Workmen's journeys operated from around 3.00am onwards, often following special routeings to work-related termini such as the Docks or Smithfield. Whilst no all-night tram routes, except route 26, operated on Saturday nights/Sunday mornings, a number of isolated very early Sunday morning journeys, operating between about 4.00am and 7.30am, gave a skeletal service over some sections of the tramway prior to the Sunday daytime schedule starting. A further, distinct category of service was provided by night time Staff tramcars whose origins dated back to the earliest days of tramway operation. Staff tramcars were principally intended to convey tramway staff needed at their depot to work early morning shifts. Tramcars on such workings carried a conductor and operated to a regular, albeit unpublicised, schedule upon which ordinary fare paying passengers could be carried. Only those persons with good 'local knowledge' would have been in a position to make use of such services if necessary.

A further major constraint upon any further expansion of the all-night network lay in the fact that, by mid-1932, London County Council Tramways' track had reached its maximum length of 158.36 miles. The final section of new tramway, apart from later diversionary tracks, to be laid by London County Council Tramways, or indeed its successor London Transport, completed the link along Westhorne Avenue, Eltham and opened to traffic on 30 June 1932. Authorised proposals to extend the tramway further south-west along Westhorne Avenue and Baring Road to link up with the tramway at Grove Park were frustrated by delay in the construction of a railway bridge along Westhorne Avenue and were later rescinded by the London Passenger Transport Board.

On Tuesday night/Wednesday morning 21/22 September 1932 the final significant route extension to London's all-night tram network was implemented when the Battersea (Prince's Head) – Blackfriars route was projected beyond Prince's Head via Wandsworth High Street and Garratt Lane to reach a new terminus at Tooting Broadway. It will be recalled that a section of this extension, between Prince's

Head and Earlsfield, had been briefly covered by this all-night tram route from its inception on 7/8 November 1909 until 30/31 January 1911. Although the route's previously prevailing hourly frequency was maintained, the 1932-dated extension increased the route's through running time considerably, from a previous 30 minutes to 55 minutes, so necessitating an increased allocation of two tramcars from Wandsworth depot to work the service, despite the fact that only three journeys worked through to Tooting Broadway, which returned thence to Blackfriars at 1.35am, 2.35am and 3.35am.

Daytime tram route 21 (North Finchley – Holborn via Caledonian Road) had been jointly operated by London County Council Tramways and Metropolitan Electric Tramways. From 29 January 1931 MET became the sole operator of this route as a result of which the two Monday–Saturday Special Early Morning Journeys on route 21 from Finsbury Park to Holborn became operated from MET's Wood Green depot and so these journeys were extended to enter service from Wood Green at 3.14am and 4.07am. The corresponding return journeys at 3.58am and 4.48am from Holborn were revised to work through to North Finchley.

LPTB 3d single ticket for daytime routes 36, 38 and 40 also incorporated fare stages for the un-numbered all night tram service to Bromley Road, Downham on its reverse side. *Dennis Cox Collection*

MODERNISATION AND REDUCED RUNNING TIMES

No new all-night bus routes were introduced during the final 4½ years remaining to the London General Omnibus Company. The emphasis during that period was on updating all-night bus operations through the introduction of new LT-type AEC Renown and ST-type AEC Regent double-deckers, equipped with more powerful engines than their predecessor types. The improved performance of the buses enabled significant reductions, ranging from five to eight minutes, to be made in all-night bus route running times as detailed in Appendix 4.

Two of the Ludgate Circus night bus routes, 4B and 189, remained operated with open-top K-type and S-type buses respectively until converted to covered top NS-type at the beginning of October 1930. This probably removed open-top bus types from the London all-night bus scene, although the theoretical possibility remained of an open-top S-type appearing on route 13B, for which the source of vehicle-type came from daytime route 13 and which retained a mixed S-type and covered-top NS-type allocation until 3/4 March 1931 when Hendon garage's allocation for route 13 became exclusively covered-top NS-type. From the night of 17/18 January 1933 all LGOC's all-night bus routes, with the exception of Special Night Journeys on routes 4B, 9C, 529B and, possibly, 13B, were operated by LT or ST-type buses.

From the night of 29/30 June 1931 buses on night-time routes 9C, 11D, 13B, 91, 94, 189 and 614 were diverted on eastbound journeys to travel via Aldwych rather than Strand as previously. This change was associated with the introduction of a gyratory traffic flow system in that vicinity. Westbound buses on those routes maintained their former routeing along Strand, whilst journeys on routes 615 and 616 were unaffected by the new gyratory system since, from inception on 17/18 July 1928, these routes had adopted a terminal working from Kingsway via Aldwych (east side), Strand and Aldgate (west side) before regaining Kingsway.

Minor timing adjustments were made to several routes. An increase in the level of frequency of route 616 to give four return journeys from the night of 10/11 May 1932, with departures from Liverpool Street Station at 4.36am, 4.37am, 4.38am and 5.11am, was particularly interesting. The first three departures, within two minutes of each other from Liverpool Street station, were evidence of the duplication necessary on this short route to cope with a surge of passengers arriving at Fenchurch Street station at 4.40am on an early morning steam train from Upminster, which also called at certain District Line stations before Underground trains started.

Whilst LGOC was not destined to introduce any further all-night bus routes, the company was responsible for two

ST 397 is seen in Cornhill, on route 617's original City routeing. This picture is evidence of the substitution of a bus other than the allocated type to an all-night bus route. Forest Gate garage's official allocation to route 617 had been 2 NS (closed top)-type since the route's inception on 17/18 July 1928 until changed to 2 LT-type from 17/18 January 1933. Forest Gate garage did have a substantial number of ST-types allocated to daytime bus routes until 1932 and it is clear that one was used on the 617 on at least this occasion. *C F Klapper/The Omnibus Society, courtesy David Ruddom*

SPECIAL NIGHT SERVICES

Route	Days / Fare	Description
4B	Mon. to Fri. Fare 5d.	*Depart at 1.0 a.m. from* LUDGATE CIRCUS to Ludgate Hill, Aldersgate St., Goswell Rd., Upper St., Blackstock Rd., **FINSBURY PARK STATION.**
9C	Mon. to Fri. Fare 8d.	*Depart at 12.45 a.m. from* LUDGATE CIRCUS to Strand, Piccadilly, Knightsbridge, Kensington Road, Hammersmith Broadway, Castelnau, **MORTLAKE GARAGE.**
13B	Mon. to Fri. Fare 9d.	*Depart at 12.32 a.m. from* LUDGATE CIRCUS to Strand, Regent Street, Oxford Street, Baker Street, Finchley Road, Golders Green Road, **HENDON GARAGE.**
39D	Sun. to Fri. Fare 6d.	CHARING CROSS, Charing Cross Road, Tottenham Court Road, Hampstead Road, Camden Road, Seven Sisters Road, **TOTTENHAM GARAGE.** Time 40 mins. *Charing X dep.* 12.52, 1.52, 2.16, 3.16, 4.11, 5.11, 5.35, 6.35 *a.m.* *Tottenham dep.* 12.10, 1.10, 1.34, 2.34, 3.29, 4.29, 4.53, 5.53 *a.m.*
91	Sun. to Fri. Fare 9d.	LIVERPOOL STREET STN., Moorgate, Bank, Cannon St., Ludgate Hill, Fleet St., Strand, Regent St., Oxford St., Edgware Rd., Harrow Rd., High St., Harlesden, Church Rd., **WILLESDEN GARAGE.** Time 54 mins. *Liverpool Street dep.* 11.56 p.m., 2.32, 4.40 a.m. *Willesden Garage dep.* 11.0 p.m., 1.36, 3.37 a.m. *See also Route 94.*
94	Sun. to Fri. Fare 7d.	LIVERPOOL STREET STN. Bank, Queen Victoria Street, Ludgate Hill, Fleet St., Strand, Trafalgar Square, Piccadilly Circus, Regent Street, Oxford Street, Edgware Rd., Maida Vale, High Road, Kilburn, Cricklewood Broadway, **CRICKLEWOOD GARAGE.** Time 46 mins. *Liverpool Street dep.* 12.30, 1.32, 3.29, 5.30 a.m. *Cricklewood Garage dep.* 11.42 p.m., 12.42, 2.41, 4.38 a.m. *See also Route 91.*
129A	Mon. to Sat. Fare 3d.	*Depart at 1.33 a.m. from* FINSBURY PARK STN. to Seven Sisters Road, Green Lanes, **PALMERS GREEN GARAGE.**
189	Sun. to Fri. Fare 7d	*Dep.—Sundays,* 12.45 a.m., *Mons. to Fris.,* 12.50 a.m. *from* LUDGATE CIRCUS to Strand, Regent Street, Oxford Street, Bayswater Road, Shepherds Bush, Goldhawk Road, **TURNHAM GREEN GARAGE.**
601	Sun. to Fri. Fare 6d.	*Depart at 1.4 a.m. from* LUDGATE CIRCUS to Cannon St., Bank, Bishopsgate, Shoreditch, Kingsland Road, Dalston Lane, Lea Bridge Road, **LEYTON** (Bakers Arms).
614	Sun. to Fri. Fare 9d.	LIVERPOOL STREET STN., Bank, Fleet Street, Charing Cross, Piccadilly, Knightsbridge, Brompton Road, Fulham Road, Dawes Road, Lillie Road, Fulham Palace Rd., King St., **TURNHAM GREEN.** Time 55 mins. *Liverpool St. dep.* 12.35, 1.52, 3.23, 4.32, 5.22, 6.27 a.m. *Turnham Gn. dep.* 11.37 p.m., 12.54, 2.25, 3.20, 4.23, 5.29 a.m.
615	Sun. to Fri. Fare 3d.	STRAND (Aldwych), Kingsway, Holborn, Bank, Moorgate, London Wall, **LIVERPOOL STREET STATION.** Time. 12 mins. *See also Route 616* *Strand dep.* 3.45, 4.22 a.m. *Liverpool Street dep.* 3.30, 3.59 a.m.
616	Sun. to Fri. Fare 3d.	STRAND (Aldwych) Kingsway, Holborn, Bank, King William Street, Gracechurch Street, Fenchurch Street, Aldgate, Houndsditch, **LIVERPOOL STREET STN.** Time 16 mins. *See also Route 615.* *Strand dep.* 5.0, 5.16, 5.32 a.m. *Liverpool Street dep.* 4.36, 4.38, 5.11 a.m.
617	Sun. to Fri. Fare 8d.	CHARING CROSS, Piccadilly Circus, Shaftesbury Avenue, New Oxford Street, Holborn, Bank, Aldgate, Bow Road, Stratford Broadway, Romford Road, Green Street, **FOREST GATE GARAGE.** Time 50 mins. *Charing Cross dep.* 12.40, 1.30, 2.25, 3.55, 4.42, 5.50 a.m. *Forest Gate Garage dep.* 11.48 p.m., 12.38, 1.32, 2.57, 3.48, 4.48 a.m.

Extract from an LGOC Bus Route Guide of 1930.

significant extensions to route 617. On the night of 14/15 February 1933 that section of the 617 along Green Street, from the junction of Romford Road to Forest Gate Garage, was withdrawn. In its place the 617 was extended eastwards along Romford Road to travel via Manor Park and Ilford to reach a new terminus at Seven Kings Garage. The increased running time, from a previous 45 minutes to 57 minutes westbound / 59 minutes eastbound, necessitated an increased allocation from two to three LT-type buses but, perhaps surprisingly in view of the 617's new outer terminus, the route's allocation continued to be provided by Forest Gate garage. The 617 was also re-routed between Aldgate and

Bank to travel via Fenchurch Street (thereby serving its station), Gracechurch Street and King William Street, thus depriving Cornhill of an all-night service.

From the night of 27/28 June 1933 the 617 was extended yet further eastwards beyond Seven Kings Garage via Chadwell Heath and Romford to reach a new terminus at LGOC's Romford Garage, actually located in Hornchurch. Route 617's running time increased yet again to become 81 minutes between Romford Garage and Charing Cross and 79 minutes in the opposite direction. Despite the considerable increase in running time to what had, by now, become LGOC's longest all-night bus route by some good margin, the schedule still allowed for the 617 to be worked by three buses which became ST-types out of Romford garage. It is fitting to note that the entry detailing route 617's extension to Romford garage was the last entry in the final Traffic Circular, No. 956 dated 28 June 1933, to be issued by the London General Omnibus Company Ltd.

FLEET COACHES

Thus far in the text, the all-night motor bus routes identified had been operated by London General. In 1930 an independent operator – Fleet Coaches – inaugurated an all-night coach service between Romford (Market Place) and Aldgate (Mansell Street). This route became noteworthy not only because it was pioneered by an independent operator but also because a schedule was operated on all seven nights of the week – giving a level of service to which neither London General nor London County Council Tramways had ever aspired over their all-night routes.

Fleet Coaches was the trading name used for the coach-related activities of Fleet Transport Services Ltd, which had been incorporated as a limited liability company in 1928 and was controlled by the Elliott family of Stratford. That business's origins were as a general haulier established in 1924 which had diversified into coaching activities in 1928. Fleet Coaches' all-night coach route between Romford and Aldgate had been inaugurated at an unknown date in 1930. The service followed the direct main road between Romford and Aldgate via Chadwell Heath, Ilford, Manor Park, Forest Gate and Stratford with a through journey time of 45 minutes. Fleet Coaches' November 1930 timetable advertised an All-Night Express Coach Service every 45 minutes from Romford to Aldgate, although, strictly speaking, the times were not at quite such regular intervals. The level of service was sufficient to deploy two Gilford 168OT coaches whose large capacity was needed to cope with heavy passenger loads encountered on some journeys. Fleet Coaches, whose office and garage was at 351 High Street, Stratford, employed two regular night crews, each comprising a driver and conductor. An element of unofficial enterprise, unauthorised by the Metropolitan Area Traffic Commissioner, is recorded in that authoritative book *London Buses Vol 2 – Country Independents 1919-1939*. Apparently the coach which was scheduled to work the Sunday morning 2am departure from Aldgate was previously despatched to the Law Courts (in Strand) where it displayed 'Private' on its destination blind as it collected passengers. On reaching Aldgate the blind display was changed to 'Romford'.

ST 649 was photographed outside Broad Street station in Liverpool Street about to set off bound for Willesden Garage on route 91.
TfL/London Transport Museum

Daytime coach services to Romford – and beyond to Brentwood – were fiercely contested by Hillman's Saloon Coaches, Sunset Saloon Coaches and, from 23 July 1930, LGOC-controlled Green Line. By November 1931 Fleet Coaches seemed to have partially joined this daytime competition with two closely-timed morning peak-hour journeys from Romford to Aldgate tacked on the end of the all-night schedule.

UPMINSTER SERVICES LTD

Upminster Services Ltd was formed on 15 June 1932 to take over an intensively-operated limited-stop daytime coach route between Upminster and Aldgate via Hornchurch, Becontree Heath, Ilford and Stratford. This service had been started by Eastward Coaches Ltd, trading as Woodgrange Coaches, on 1 December 1930. Woodgrange's route became subject to competition from Hillman's Saloon Coaches from

11 February 1931. An acrimonious, complicated and protracted legal dispute arose between these two operators which eventually led to the formation of Upminster Services Ltd, in which company Hillman's controlled 50% of the shares, the balance of equity being held by Fairway Coaches Ltd, an assignee of Eastward Coaches Ltd.

Upminster Services Ltd introduced extremely early and late journeys to the Upminster – Aldgate route which effectively gave it a night service element. These operated on a daily basis and comprised:

First journey   3.30am Upminster to Aldgate
Last journey   1.00am Aldgate to Upminster

These journeys may have originated on either 29 July 1932, when Upminster Services Ltd obtained the former Woodgrange road licence, or 15 August 1932, when Upminster Services Ltd formally took over the Woodgrange route, using Gilford coaches transferred from Hillman's fleet.

FORMATION OF LONDON TRANSPORT

On 1 July 1933 the London Passenger Transport Board absorbed the assets and operations of the London General Omnibus Company Ltd, London General Country Services Ltd, Green Line Coaches Ltd, Tramways (MET) Omnibus Company Ltd, London County Council Tramways, seven other municipally-owned and three company-owned tramway systems, one company-owned trolleybus system, the operations, or elements of the operations of six other bus or coach undertakings along with 139 buses and coaches, as well as the Metropolitan and Underground railways. Provisions in the London Passenger Transport Act 1933 allowed for the acquisition by the LPTB of Thomas Tilling Ltd's London bus operations, which occurred on 1 October 1933, as well as for the mandatory acquisition of all independent bus proprietors operating within the Metropolitan Police District which process, due to arbitration, took from 1 November 1933 to 5 December 1934 to complete. The operations of certain other independent operators, as well as elements of the operations of certain group-owned operators outside the Metropolitan Police District but within the London Passenger Transport Area, were also acquired by the LPTB. The Board also had powers to negotiate to acquire any road passenger transport operators within, or mainly within, the London Passenger Transport Area.

The London Passenger Transport Board was granted a monopoly status for the provision of public road passenger transport services within the London Special Area, with the exception of long-distance express services, excursions and tours and private hire. In the 'outer' areas, between the boundary of the London Special Area and the boundary of the London Passenger Transport Area, the London Passenger Transport Board had to apply to the Metropolitan Traffic Area Commissioner for road service licences, as could other operators.

The LPTB formed a Central Omnibus Department, a Country Omnibus Department and a Tram and Trolleybus Department to operate its road passenger transport services. Although all acquired buses, coaches, trams and trolleybuses received LPTB legal lettering immediately following acquisition, there was a void whilst a new fleet name was devised. In May 1934 LPTB announced that a new 'London Transport' fleet name would be adopted across the fleet, embracing bus, tram, trolleybus as well as railway operations, whilst 'Green Line' would be perpetuated on coaches.

FOUR NEW ALL-NIGHT BUS ROUTES

The LPTB was quick off the mark in expanding London's all-night bus work by introducing four new routes within the first eight weeks of its assumption of operating powers – although route planning must have dated back to the London General period. All four new routes were introduced on Tuesday night/Wednesday morning 22/23 August 1933 and opened up significant new territory to all-night bus services. The new routes resulted in a net increase of eight LT-type buses out on the streets of London overnight for six nights of the week since, following established practice, none of the new routes operated on Saturday nights/Sunday mornings.

Route 184: Southall (Western Road) – London Bridge Station

Timetable		*first pm*	*last am*
Southall	dep	11.34	TH 6.50
London Bridge	dep	FH 11.17	5.40

Running Time 68 mins. **Garage** Hanwell.
Allocation 3 LT-type.
Key: FH – From Hanwell Garage at time shown. TH – To Hanwell Garage.
Frequency 6 return journeys plus garage journeys.

Route 611: Barking Garage – Charing Cross (Trafalgar Square)

Timetable		*first pm*	*last am*
Barking Garage	dep	12.15	5.45
Charing Cross	dep	1.15	6.45

Running Time 56 mins. **Garage** Barking.
Allocation 2 LT-type.
Frequency 6 return journeys.

Route 613: Leyton Garage – Waterloo Station (Alaska Street)

Timetable		*first pm*	*last am*
Leyton Garage	dep	12.15	5.38
Waterloo Station	dep	1.05	6.28

Running Time 47 mins. **Garage** Leyton. **Allocation** 2 LT-type.
Frequency 6 return journeys.

Route 619: Edmonton (Park Road) – Pimlico (King William IV)

Timetable		*first pm*	*last am*
Edmonton	dep	11.46	5.23
Victoria	arr	12.36	6.13
Pimlico	arr	12.44	6.21
Pimlico	dep	12.50	6.23
Victoria	arr	12.58	6.31
Edmonton	arr	1.48	7.21

Shortworkings: 11.33pm, 12.26am, 12.48am Tottenham Garage – Edmonton
5.56am, 6.26am, 7.23am Edmonton – Tottenham Garage

Running Time 58 mins. **Garage** Tottenham.
Allocation 3 LT-type.
Frequency 5 return journeys Edmonton to Pimlico, plus 3 return journeys Edmonton to Victoria.

Route 184 displayed the same route number as its daytime counterpart which operated over exactly the same route between Southall and London Bridge Station. The all-night service on the 184 provided a completely new facility along the Uxbridge Road and almost so through Shepherds Bush and up Bayswater Road, along which the only prior night bus service had been the single return journey on route 189 between Turnham Green and Ludgate Circus. The 184 traversed the full length of Oxford Street, passed Tottenham Court Road station and headed through Holborn to Bank, thence following King William Street to London Bridge and its terminus. The 184 was the first all-night bus service to cross London Bridge since the Elephant & Castle early morning supplementary journeys on route 94A which had been withdrawn after operation on 14/15 July 1916, during the First World War.

Route 611 offered a new all-night service over the entire length of Barking Road. Along East India Dock Road the 611 joined the route of the Poplar–Bloomsbury all-night tram service, continuing in parallel with the tram route along the length of Commercial Road. From Aldgate (Gardiner's Corner) to its Charing Cross terminus the 611 followed identical routeing to that used by the other east London all-night bus route, the 617 from Romford. After setting passengers down at Trafalgar Square, routes 611 and 617 both used a bus stand located on the right hand side of the carriageway on the north side of the Square, on the opposite side of the road to the National Gallery. As a result, boarding passengers had to walk into the carriageway to board 611 and 617 buses.

Route 613 brought a regular all-night bus facility to Leyton and along Lea Bridge Road which previously had only been served by the single return journey on Ludgate Circus route 601. Although both the 601 and 613 were worked by Leyton garage, a subtle distinction in terminal points existed between the two routes. The 601 terminated at the Bakers Arms whilst the 613 was scheduled to work through to Leyton garage. After Clapton Pond the 613 was routed through the centre of Hackney and along Graham Road, meeting again the 601, which was routed via Hackney Downs, in Dalston Lane. The routeing followed by the 613 along Balls Pond Road and Essex Road gave these roads their first all-night bus service. From Islington and along Rosebery Avenue as far as Mount Pleasant, the 613 ran in parallel to the Highgate – Bloomsbury all-night tram service. The 613 then travelled via Farringdon Road and Farringdon Street to Ludgate Circus, also the terminal point of route 601. Route 613 then followed that, by now, time-honoured route for all-night buses along the length of Fleet Street to Strand (returning via Aldwych) and then became the first all-night bus route to cross Waterloo Bridge before reaching its terminus at Waterloo Station.

The fourth new route, numbered 619, was correctly described in London Passenger Transport Board's Traffic Circular No. 5 dated 23 August 1933 as 'Route 39D (Night Service) extended (at) both ends and intermediately diverted, Tuesday Night August 22/23 1933'. Route 39D operated between its Tottenham (LPTB garage) and Charing Cross (Trafalgar Square) termini for the last time on the night of 21/22 August 1933. From the following night it was incorporated into route 619 which operated between Edmonton (Park Road) and Pimlico (King William IV). The northward extension of the 619 beyond Tottenham to Edmonton represented new territory for night bus operations. The intermediate diversion referred to in the Traffic Circular diverted the 619 away from route 39D's previous direct routeing between Tottenham and Manor House via Seven Sisters Road. Instead the 619 continued via South Tottenham to Stamford Hill, thereafter proceeding along Amhurst Park to join Seven Sisters Road. At Stamford Hill the 619 met up the now LPTB-operated 30-minute frequency all-night tram service to Holborn. By interchanging between all-night bus 619 and the Holborn all-night tram at Stamford Hill passengers from Edmonton and Tottenham were offered good access to the City.

This re-routeing was evidence of the opportunities that were available better to integrate all-night bus and tram services now that the formerly competitive London General bus operations and London County Council Tramways operations were united under the London Passenger Transport Board. Having joined Seven Sisters Road above Manor House, route 619 then followed an identical routeing to former 39D via Finsbury Park, Holloway, Camden Town, Tottenham Court Road and Charing Cross Road to Trafalgar Square. From Trafalgar Square, former terminus of route 39D, the 619 was projected via Whitehall, Parliament Square, Victoria Street, Wilton Road, Belgrave Road and Lupus Street where the 619 formed a circular working to its terminal point on the north bank of the River Thames outside the King William IV public house in Pimlico's Grosvenor Road. The link beyond Victoria to Pimlico opened up entirely new territory to an all-night bus facility. The end-to-end running time of route 619, 58 minutes, necessitated an increase in allocation from two to three LT-type buses, compared with the 39D, from Tottenham garage. Tottenham was one of the first garages to receive a substantial allocation of new STL-type AEC Regents, leading to the 619's allocation becoming three STL-type buses from Tuesday night/Wednesday morning 27/28 February 1934.

Romford garage's operation of route 617 with ST-type double deckers lasted barely three months before that route's allocation was changed to Seven Kings garage from the night of 3/4 October 1933, using three LT-type double-deckers. On Wednesday morning, 28 March 1934, an additional short working was introduced on route 617 which departed Mile End Station at 4.03am for Charing Cross with return from Charing Cross at 4.32am bound for Mile End. This duty was covered by a Tottenham garage based STL-type off day route 76.

From the night of 10/11 April 1934 route 614's allocation was switched from Turnham Green garage to Hammersmith garage, which was located on the line of route 614. A vehicle type change was also involved as Turnham Green's two ST-types formerly used on the route were replaced by two LT-types from Hammersmith. Apart from short-workings into, and out of, service from Hammersmith Garage the 614's timetable remained essentially unchanged.

INDEPENDENTS' ALL-NIGHT SERVICES ACQUIRED BY LPTB

The London Passenger Transport Board acquired the greater part of Edward Hillman Saloon Coaches Ltd's business on 10 January 1934 including Hillman's daytime Bow to Romford and Brentwood coach services along with 65 coaches, 320 staff and Hillman's garage in London Road, Romford. Upminster Services Ltd, in which Hillman's Ltd had a 50% shareholding, was acquired by the LPTB on the same date. The former independents' operations became the responsibility of LPTB's Country Omnibus Department. Hillman's Bow – Brentwood service was merged with existing Green Line route Y, which in entirety worked between Horse Guards Avenue and Brentwood, whilst Upminster Services Ltd's Upminster – Aldgate route became route AY in the burgeoning Green Line network. Both routes Y and AY had very intensive daytime frequencies of up to three or five minutes respectively along sections of each route. On assumption of operation by the LPTB neither route had an officially designated night service. However, Green Line route AY maintained some very early and very late journeys (3.17am first departure from Romford (Roneo Corner), 2.08am last arrival at Roneo Corner, which meant that at least one coach was in service at some point along route AY for about 23 hours of the clock on all seven days/nights of the week. Initially route AY continued to use the Mansell Street, Aldgate terminus of predecessor Upminster Services Ltd. The Aldgate terminus became Minories coach station from 19 April 1934, although a contemporaneous Traffic Circular indicated that when the coach station was closed at night, between 1.50am and 6am, coaches stood in nearby Jewry Street. It is not clear for how long this night-time terminal arrangement lasted.

Fleet Coaches' all-night route between Romford and Aldgate officially passed into LPTB control at noon on Wednesday 21 February 1934, along with the night service crews. In a similar manner to the former Hillman's and Upminster Services' routes operational responsibility passed to LPTB's Country Omnibuses who thus first operated the Romford-Aldgate all-night service from Wednesday night/Thursday morning 21/22 February 1934, most probably using Gilford coaches based at the former Hillman's garage in London Road, Romford. Fleet Coaches' timetable was merged with that of existing Green Line route Y which operated between Brentwood, Romford and Aldgate – with an extension to Horse Guards Avenue during late evenings, on Saturdays after 1.45pm, and all day on Sundays. The identity of the former Fleet Coaches all-night service became harder to discern upon its integration into Green Line route Y, over which route a 15-minute late evening frequency prevailed right up until last departures from Aldgate to Romford at 1.37am on weekdays and 1.42am on Sundays. However, the core all-night service remained identifiable with nightly departures from Romford at 1.20am, 2.05am, 2.55am, 3.50am and 4.25am and return journeys from Aldgate at 2.10am, 3.20am, 3.40am, 4.36am and 5.21am. These journeys required an allocation of two coaches.

Operation of the former Fleet Coaches Romford–Aldgate all-night service as an element of Green Line route Y was destined to last for less than four months, running for the last time in that guise on the night of 11/12 June 1934. Thereafter operational responsibility for the all-night service passed from London Transport's Country Omnibus Department to its Central Omnibus Department, which incorporated the Sunday night to Friday night element of the service into a revised schedule introduced on existing route 617 with effect from Tuesday night/Wednesday morning 12/13 June 1934. The new timetable necessitated an increased allocation of four LT-type buses from Seven Kings garage, whilst the single return journey at 4.03am from Mile End Station to Charing Cross and return continued to be worked by a Tottenham garage-based STL-type, which meant that five buses were used on weekday workings of route 617. Operation of the former Fleet Coaches, latterly Green Line Y, Saturday night/Sunday morning all-night service between Romford and Aldgate was maintained by Central Omnibuses. However, workings on that night of the week, first introduced on 16/17 June 1934, were designated as route 617F in the Official Allocation Book entry, which detailed that three LT-type buses from Seven Kings garage were allocated to the 617F. The operation of a true all-night service on Saturday nights/Sunday mornings by the London Passenger Transport Board broke all established precedents set by its predecessors, London General, London County Council Tramways and The North Metropolitan Tramways Company. Since the inception of all-night services in 1899, those operators had, with minor exceptions, avoided the practice of running all-night services on Saturday nights/Sunday mornings. Sustained operation on that night of the week over the Romford – Aldgate route had been pioneered by independent Fleet Coaches who, like all private operators, had to make a profit or succumb. Clearly London Transport considered it worthwhile to continue the service. Nonetheless Saturday night/Sunday morning operation of a true all-night service over route 617F, later renumbered 298 and which subsequently became route N98, remained a unique phenomenon of London Transport's all-night bus and tram network for many years. Although a handful of all-night bus routes did gain a Saturday night/Sunday morning service in the post-Second World War years, universal operation by London Transport of all-night bus routes on that night of the week was not achieved until 29/30 October 1983, over 50 years after the LPTB had acquired Fleet Coaches pioneering seven nights of the week Romford – Aldgate route.

Table E opposite shows that the numbers of vehicles allocated to London's all-night road passenger transport services had doubled over the ten years between 1924 and 1934 with 56 trams, buses and one coach in service on Monday–Friday nights at 29/30 June 1934, compared with 28 trams and buses in service on similar nights at 29/30 June 1924. Another significant difference was that, in 1934, all the vehicles were operated by the London Passenger Transport Board whilst ten years earlier the buses had been provided by the London General Omnibus Company and the trams by London County Council Tramways. The increase in vehicles on night service duties reflected a substantial increase in the scope of the service provided, largely attributable to the introduction in 1928 and 1933 of bus routes 184, 611, 613, 614, 617 and 619,

Table E: All-Night Bus and Tram Routes. Vehicle Allocations 29/30 June 1934

Route	Tram Allocation			Depot
	Su	M–Fr	Sa	
Tram routes north of River Thames:				
Stamford Hill–Holborn	2	2	–	Stamford Hill
Hampstead–Holborn	1	1	–	Hampstead
Poplar–Bloomsbury	2	2	–	Poplar
Highgate–Bloomsbury	1	1	–	Highgate
Wood Green–Holborn (21)	2	2	–	Wood Green
Sub Total	8	8	–	
Tram routes south of River Thames:				
Downham–Victoria Embankment	3	3	–	New Cross
New Cross Gate–Victoria Embankment	2	2	–	New Cross
Tooting Broadway–Victoria Embankment loop	3	3	–	Clapham
	3	3	–	Streatham
Tooting Broadway–Victoria Embankment via Battersea	2	2	–	Wandsworth
Hammersmith–Vauxhall (26)	1	1	1	Wandsworth
Sub Total	14	14	1	
Tram Total	22	22	1	

No	Route	Bus Allocation			Garage
		Su	M–Fr	Sa	
4B	Ludgate Circus–Finsbury Park	–	1 NS	–	Holloway
9C	Ludgate Circus–Barnes	–	1 NS	–	Mortlake
11D	Hammersmith–Liverpool Street Station	2 LT	2 LT	–	Hammersmith
13B	Ludgate Circus–Hendon	–	1 NS/ST	–	Hendon
91	Willesden–Liverpool Street Station	1 ST	1 ST	–	Willesden
94	Cricklewood–Liverpool Street Station	2 LT	2 LT	–	Cricklewood
184	Southall–London Bridge Station	3 LT	3 LT	–	Hanwell
189	Ludgate Circus–Turnham Green	1 ST	1 ST	–	Turnham Green
529B	Finsbury Park–Palmers Green	–	1 NS	1 NS	Palmers Green
601	Ludgate Circus–Leyton	1 ST	1 ST	–	Leyton
611	Barking Garage–Charing Cross	2 LT	2 LT	–	Barking
613	Leyton Garage–Waterloo Station	2 LT	2 LT	–	Leyton
614	Turnham Green–Liverpool Street Station	2 LT	2 LT	–	Hammersmith
615	Liverpool Street Station–Aldwych	1 LT	1 LT	–	Dalston
616	Liverpool Street Station–Aldwych	4 LT	4 LT	–	Dalston
617	Romford Garage–Charing Cross	4 LT	4 LT	–	Seven Kings
		1 STL	1 STL	–	Tottenham
617F	Romford Garage–Aldgate	–	–	3 LT	Seven Kings
619	Edmonton–Pimlico	3 STL	3 STL	–	Tottenham
AY	Upminster–Aldgate	1 Coach	1 Coach	1 Coach	Romford (London Road)
Bus and Coach Total		30	34	5	
TRAM, BUS AND COACH GRAND TOTAL		52	56	6	

all of which operated a full all-night service. As always with statistical figures, care needs to be exercised in their interpretation. It should be borne in mind that several night bus routes did not operate a full all-night service. Ludgate Circus routes 4B, 9C, 13B and 601, as well as route 529B, only operated single return journeys whilst the 11D worked two early morning return journeys only. The allocation of four LT-type buses to Liverpool Street Station–Aldwych route 616 was, in numerical terms, most impressive but each bus worked only one return trip over the 16-minute journey time route before taking up duties on daytime route 11E. The vehicle type mix is most interesting and shows the modernisation of London's then-current bus fleet which had started in 1930 with the introduction of the LT and ST-types, followed by the extended wheelbase STL-type AEC Regents which first entered service in 1933. Older generation NS-type buses were still to be found on night service duties, but by 29/30 June 1934 their appearances were confined to Special Night Journeys on routes 4B, 9C and 529B as well as, possibly, 13B. The NS were petrol-engined buses, as were the ST-types to be found on routes 91, 189 and 601. Tottenham garage's four STL-types allocated to all-night service duties (one on route 617 and three on route 619) would have been petrol-engined examples, very likely having been fitted with petrol engines removed from LT-types which latter type, from October 1933 onwards, was subject to an extensive conversion programme from petrol to oil (diesel) engines. The LT-type dominated contemporary all-night bus operation and, at 29/30 June 1934, would have comprised a mixture of petrol and diesel-engined models.

The all-night tram network showed a net increase of four tramcars in use, with 22 in use on Sunday – Friday nights at 29/30 June 1934 compared with 18 tramcars in use over the same nights at 29/30 June 1924. The all-night tram network had experienced two significant route extensions in 1928 – from Catford to Downham on 29/30 April and the establishment of the Tooting Broadway–Victoria Embankment dual direction cyclical working via Brixton and via Clapham from 17/18 July – which, due to scheduling efficiencies, succeeded in covering an additional 5½ route miles of tramway with an all-night service whilst avoiding any increase in tramcar allocation. The increase was a result of the need for one additional car on the Battersea (Prince's Head) route when it was extended to Tooting Broadway on 21/22 September 1932, two tramcars which worked the week-days early morning journeys on route 21 between Wood Green and Holborn, and one tram needed for the all-night route 26 between Hammersmith and Vauxhall.

Route 189 was withdrawn after operation on Tuesday night/Wednesday morning 3/4 July 1934. The advent of route 614, from 16/17 July 1928, offered an alternative and full all-night service between route 189's two terminal points, whilst the introduction of an all-night service, from the night of 22/23 August 1933, on route 184 provided a full all-night service along a lengthy section of route from Oxford Circus to Shepherds Bush also covered by the 189's single night time return journey. It would seem that these two newer night routes had abstracted traffic from the 189 which led to its withdrawal. However, matters do not appear to have been quite so straightforward as that since the Official Allocation Book recorded the introduction, from Tuesday night/Wednesday morning 7/8 August 1934, of an additional Sunday night–Friday night return journey, numbered 614A, leaving Turnham Green at 12.33am for Ludgate Circus, from which latter point the bus set off at 1.16am on its return trip to Turnham Green. The 614A duty, effectively a short working of route 614, had terminal point departure times similar to those of the withdrawn route 189 and also maintained Turnham Green garage's presence on all-night bus work through the one ST-type bus allocated from that garage to work the journeys.

By the time the LPTB issued its first-ever London Area Timetable in July 1934, many daytime bus routes had last departures from central London timed between 12 midnight and 1.0am. In a few cases last journeys left even later, such as those in both directions on route 15 to Ladbroke Grove and to Upton Park, and route 32 whose last journey on weekday

nights left Oxford Circus at 1.15am bound for Merton garage via Whitehall, Vauxhall Bridge, Stockwell and Tooting. The very latest daytime route departure from central London was the Saturday night/Sunday morning 1.40am journey on route 60 from Strand to Cricklewood (arrival 2.19am) which gave a partial night time service along the Edgware Road on that night of the week when all-night route 94 did not operate. The foregoing departures were last journeys which formed part of a preceding regular daytime schedule. Certain other routes were annotated as having 'Special Night Journeys' which operated some time after the regular daytime schedule had finished on the appropriate route. These are shown in the table opposite.

The Monday–Saturday night Palmers Green to Finsbury Park only return journey on route 529B had been renumbered 29C from the night 29/30 March 1934. The return journey from Finsbury Park on the 29C at 1.33am had, by then, become very closely timed to the last scheduled daytime journey from Finsbury Park on route 29 at 1.29am.

On Tuesday night/Wednesday morning 7/8 August 1934 route 91's allocation from Willesden garage changed from one ST-type to one STL-type bus, coincident with the conversion of Willesden garage's allocation on daytime route 8 to STL-type.

Two minor extensions to the all-night tram network were evident from the July 1934 timetable. On the Downham – Victoria Embankment (Savoy Street) route the 2.09am departure ex Downham was projected further around Victoria Embankment to terminate at Charing Cross Station whence the return journey to Downham started at 3.01am. The New Cross Gate–Savoy Street via Peckham route gained an extra working at 5.27am from New Cross Gate which terminated 30 minutes later at St. George's Church in Borough High Street whence the return journey set off at 6am back to New Cross Gate. The section of tramway covered between Elephant & Castle and Borough High Street via Newington Causeway represented new territory to the official all-night tram network.

Whilst all-night trams benefited those persons who had occasion to make use of them, their popularity was not universal. Stoke Newington Borough Council resolved at its meeting on 18 September 1934 to write to the London Passenger Transport Board suggesting that buses should replace trams between the hours of 11pm and 6am. This, the Council claimed, would lessen noise at night about which residents, living on the line of the Stamford Hill – Holborn all-night tram route, had complained. London Transport replied that it would be uneconomic to do so.

London's public all-night road passenger transport network, built up over the preceding 36 years, would prove to be enduring. The network established by summer 1934 would continue in substantially unchanged and quite recognisable form for the next half century – despite two route renumberings, the Second World War, conversion of both tramway and trolleybus networks to bus operation, the Chambers Report, the Bus Reshaping Plan, the spread of one-man operation – as well as the vicissitudes associated with 14 changes of government – until finally expanded from 13/14 April 1984 as will be covered in Volume 2.

Route 9B/9C : Special Night Journeys

| | | Mon–Fri nights | | | Saturday nights | | | |
		pm/am	am	am	pm/am	pm/am	am	am
Barnes	dep	11.50	12.05	12.12	11.41	11.56	12.06	12.16
Strand (Aldwych)	arr	12.41	12.48	12.55	12.24	12.39	12.49	12.59
Ludgate Circus	arr	12.44	-	-	-	-	-	-
Ludgate Circus	dep	12.45	-	-	-	-	-	-
Strand (Aldwych)	dep	12.48	12.52	12.57	12.32	12.45	12.53	1.01
Barnes	arr	1.31	1.36	1.41	1.16	1.29	1.37	1.45

Garage: Mortlake. **Allocation:** 3 NS-type Mon–Fri nights, 4 NS-type Saturday nights.

Route 12B: Special Night Journeys

| | | Mon–Fri nights | | Saturday nights | |
		pm/am	am	pm/am	am
Dulwich	dep	11.48	-	-	-
Peckham Rye	dep	11.53	12.56	11.54	12.54
Oxford Circus	arr	12.25	1.28	12.28	1.28
		am	am	am	am
Oxford Circus	dep	12.30	1.30	12.30	1.30
Peckham Rye	arr	1.02	2.02	1.04	2.04

Garage: Nunhead. **Allocation:** 2 LT-type. **Note:** First listed in August 1934 timetable.

Route 24: Special Night Journeys

| | | Mon–Fri nights | | Saturday nights | |
		am	am	am	am
Pimlico	dep	12.22	12.34	12.28	12.40
Hampstead Heath	arr	1.05	1.14	1.08	1.20
Hampstead Heath	dep	1.05	1.17	1.11	1.23
Camden Town *	arr	1.14	1.26	1.20	1.32

* Arriving journeys continued 2 minutes later to Chalk Farm garage.
Garage: Chalk Farm. **Allocation:** 2 NS-type.

Route 25C: Special Night Journeys

| | | Mon–Fri nights | | | | |
		pm	pm	pm/am	pm/am	pm/am
Seven Kings	dep	10.56	11.08	11.20	11.32	11.49
Bank	arr	11.47	11.59	12.11	12.23	12.40
		pm/am	am	am	am	am
Bank	dep	11.49	12.01	12.13	12.25	12.42
Seven Kings	arr	12.40	12.52	1.04	1.16	1.33

Garage: Seven Kings. **Allocation:** 5 LT-type.

Route 159C : Special Night Journey

| | | Mon-Fri nights |
		pm/am
Oxford Circus	dep	11.57
South Croydon	arr	1.07

Garage: Croydon. **Allocation:** 1 ST-type. **Note:** SNJ operated outbound only.

For the first year or so following the formation of the London Passenger Transport Board the average bus or tram passenger might have formed the impression that not too much had changed in respect of operations and services. Central Buses, including vehicles acquired on or after 1 July 1933, still sported 'General' fleetnames although the more observant bystander would have noticed that such vehicles' legal lettering now referred to the recently created Board. Tramcars continued to operate in a variety of liveries originally applied by their former municipal or company owners. The adoption of a new 'London Transport' fleetname in May 1934, combined with the announcement that a standard livery of red and white was to be applied to Central Area buses, trams and trolleybuses, were amongst the first externally-visible manifestations that profound changes to the operation and style of London's public road passenger transport were in hand.

ALL-NIGHT BUS ROUTE RE-NUMBERING
Route numbers in the Central Buses area ranged from 1 to 629A with a bewildering array of suffix-lettered route numbers that had originated in attempts to adhere to the principles of the 1924 Bassom System. On 3 October 1934, coincident with the start of that year's Winter Schedules, London Transport introduced a new route numbering system for its Central Buses, as well as for its Country Buses. The main principle behind the renumbering of Central Buses routes was to bring together the pre-existing complex and scattered route numbers into a compact group more easily capable of being remembered by the public. The tenets of the Bassom System were abandoned and, in their place, all journeys on a route, including shortworkings, were to use the same route number whilst the application of route suffix letters became restricted to route deviations and bifurcations. Under the new route numbering system Central Bus routes were grouped numerically according to vehicle-types used as well as providing the first ever dedicated numbering series for all-night buses from 299 downwards.

Table F: All-Night Bus Route Renumbering 3 October 1934

Special Night Journeys or all-night service covering part or all of Daytime Bus Routes

New Route Numbers	Former Route Numbers	Termini
4	4B	Ludgate Circus – Finsbury Park
9	9B/9C	Ludgate Circus – Mortlake Garage
11	11D	Hammersmith – Liverpool Street
12	12B	Oxford Circus – Peckham Rye
13	13B	Ludgate Circus – Hendon
17	184	Southall – London Bridge Station
24	24	Pimlico – Hampstead Heath
25	25C	Bank – Seven Kings Garage
29	29C	Finsbury Park – Palmers Green
159	159C	Oxford Circus – South Croydon

Renumbering of all-night bus routes into a numerically-descending series from 299 was only applied to those services which followed a unique night time route. Special Night Journeys which worked over the length of, or a section of, a daytime route continued the practice of using the same route number base as the equivalent daytime service but without a route number suffix-letter.

All-Night Bus Route Number Series (in descending order)		
New Route Numbers	Former Route Numbers	Termini
299	601	Ludgate Circus – Leyton, Bakers Arms
298	617	Romford Garage – Charing Cross
298	617F	Romford Garage - Aldgate
297	614	Turnham Green – Liverpool Street
297	614A	Turnham Green – Ludgate Circus
296	613	Leyton Garage – Waterloo Station
295	611	Barking Garage – Charing Cross
294	94	Cricklewood Garage – Liverpool Street
293	616	Liverpool Street Station – Aldwych
292	615	Liverpool Street Station – Aldwych
291	91	Willesden Garage – Liverpool Street
290	619	Edmonton – Pimlico

Route numbers 299 to 290, as well as 11, first came into use on Tuesday night/Wednesday morning, 2/3 October 1934 whilst Special Night Journeys over other daytime routes were renumbered from Wednesday night/Thursday morning 3/4 October 1934 since such workings finished any particular day's schedule. London Transport also renumbered elements of its daytime tram routes from 3 October 1934 but all-night tram routes continued to be excluded from numbering, so still ran as unnumbered routes, with the possible exception of the night journeys on routes 21 and 26. In a separate exercise, Green Line coach routes were re-lettered in June 1935. The night journeys on route AY (Upminster – Aldgate) were re-designated as route Y2 from 26/27 June 1935, coincident with that route's extension beyond Upminster to Corbets Tey.

From 3/4 October 1934 the daytime schedule on route 12 was extended to absorb the earlier of the two former Special Night Journeys, leaving just a single return journey on Monday–Saturday nights at 12.54am from Peckham Rye to Oxford Circus and return journey from Oxford Circus at 1.30am as a Special Night Journey, worked by one LT-type bus from Nunhead garage. From the same night a daily Special Night Journey was introduced to daytime route 6.

Left STL 332, on route 291, awaits departure time from Liverpool Street in August 1936. A background poster advertises summer seasonal overnight train excursions from St Pancras Station to the Peak District. TfL/London Transport Museum

| Route 6 : Special Night Journey |
Willesden Garage – Oxford Circus via Kensal Rise, West Kilburn, Edgware Road, Marble Arch

		M–Sa Nights	Sun Night
		am	am
Willesden Garage	dep	12.44	12.45
Oxford Circus	arr	1.20	1.20
Oxford Circus	dep	1.30	1.30
Willesden Garage	arr	2.06	2.05

Garage: Willesden. **Allocation:** 1 STL-type.

On route 294 an additional Sunday night/Monday morning only journey was introduced from the night of 7/8 October 1934 which increased the allocation from Cricklewood garage to three LT-type on that night of the week, though it remained at two LT-type on other nights of operation.

Two further daytime bus routes gained Special Night Journeys from December 1934. The Saturday night journey on route 12 at 12.54am from Peckham Rye to Oxford Circus with its corresponding return journey at 1.30am from Oxford Circus back to Peckham Rye was transferred to route 121's schedule worked, as formerly, by one LT-type bus from Nunhead garage. Monday – Friday night Special Night Journeys continued to operate as route 12. The January 1935 London Area Timetable detailed, for the first time, two Special Night Journeys which operated on route 38. It is likely that these journeys were introduced on Saturday night/Sunday morning 5/6 December 1934, coincident with Dalston garage gaining an allocation-share on route 38.

| Route 38: Special Night Journeys |
		M–Fr nights		Sa nights	
		pm	pm	pm	pm
Victoria Station	dep	11.09	11.19	11.08	11.18
Chingford Mount	arr	12.20	12.30	12.20	12.30
		am	am	am	am
Chingford Mount	dep	12.23	12.33	12.23	12.33
Dalston (Queens Road)	arr	12.58	1.08	12.59	1.09

Garage: Dalston. **Allocation:** 2 LT-type (M–Sa). Last departure on the daytime schedule was at 12.32 am (M–Sa nights) from Victoria Station to Leyton, Bakers Arms.

The Saturday night return Special Night Journeys on route 38 were shortened to terminate at Leyton, Bakers Arms from 2/3 February 1935 coincident with the transfer of Saturday's allocation from Dalston to Leyton garage. Monday to Friday night return journeys continued to work through to Dalston, Queens Road until October 1935 by which date Leyton garage had taken over operation on all weekday nights and all journeys terminated at Bakers Arms. Dalston garage's Saturday allocation on route 38 was replaced by Leyton garage from 2/3 February 1935.

LT 376 was photographed at an unknown location, possibly in the vicinity of Cricklewood garage, displaying new all-night series route number 294. This shot is possibly attributable to the period between 3 October 1934, when route 94 was re-numbered to 294, and 7/8 December 1936, after which latter date the 294's allocation from Cricklewood garage changed from LT to STL-type. *Alan Cross*

The Silver Jubilee of His Majesty King George V was celebrated in May 1935. An extended Jubilee weekend, which started on Saturday 4 May, culminated with Jubilee Day on Monday 6 May. To cope with the flood of well-wishers and visitors, many all-night bus routes had their service levels enhanced on both Sunday night/Monday morning 5/6 May 1935 and Monday night/Tuesday morning 6/7 May 1935. All-night bus routes 17, 290, 291, 294, 295, 296, 297 and 298 had additional journeys scheduled to run approximately 15 minutes after most, but not all, of their regular timetabled journeys.

Dalston garage's allocation type on Liverpool Street Station – Aldwych early morning routes 292 and 293 changed from a total of five LT-type to five STL-type from Wednesday morning, 31 July 1935. The operation of these two routes came even closer together from Wednesday morning 11 September 1935 when their allocation was officially combined and was reduced by one bus to four STL-type.

In order to provide all-night facilities for the Becontree Estate route 295 was projected beyond Barking garage via Longbridge Road to reach a new terminal at Becontree Heath on 10/11 September 1935. The 295's allocation was increased to three LT-type buses from Barking garage. Route 298, now correctly described as operating between Hornchurch Garage and Charing Cross as a consequence of the re-naming of Romford garage on 1 September 1935, had an additional early morning short-working return journey introduced between Mile End Station and Charing Cross by December 1934. Tottenham garage's allocation on the 298 increased from one to two STL-type buses to cover the two Mile End short-working duties.

The period between 15/16 October 1935 and 8/9 December 1936 saw the highest-to-date numbers of vehicles allocated to London's night time road passenger transport services with 49 buses, 21 trams and one Green Line coach, a total of 71 vehicles, so employed on Monday – Friday nights. Dilution of this record vehicle requirement began from the night of 9/10

December 1936 when rescheduling of the 25 group of routes absorbed that route's Special Night Journeys into an extended schedule on daytime route 25A.

Table G summarises changes to all-night bus routes' garage allocations and vehicle types between 1/2 January 1936 and 2/3 September 1939, the eve of the outbreak of the Second World War. Of particular note amongst the vehicle-type changes was the withdrawal from night bus service of the last NS-type bus which ran out of service after completing route 4's Ludgate Circus – Finsbury Park journey at 1.33am on Wednesday 3 November 1937. Also noteworthy was the introduction of the STD-type to night bus duties with the conversion of route 13 to that type from 4/5 August 1937. The expansion of the Mortlake Garage to Ludgate Circus, and return, Special Night Journey on route 9 to operate additionally on Saturday nights, from 5/6 February 1938, was significant in view of the future longevity of such journeys. All-night route 17 abandoned the use of its circular terminal working off Western Road, Southall, via Albert Road, Florence Road and Leonard Road from the night of 26/27 May 1936 as a consequence of that route's projection approximately 500 yards further down Western Road to reach a new terminal point at Brent Road. Whilst this extension to route 17 was, in itself, relatively insignificant, the event merited greater distinction in being the last route innovation to London's all-night bus network for the next 7½ years.

Table G: Changes to Allocations and Vehicle Types on All-Night Bus Routes, Period: 1/2 January 1936 – 2/3 September 1939

Route Number	Effective Date	Garage/Commentary	Su	M–Fr	Sa
4	3/4 Nov 1937	Holloway	-	1 ST	-
	12/13 Oct 1938	Tottenham *	-	1 ST	-
9	4/5 Mar 1936	Mortlake	-	3 LT	3 LT
	By Apr 1936	Additional Saturday journey	-	3 LT	4 LT
	2/3 Feb 1938	Reduction in night journeys	-	2 LT	1 LT
13	4/5 Aug 1937	Hendon	-	1 STD	-
17	7/8 April 1936	Hanwell	3 STL	3 STL	-
24	4/5 Aug 1937	Chalk Farm	-	2 STL	2 STL
	5/6 Jan 1938	Mon–Fri night journeys absorbed into extended daytime schedule	-	-	2 STL
25	9/10 Dec 1936	Seven Kings	-	-	-
		Night journeys absorbed into extended daytime schedule on route 25A			
29	24/25 Mar 1937	Palmers Green	-	1 NS/LT	1 NS/LT
	4/5 Aug 1937		-	1 LT/STL	1 LT/STL
	8/9 Sept 1937		-	1 STL	1 STL
38	3/4 Aug 1938	Leyton	-	2 LT/ST	2 LT/ST
159	29/30 Apr 1936	Streatham *	-	1 LT	-
	7/8 Oct 1936		-	1 LT/ST	-
292/293	23/24 Mar 1936	Hackney	1 LT	1 LT	-
294	8/9 Dec 1936	Cricklewood †	4 STL	3 STL	-
299	3/4 Mar 1936	Leyton	1 LT	1 LT	-

* Change of garage
† Allocation to route 294 increased to 3 LT-type (M–Fr nights) and 4 LT-type (Su nights) from 30/31 July 1935. This exceeded timetable requirements by one vehicle on each night of operation unless duplication of certain journeys occurred.

A strike by Central Bus crews between 1 May and 27 May 1937 caused the suspension of both daytime and all-night bus services. This action frustrated prepared plans to enhance all-night routes 17, 290, 291, 294, 295, 296, 297 and 298 with 15-minute frequency headways throughout Tuesday night/Wednesday morning 11/12 May 1937, the eve of the Coronation of His Majesty King George VI. In the absence of buses on the streets of London, the LPTB's tram network bore the brunt of the crowds. An outcome of negotiations between LPTB and the trade union to settle the 1937 strike was LPTB's agreement not to extend joint compilation of service schedules on Central Buses. This meant that crews on comparatively short duty period all-night bus routes could not be made to work part of their shift on another route, such as late evening or early morning daytime routes. This created a high wage cost base for all-night rosters and may well have acted as a significant inhibitory factor on the development of all-night bus services for many years to come. The comparatively short working hours of some shifts also accounted for the attraction of all-night work to some crews.

One minor route extension to the all-night tram network was evident by the time of issue of the November 1935 timetable. The 4.45am journey from New Cross Gate via Peckham was projected beyond that route's usual terminal point at Victoria Embankment, Savoy Street, to terminate at Charing Cross Underground Station, whence the return journey back to New Cross Gate set off at 5.17am.

STL 1950 stands posed in front of the Cumberland Hotel and Marble Arch Underground station entrance whilst working route 294 in August 1938. *TfL/London Transport Museum/courtesy Malcolm Papes*

Feltham tramcar 2138 is seen at Tooting Broadway in 1938 whilst working the all-night route to Victoria Embankment. The car had arrived in Tooting after travelling from Victoria Embankment via Blackfriars Bridge, Elephant & Castle, Brixton and Streatham and would return to Victoria Embankment via Clapham, Elephant & Castle and Blackfriars Bridge. It would then leave Victoria Embankment via Westminster Bridge and return to Tooting via Clapham, after which it would work back to Victoria Embankment via Streatham, Brixton and Westminster Bridge, thus completing its 3 hour long 'figure of eight' cycle. *TfL/London Transport Museum*

ALL-NIGHT TRAM AND TROLLEYBUS ROUTES

Commercial operation of trolleybuses in London had been started by London United Tramways, an Underground-group company, with the inception of a daytime Twickenham – Teddington route on 16 May 1931. LUT's fleet quickly built up to 61 trolleybuses operating a network of routes based around Kingston-upon-Thames and which was acquired by the London Passenger Transport Board on 1 July 1933. On that same date the newly-created Board became responsible for the operation of 2,625 tramcars taken over from a variety of municipal and company operators. A significant element of the LPTB's acquired tram fleet was elderly and in need of replacement, whilst much of the tram track was well-worn. On the other hand, the tramways' electrical generating installations and supply systems had many more years' economic life remaining, and could readily be adapted to power a trolleybus network. London Transport quickly decided to adopt trolleybus operation on a massive scale with the intention, at that time, of converting its entire tramway system to trolleybus operation. A rapid tram to trolleybus conversion programme started on 27 October 1935.

All-night tram routes remained unaffected by the tram to trolleybus conversion programme until 12 September 1937 when the last vestiges of tram operation were removed from Hammersmith, from west of Clapham Junction and from Garratt Lane. Two all-night tram routes were affected by this stage of the conversion programme. These comprised the Tooting Broadway – Victoria Embankment (Blackfriars) and Hammersmith – Vauxhall (route 26) all-night tram routes which operated for the final time, in their original form, on

Friday night/Saturday morning 10/11 September 1937. That particular stage of the tram to trolleybus conversion programme affected only the westernmost sections of these two all-night tram routes, between Tooting Broadway and Battersea (Prince's Head) and between Hammersmith and Clapham Junction respectively. The tramway infrastructure remained intact over those two routes' easternmost sections, between Battersea (Prince's Head) and Victoria Embankment (Blackfriars) and between Clapham Junction and Vauxhall respectively. As a consequence operation of these two all-night tram routes was divided, with the westernmost sections of each route being converted to trolleybus operation whilst trams continued to provide an all-night service over the easternmost sections. Such partial conversion to trolleybus operation of all-night tram routes was to remain unique to this pair of routes.

The now-divided routes first operated in this form from Sunday night/Monday morning 12/13 September 1937. The opportunity was also taken to extend what would otherwise have been a stump of a tram route between Clapham Junction and Vauxhall onwards to Westminster station on Victoria Embankment, thereby affording passengers access to and from central London. Each 'pair' of night tram and trolleybus routes was scheduled to provide connections at their points of divide, Battersea (Prince's Head) and Clapham Junction respectively. The Sunday to Friday nights allocation to the two new trolleybus routes comprised one trolleybus from Hammersmith depot for the Clapham Junction service and one trolleybus from Wandsworth depot for the Tooting Broadway service. Timetables are in Appendix 5.

The newly-introduced all-night trolleybus routes maintained the established tramway practice of working all-night services as unnumbered routes. The former all-night tram service over route 26 between Hammersmith and Vauxhall had never been specifically classified by London County Council Tramways or the LPTB as an 'official' all-night service so may have possibly displayed route number 26 on night workings. Upon that route's division at Clapham Junction and extension to Westminster Station from 12/13 September 1937 it gained the status of an 'official' all-night tram service and operated as an unnumbered route.

The next three all-night tram routes to become involved in the tram to trolleybus conversion, in 1938 and 1939, operated north of the River Thames and shared Holborn as a common terminal point. These comprised the early morning journeys on tram route 21 from Wood Green (return to North Finchley) and the all-night tram routes from both Hampstead Heath and Stamford Hill.

Conversion of tram routes to trolleybus operation often presented problems with turning arrangements for trolleybuses at termini. The reversible driving positions inherent in most tramcars' design meant that stub-end terminal workings could be undertaken in many streets. Trolleybuses had only one driving position and, although capable of being reversed under power, travelling for short distances on battery power or coasting if the gradient was favourable, operators, in general, adopted loop terminal workings for trolleybus routes. Such loop workings might encompass a short circuit around adjacent side streets or, if space permitted, might involve the construction of a purpose-built turning circle. In the case of Holborn tram terminus, situated at the south end of Gray's Inn Road in a heavily built up area of London, such options were not practicable. On the conversion of the Holborn tram routes to trolleybus operation London Transport instituted a lengthy, dual-direction loop

terminal working with trolleybuses either approaching Holborn via Gray's Inn Road or Farringdon Road.

Two early morning trolleybus journeys on route 521, at 3.01am and 4.02am from North Finchley to Holborn with return journeys from Holborn at 4.05am and 4.57am respectively, replaced, from 7 March 1938, the former Wood Green – Holborn early morning tram journeys over route 21 which had last operated on 5 March 1938. The trolleybus journeys, which operated on Monday to Saturday mornings, required an allocation of two trolleybuses from Finchley depot.

The all-night tram service between Hampstead Heath and Holborn, which had last operated on the night of 8/9 July 1938, was replaced by a Hampstead Heath to Holborn all-night trolleybus service from the night of 10/11 July 1938. This trolleybus route had an approximately hourly frequency, with first and last departures from Hampstead Heath at 12.24am and 5.35am respectively and corresponding first and last return journeys from Holborn at 12.44am and 5.56am respectively, which required an allocation of one trolleybus from Holloway depot on Sunday to Friday nights.

The all-night tram service between Stamford Hill and Holborn last operated on the night of 3/4 February 1939. It was replaced from Sunday night/Monday morning 5/6 February 1939 by an all-night trolleybus route between Stamford Hill (Amhurst Park) and Holborn. This trolleybus service operated to a 30-minute headway for much of the night, with first and last departures from Stamford Hill at 12.30am and 5.03am respectively and corresponding first and last return journeys from Holborn at 1am and 5.34am respectively. An additional departure from Stamford Hill at 3.20am, with corresponding return journey from Holborn at 3.53am, on Sunday to Thursday nights necessitated an allocation from Stamford Hill depot of three trolleybuses on those nights of the week with a reduced allocation requirement of two trolleybuses on Friday nights.

Table H: All Night Bus Routes
Route and/or Garage and/or Vehicle-type Changes, Period 1 September 1939 – 31 August 1940

Route Number	Garage	Allocation Type			Date Effective/Notes
		M–F	Sa	Su	
4	J	1 STL	-	-	By 13/14 Dec 1939. Change of Garage and vehicle type.
6	AC	-	-	1 STL	Weekday nights SNJ last operated 24/25 Oct 1939. Continued to run on Sun nights.
9	M	2 LT	2 LT	1 LT	Mortlake – Aldwych SNJs introduced Sat and Sun nights from 21/22 Oct 1939.
12	AH	1 LT	-	-	Oxford Circus – Peckham Rye SNJ extended to Forest Hill from 14/15 May 1940.
17	R	3 LT	-	3 LT	By 12/13 December 1939. Changes of Garage and vehicle type.
24	CF	-	-	-	SNJ withdrawn after operating 30/31 Dec 1939.
29	AD	1 STL	1 STL	-	2/3 Jan 1940. Palmers Green – Finsbury Park SNJ projected to start from Hadley Woods.
38	T	1 LT	1 LT	-	6/7 Dec 1939. Reduction from 2 to 1 SNJs. Type change.
121	AH	-	-	-	SNJ withdrawn after operating 14/15 Oct 1939.
159	AK	-	-	-	SNJ withdrawn after operating 20/21 Nov 1939.
290	AR	3 LT	-	3 LT	19/20 March 1940. Type change.
292/293	H	3 STL	-	3 STL	14/15 May 1940. Combined allocation reduced by 1 bus.
294	W	2 STD	-	2 STD	19/20 May 1940. Type change.
298	AP	4 LT	3 LT	4 LT	14/15 May 1940. One Mile End – Charing Cross (and return) journey withdrawn. AR
	AR	1 STL	-	1 STL	allocation reduced from 2 to 1 bus.

THE PHONEY WAR

At 11.15am on Sunday 3 September 1939, Prime Minister Neville Chamberlain announced that Britain was at war with Germany. The outbreak of the Second World War had been anticipated over the previous two years, which had given the Authorities some scope to prepare contingency plans. London Transport, along with the main line railway companies, had been brought under direct Government control from 1 September 1939 under the terms of the Emergency Powers (Defence) Act 1939, with control exercised through the Railway Executive Committee. In expectation of casualties arising from an aerial bombardment, Green Line coaches were earmarked for conversion to ambulances, which led to the official withdrawal of Green Line coach routes after service on Thursday 31 August 1939. In practice, some Green Line services continued to operate for a short while longer, including those routes serving East London along the Romford Road. The 3.23am Corbets Tey – Aldgate journey on route Y2 probably operated for the last time on Friday 1 September 1939 whilst the 1.18am Aldgate – Corbets Tey journey on that route was likely to have run for the last time on Saturday 2 September 1939, thus marking out route Y2's night service as the first all-night road passenger transport service 'casualty' of the Second World War. Route Y2 was reinstated from 13 December 1939 but without its former all-night service element.

The four months from September to December 1939 represented a period of unprecedented logistical, planning and operational activity for London Transport's Central Buses Department. Wartime Blackout Regulations were introduced which made the operation of buses, by now equipped with masked headlights and reduced interior lighting, much more difficult at night when drivers also had to cope with the additional hazard of driving along darkened streets. The operational difficulties caused by Blackout conditions led to increased running times becoming applied to most all-night services, as detailed in Table J. No evidence has been traced of increased running times having been applied to all-night tram and trolleybus routes, although their crews would also have had to contend with the difficulties associated with Blackout conditions.

In pursuit of fuel savings daytime bus route schedules were cut, particularly where bus routes ran in parallel with tram or trolleybus services. Some lightly used daytime routes, sections of routes, and journeys, were withdrawn which impacted the all-night network when Special Night Journeys operating over daytime routes were pruned. Garage allocation changes were made in efforts to improve efficiency by reducing dead mileage incurred by buses running into and out of service. The pace of allocation changes in those final four months of 1939 was frantic and could only be comprehensively summarised in the Official Allocation Book issued on 13 December 1939. Under the pressure of the prevailing emergency conditions it is not always possible to be certain about exact dates of change.

Prominent amongst the changes effected in the last four months of 1939 was the re-allocation of all-night bus route 17 away from Hanwell garage to Hammersmith garage by Tuesday night/Wednesday morning 12/13 December 1939,

Table J: All-Night Bus Routes – Increased Terminus to Terminus running times			
Route Number	Running Time Increase in Minutes		Effective Date
	From	To	
4	26	29	1/2 November 1939
9	44	48	18/19 October 1939
11	48	52	24/25 October 1939
13	49	53	30 April/1 May 1941
17	70	74	5/6 December 1939
29	20	21	5/6 December 1939
290	58	62	5/6 December 1939
291	47	50	5/6 December 1939
292	12	14	21/22 November 1939
293	16	18	21/22 November 1939
294	40	43	5/6 December 1939
295	66	70	5/6 December 1939
296	47	50	5/6 December 1939
297	49	52	5/6 December 1939
298	79	86	5/6 December 1939
299	35	37	31 October/1 November 1939

which move introduced LT-type buses to that route. The reason for this change of garage was related to contractions in the length of the daytime element of route 17. From 24 March 1937 the weekday daytime service on the 17 had been withdrawn from Southall and reduced to operate between Hanwell Garage and London Bridge Station. The daytime Sunday service, as well as the Sunday to Friday nights all-night service, had continued to operate between Southall (Brent Road) and London Bridge Station. As a wartime economy measure that section of the weekday daytime service on the 17 between Hanwell Garage and Shepherds Bush was

This route 290 ld Child ticket carries a reminder about gas masks on its reverse side. Although printed during wartime it may well have been issued after the Second World War to use up stocks. *Dennis Cox Collection*

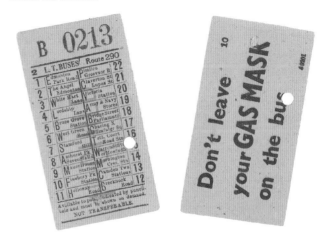

withdrawn from Wednesday 18 October 1939, since it ran in parallel with the 607 trolleybus route. The entire Sunday service over route 17 was also withdrawn. This left the 17 as a weekdays-only daytime route operating between Shepherds Bush (Princess Victoria) and London Bridge Station whilst route 17's all-night service still operated between Southall (Brent Road) and London Bridge Station. Hanwell garage, 5½ miles west of Shepherds Bush, along the Uxbridge Road, became remote from the truncated daytime route 17 and clearly considerable 'dead' mileage savings were achieved by switching the daytime service's allocation to Hammersmith garage, little over one mile away from Shepherds Bush. The allocation for the all-night service on route 17 simply went with its daytime counterpart to Hammersmith garage.

Completely bucking the general trend towards retrenchment, Mortlake Garage – Aldwych Special Night Journeys on route 9 were introduced additionally on Saturday and Sunday nights with effect from the weekend 21/22 October 1939.

Route 9 Special Night Journeys
Timetable effective 18/19 October 1939

		M–Fr pm/am	M–Sa am	Su am	Sa am
Mortlake	dep	11.51	12.14	12.21	12.31
Aldwych	arr	12.35	12.58	1.03	1.05
Ludgate Circus	arr	12.39	-	-	1.19
		am	am	am	am
Ludgate Circus	dep	12.45	-	-	1.24
Aldwych	dep	12.49	1.03	1.08	1.28
Mortlake	arr	1.33	1.49	1.52	2.12

Although the authorities and the nation itself expected an early and devastating assault by Germany, the early months of the Second World War became dubbed 'The Phoney War' since Germany made no aggressive strikes against mainland Britain. Elsewhere, though, British Forces were involved in heavy fighting. German U-Boats wreaked havoc with shipping, squeezing supplies of vital commodities such as fuel and rubber. On 20 September 1939 a British Expeditionary Force was despatched to France. The British Army, along with its French allies, was destined to be overwhelmed by German Forces which episode culminated, in June 1940, in the almost miraculous evacuation of much of that Army from the beaches around Dunkirk. On 10 May 1940 an All-Party Coalition Government was formed when Winston Churchill became Prime Minister.

FINAL ALL-NIGHT TROLLEYBUS CONVERSION
The tramway to trolleybus conversion programme initiated by London Transport in October 1935 involved long term planning with orders for replacement trolleybuses and related infrastructure equipment having to be placed considerably in advance of targeted conversion dates. The supply chain was complex with orders already in the pipeline and the whole conversion process could only be wound down gradually after the outbreak of hostilities. So it came about that what was

destined to be London's final tranche of the tramway to trolleybus conversion programme was implemented nine months into the Second World War when, on Sunday 9 June 1940, those former daytime tram routes serving East London's Commercial Road became operated by trolleybuses. This conversion affected the all-night tram route between Poplar and Bloomsbury which was last operated by London Transport tramcars on Friday night/Saturday morning 7/8 June 1940. The replacement all-night London Transport trolleybus service first ran on Sunday night/Monday morning 9/10 June 1940. This Sunday to Friday night trolleybus route's time-table was very similar to that of the replaced tram route, even to the extent of maintaining an alternate 30-minute and 60-minute service frequency, whose origins went right back to the LCC Tramway's emergency timetable introduced by February 1916, with the aim of reducing the then-tram route's allocation by one tramcar, during the First World War. Consequently an allocation of two trolleybuses from Poplar depot, which had been converted from tram to trolleybus, sufficed to cover the all-night service. Conveniently situated side streets allowed terminus workings at Poplar (Benledi Street) and at Bloomsbury (Red Lion Square). First and last departures from Poplar were at 11.46pm and 4.44am repectively with corresponding first and last return journeys from Bloomsbury at 12.26am and 5.25am. This new all-night trolleybus service followed established practice and operated as an unnumbered route – its daytime counterpart route was numbered 665 and continued to Barking Broadway.

THE BLITZ
The Battle of Britain started in July 1940 and aerial bombardment of London began on 15 August 1940 when Croydon Aerodrome was bombed, whilst the first bomb fell on the City of London at 12.15am on 25 August 1940. These spasmodic, early raids were but harbingers for the onslaught that was to follow. On Saturday afternoon 7 September 1940 the German *Luftwaffe* launched a wave of heavy bomber aircraft against London. Such raids intensified, continuing throughout the remainder of 1940 and into the early months of 1941. This method of aerial assault became known to Londoners as 'The Blitz', their defiant retort to the German word *Blitzkreig* literally meaning 'Lightning War'. The Royal Air Force resisted the German assault during the Battle of Britain which was fought in the skies above southern England during the summer and autumn of 1940 and, displaying much heroism and suffering sacrifice, prevailed in that critical struggle to achieve mastery of the skies over Britain. Thwarted of the capability of continuing with daylight bombing raids, the *Luftwaffe* switched its tactics to devastating night time bombing raids. No area of the capital was immune from the prospect of being bombed but the City, the Docks and the East End were particularly severely attacked.

Clearly under such Blitz conditions normal day-to-day life and routines were severely disrupted. London Transport's scheduling staff was dispersed from 55 Broadway when the Central Bus Department moved into temporary offices at Manor House where they were joined in Spring 1940 by their Tram and Trolleybus Department colleagues, following the latter's brief sojourn working out of Sutton trolleybus depot.

Their numbers were, by then, depleted by colleagues called up for service in the armed forces. All these factors give an insight into the difficulties of maintaining precise records during a period of great change and stress. Further difficulties were caused by operating conditions on the streets of London. London commentator Dennis Cox, who lived through the Blitz, recalls that during night bombing raids in 1940/1941 it was often physically impossible for buses to operate on City streets, which were blocked with debris, hosepipes and the Emergency Services dealing with bomb and fire damage. A further hazard was posed by unexploded bombs. Thus several nights might pass without any service at all until, during a lull in the bombing, services might restart only to be suspended again when the Blitz resumed. Such 'cat and mouse' operations eventually fizzled out after long periods of bombing and a decision was made to suspend operations until further notice. An example of the uncertainty surrounding all-night bus operations at this time is illustrated by Liverpool Street station to Aldwych route 292 which was officially withdrawn on Wednesday 1 January 1941. The City experienced

a particularly heavy bombing raid over Sunday night and Monday morning 29/30 December 1940, during which that well-known, iconic image of the dome of St Paul's Cathedral standing undamaged above the flames and smoke which engulfed Ludgate Hill, was captured on film. That raid blocked City streets with debris and UXBs for several days during which no bus services could possibly have run although diversionary routes were formed as soon as possible. In any event, route 292's buses would probably have been confined to Hackney garage during the period of air raid alerts since, during the Blitz, air raid warnings were normally sounded by siren in the late evening as the first raids took place. The All Clear was not sounded until much later, towards dawn, even though there might not have been enemy activity for several hours. The authorities used this delay as a form of curfew. In summary, the withdrawal dates of all-night bus routes quoted in Traffic Circulars between late 1940 and during 1941 can only be regarded with certainty as the date when the situation was formally reviewed. Actual last nights of operation may have occurred earlier.

Table K: All-Night Bus Routes
Principal Route and/or Vehicle Type Changes
Period 1 September 1940 – 31 December 1941

Route Number	Garage	Allocation Type			Date Effective/Notes
		M–Fr	Sa	Su	
4	-	-	-	-	SNJ officially withdrawn 10/11 June 1941
6	-	-	-	-	Sunday night SNJ withdrawn after 17/18 Nov 1940
9	M	1 LT	1 LT	-	Mortlake Garage-Aldwych SNJs withdrawn after 10/11 Dec 1940. Ludgate Circus journeys continued
12	-	-	-	-	SNJ officially withdrawn after 18/19 Nov 1940
13	-	-	-	-	SNJ officially withdrawn after 12/13 Aug 1941
17	R	3 LT	-	3 LT	Renumbered route 289 from 5/6 Nov 1940
29	-	-	-	-	Hadley Woods-Finsbury Park- Palmers Green Garage SNJ withdrawn after 10/11 Dec 1940
	AD	1 STL	1 STL	-	Palmers Green-Charing Cross and return SNJ introduced from 11/12 Dec 1940. Mixed STL/LT-type allocation 11/12 June – 28/29 October 1941.
292	-	-	-	-	Route officially withdrawn 31 Dec 1940/1 Jan 1941
293	H	3 STL	3 STL	-	Officially reduced from 4 to 3 return journeys from 31 Dec 1940/1 Jan 1941
	H	3 STL	3 STL	-	Route suspended from 13/14 May 1941
	-	-	-	-	Route officially withdrawn 8/9 Aug 1941
294	W	3 STL	-	4 STL	1/2 April 1941 – Type change. Sunday night 12.39 am journey ex Cricklewood and return withdrawn after 11/12 May 1941
298	AP	5 LT	4 LT	5 LT	AR allocation withdrawn after operation 27/28 Oct 1941. Entirely operated by AP from 28/29 Oct 1941 with increased allocation
299	-	-	-	-	Route officially withdrawn 13/14 May 1941

All-night bus route casualties of the Blitz comprised Special Night Journeys operating over sections of daytime routes 4, 6, 12 and 13 as well as all-night bus routes 292, 293 and 299. These withdrawals decimated the Ludgate Circus group of 'press journeys', which had originated in 1921, leaving the Monday–Saturday night return journey between Mortlake Garage and Ludgate Circus on route 9 as the sole survivor, although all-night routes 291, 294, 296 and 297 continued to serve Ludgate Circus. The withdrawal of the Ludgate Circus – Finsbury Park press journey on route 4 left a significant section of road along Aldersgate and Goswell Road, between St Paul's and The Angel, without a night bus service, a deficiency which continues up to the date of writing this book. The withdrawal of early-morning routes 292 and 293 between Liverpool Street Station and Aldwych was influenced by a reduction in demand for early-morning cleaning ladies due to bomb-damaged offices remaining closed, along with a switch to the practice of cleaning offices in the evening, to reduce the risk from bombing raids.

The all-night service over route 17 between Southall (Brent Road) and London Bridge Station was renumbered as route 289, the next vacant number in the descending all-night bus route number series, from 5/6 November 1940. This happened because the imminent extension of the peak hour service on route 17 beyond Shepherds Bush to Park Royal, Coronation Road, implemented on 13 November 1940, was off the line of route of all-night journeys. Renumbering as 289 formally acknowledged the unique routeing of the all-night service.

On route 29 a subtle distinction occurred to the profile of that route's Special Night Journey. After 10/11 December 1940 the Hadley Woods to Finsbury Park and return to Palmers Green Garage Special Night Journey, which had originated on 6/7 November 1921, was withdrawn. A different Special Night Journey was introduced from Wednesday night/Thursday morning 11/12 December 1940 which is of particular interest in view of its future longevity and ultimate incorporation into all-night bus route N29 from 27/28 February 1982.

Extract from Timetable Route 29 Special Night Journey with effect 11/12 December 1940: Monday – Saturday nights		
		am
Palmers Green Garage	dep	12.06
Charing Cross (Trafalgar Square)	arr	12.55
Charing Cross (Trafalgar Square)	dep	1.09
Palmers Green	arr	1.58
Garage: Palmers Green. **Allocation**: 1 STL-type.		

During 1941 a number of provincial bus operators loaned buses to London Transport in order to bolster the number of buses available for London service due to the depletion in London Transport's own fleet caused by enemy action. Loaned provincial buses might have made appearances on Special Night Journeys on routes 9, 11 and 29 between early April and late October 1941.

There were no alterations to all-night tram and trolleybus routes during the Blitz, although such services would have been subject to disruption and suspension as a result of enemy action. London Transport's conduit-equipped tramway showed itself to have two inherent advantages over overhead power supply wiring, which latter system was more easily damaged by bomb blast than sub-surface conduit power supply. The ability of tramcars to reverse anywhere on the conduit-equipped tramway, unimpeded by any need to change power-supply poles, gave great flexibility of operation during Blitz conditions.

From 24/25 March 1942 Turnham Green garage's allocation on route 297 changed to STL-type so removing (for the time being) the ST-type bus from the all-night network. From 29/30 March 1942 that garage's short-working journey on route 297, between Turnham Green and Ludgate Circus, was reduced to operate on Sunday nights/ Monday mornings only and this working was withdrawn entirely after operation on 6/7 December 1942. The core 297 service continued to be worked on Sunday to Friday nights by two of Hammersmith garage's LT-types. The Monday–Saturday Special Night Journey on route 38 between Victoria Station and Chingford Mount, with return to Leyton Garage, was withdrawn at an unknown date between the issue of the 6 January 1943 timetable, which listed it, and the 21 April 1943 timetable, when that working was no longer detailed. From 20/21 April 1943 the last two outbound journeys from London Bridge Station on route 289 were diverted at Shepherds Bush via Shepherds Bush Road to terminate at Hammersmith Garage.

With effect from Tuesday night/ Wednesday morning 31 March/1 April 1942, additional early morning journeys appeared in the timetables of one all-night tram and one all-night trolleybus route in south London. These journeys had originated at earlier dates before the War and had previously been treated as part of the daytime service. The tram route concerned was the all-night service between Clapham Junction and Westminster Station which gained two additional departures from Clapham Junction at 4.52am and 6.11am. Instead of terminating at Westminster Station these two journeys were projected along Victoria Embankment, across Blackfriars Bridge and down Southwark Street to terminate at London Bridge, Borough, whence the return journeys to Clapham Junction departed at 5.31am and 6.51am, although the later return journey was withdrawn from 18/19 April 1944. Also with effect from 31 March/1April 1942 the previously rather limited all-night trolleybus service between Tooting Broadway and Battersea (Prince's Head) was considerably bolstered by starting its service an hour earlier, as well as by the addition of three early morning journeys which extended beyond Tooting Broadway to Mitcham (Fair Green). These additional journeys departed from Battersea (Prince's Head) at 4.4am, 5.13am and 6.23am and returned from Mitcham (Fair Green) at 4.42am, 5.48am and 6.54am. These two routes' extensions led to the all-night services operating over the full length of daytime tram route 26 and daytime trolleybus route 612 respectively. No increase in allocation was necessary since the workings were achieved by the simple expedient of keeping the single tram and single trolleybus already allocated to each route in service for longer hours. The Tram and Trolleybus Departmen's characteristic timing overlap between the finish of the all-night service and the beginning of the daytime schedule was particularly evident in the case of the Mitcham – Battersea trolleybus service over which the regular weekday daytime schedule, as route 612, began with a 5am departure from Mitcham and a 5.40am departure from Battersea.

By, or from, the 21 April 1943 issue of the LPTB's Tram and Trolleybus timetable, and effective on Sunday nights/Monday mornings only, the 11.54pm departure from Stamford Hill on the all-night trolleybus service to Holborn Circus was diverted at Shoreditch to operate to Bishopsgate, for Liverpool Street Station. This journey returned at 12.22am from Liverpool Street Station to Stamford Hill. On Monday to Friday nights this journey followed the standard all-night route between Stamford Hill and Holborn Circus.

A selection of all-night bus route tickets from the 1940s.
Dennis Cox Collection

INTER-STATION ROUTE ALL-NIGHT SERVICE

The disparate locations of London's main line railway termini, on the periphery of central London, meant that cross-London rail passengers had to find an alternative means of conveyance between terminal stations. Daytime inter-station horse-coach services have been traced back to 1851 and, as recorded in Chapter 1, London General operated two all-night inter-station motor bus services between 1915 and 1916, during the First World War. These services were identified by their route numbers – 93 (Victoria Station – Liverpool Street Station) and 95 (Victoria Station – King's Cross Station) – and were primarily intended for the conveyance of military personnel. A daytime inter-station motor coach service was inaugurated in July 1928 by P. Hearn, trading as Gray's Inn Coaches, apparently with sponsorship provided by the London & North Eastern and Southern Railways. Hearn's service expanded and became known as the 'Inter-Station Autobus Service'. It was not acquired by the London Passenger Transport Board upon its formation in July 1933, probably because of continued railway sponsorship. Hearn's Inter-Station Autobus Service continued to expand but it would seem this growth, allied with the prospect of having to provide a Sunday service in Coronation Year 1937, stretched the independent coach operator's resources too far. London Transport took over Hearn's service on Thursday 1 October 1936, designating the route as the 'Inter-Station Bus Service'. Eight forward control petrol-engined Leyland Cubs with 20 seat observation coach bodies (1½ deck) by Park Royal were especially built to work London Transport's Inter-Station Bus Service. Numbered C 106–113, the Cubs were painted in a dedicated livery of sky blue and cream and were based at Old Kent Road garage. Their design included a capacious luggage boot located below the raised rear portion of the bodywork. The Inter-Station Bus Service continued as a daytime and evening operation, without any all-night service element, until withdrawn in entirety after operation on Saturday 16 September 1939, an early victim of wartime economies. The Leyland Cubs subsequently saw wartime service with ENSA, the armed forces' entertainment organisation.

In response to a direct request from the Minister of War Transport, London Transport reinstated a re-designated 'Inter-Station Route' from Monday 20 December 1943 to cope with a considerable increase in troop movements across London. This comprised a daily 30-minute frequency evening service, starting at 6.06pm, as well as incorporating a limited all-night service element worked by one vehicle. Four of the Inter-Station Leyland Cubs had been returned from loan to ENSA by this date and went back into service on their old route. However, since the full evening schedule required five buses, double-deck ST 613 was repainted into sky blue and cream Inter-Station livery, had eight transverse seats in its lower deck removed to create a luggage space and entered service as the fifth Inter-Station bus – thereby potentially restoring an ST-type bus presence to London's all-night bus network.

The all-night element of the Inter-Station Route comprised a 2.54am departure from Waterloo Station to King's Cross Station via Euston Station. After layover the vehicle departed from King's Cross Station at 3.30am and re-traced its outbound journey back to Waterloo Station via Euston Station. Following layover it left Waterloo Station at 4.25am and travelled via Victoria Station to Paddington Station. It then completed a 4.59am trip from Paddington Station to King's Cross Station whence it set off at 5.17 am on a journey directly back to Waterloo Station.

From Wednesday 19 April 1944 the timetable of the Inter-Station Route was recast to create a bi-directional circular service starting from and terminating at Waterloo Station. The main reason for this change was to facilitate buses entering and leaving service at Waterloo Station, the nearest main line railway station to Old Kent Road garage. Basic operation continued to comprise a daily 30-minute frequency evening service, starting at 6.11pm, along with an all-night service element. The route's evening allocation remained constant at five vehicles, reducing to one vehicle required for the all-night service.

Inter-Station Route
Extract from Timetable dated 19/20 April 1944
Late Evening and All-Night Service Elements:
Operated Nightly

Last Journeys – Evening Service				All-Night Service		
		pm	pm	am	am	am
Waterloo	dep	11.11	11.41	12.11	-	4.26
Victoria	arr	11.21	11.51	12.21	-	4.36
	dep	11.25	11.55	12.25	-	4.40
Paddington	arr	11.38	12.08	12.38	-	4.53
	dep	11.43	12.13	12.43	-	4.58
Euston	arr	11.53	12.23	12.53	-	5.08
	dep	11.58	12.28	12.58	-	5.13
Kings Cross	arr	12.02	12.32	1.02	-	5.17
	dep	12.07	12.37	1.07	3.22	5.22
Waterloo	arr	12.21	12.51	1.21	3.36	5.36
		pm	pm	pm	am	am
Waterloo	dep	10.56	11.26	11.56	3.03	3.41
Kings Cross	arr	11.10	11.40	12.10	3.17	3.55
	dep	11.15	11.45	12.15	-	4.00
Euston	arr	11.19	11.49	12.19	-	4.04
	dep	11.24	11.54	12.24	-	4.09
Paddington	arr	11.34	12.04	12.34	-	-
	dep	11.39	12.09	12.39	-	-
Victoria	arr	11.52	12.22	12.52	-	-
	dep	11.56	12.26	12.56	-	-
Waterloo	arr	12.06	12.36	1.06	-	4.21

Garage: Old Kent Road. **Allocation** (All-Night Service): 1 C-type or ST 613.

The Official Allocation Book indicated that the Inter-Station Route's evening service vehicle allocation became five double-deck ST-type buses from 2/3 May 1945. According to The PSV Circle's *Fleet History LT7*, only three ST-types had been converted to Inter-Station layout by that date – these comprised ST 454, 613 and 757. Three others were so converted at later dates – ST 470 and 771 in September 1945 and ST 164 in February 1946. Until these latter three buses were available for Inter-Station Route use it is assumed that the shortfall in allocation requirements was met by either Leyland Cubs or standard London Transport ST-type buses. One vehicle remained sufficient to cover the all-night service.

The most notable change in vehicle-type allocations to all-night road passenger transport services at 29/30 June 1944, as shown in Table L, when compared with vehicle allocation 10 years earlier at 29/30 June 1934, had been the emergence of all-night trolleybus routes with nine trolleybuses allocated to all-night services on Sunday–Friday nights at 29/30 June 1944. An almost corresponding decrease in the number of trams allocated to all-night routes (22 in 1934 and 14 in 1944) reflected the direct replacement of certain all-night tram routes by all-night trolleybus routes. Over the same period the numbers of buses on all-night service showed a significant decrease from 34 buses on Monday–Friday night service at 29/30 June 1934 to 27 buses working on the same nights of the week at 29/30 June 1944. This reduction had been caused by the withdrawal of all-night bus routes 292, 293 and 299, along with the all-night coach service to Upminster on Green Line route AY, as well as a reduction in the number of Special Night Journeys worked over the sections of daytime bus routes – by 29/30 June 1944 such workings were confined to routes 9, 11 and 29. The only new route to be added to the all-night bus network had been the Inter-Station Route, introduced on 20/21 December 1943. This latter route provided the only example of a petrol-engined vehicle on all-night service with either a C-type Leyland Cub or possibly ST 613. At 29/30 June 1944 the three-axle AEC Renown LT-type double-decker dominated all-night bus route operations. A total of 50 trams, trolleybuses and buses was allocated to all-night service on Monday-Friday nights at 29/30 June 1944, which compared with 56 trams and buses allocated to such duties on the same nights of the week ten years previously at 29/30 June 1934.

London Transport's all-night road passenger service network's profile remained unchanged for the rest of the War. Occasional minor timing adjustments were made to individual bus routes whilst a more comprehensive re-timing scheme affected several all-night bus routes from 18/19 April 1944. On 29 October 1944 one return early Sunday morning journey on route 298 was projected beyond Aldgate, that route's inner terminus on Saturday nights/Sunday mornings, to Holborn Circus, for the benefit of night press workers. An early Sunday morning working was introduced over the North Finchley – Holborn Circus trolleybus route with effect from 4 February 1945. This journey departed North Finchley at 4.47am and returned from Holborn Circus at 5.45am and traversed the Holborn loop as route number 621, in the opposite direction to its weekday 521 counterparts, approaching Holborn Circus via Farringdon Road and departing via Gray's Inn Road.

Table L: Vehicle Allocations 29/30 June 1944

Tram Routes	Tram Allocation			Depot
	Su	M–Fr	Sa	
Highgate – Bloomsbury	1	1	-	Highgate
Downham – Victoria Embankment	3	3	-	New Cross
New Cross Gate – Victoria Embankment	2	2	-	New Cross
Tooting Broadway – Victoria Embankment loop	6	6	-	3 ex Clapham
				3 ex Streatham
Battersea – Victoria Embankment	1	1	-	Wandsworth
Clapham Junction – London Bridge, Borough	1	1	-	Wandsworth
Tram Total	**14**	**14**	**-**	

Trolleybus Routes	Trolleybus Allocation			Depot
521 North Finchley – Holborn Circus	2	2	-	Finchley
Hampstead Heath – Holborn Circus	1	1	-	Holloway
Stamford Hill – Holborn Circus	2	2	-	Stamford Hill
Poplar – Bloomsbury	2	2	-	Poplar
Mitcham – Battersea	1	1	-	Wandsworth
Hammersmith – Clapham Junction	1	1	-	Hammersmith
Trolleybus Total	**9**	**9**	**-**	

No	Bus Routes	Bus Allocation			Garage
9	Ludgate Circus – Mortlake Garage	-	1 LT	1 LT	Mortlake
11	Hammersmith – Liverpool Street Station	2 LT	2 LT	-	Hammersmith
29	Palmers Green – Charing Cross	-	1 STL	1 STL	Palmers Green
289	Southall – London Bridge Station	3 LT	3 LT	-	Hammersmith
290	Edmonton – Pimlico	3 LT	3 LT	-	Tottenham
291	Willesden – Liverpool Street Station	1 STL	1 STL	-	Willesden
294	Cricklewood – Liverpool Street Station	3 STL	3 STL	-	Cricklewood
295	Becontree Heath – Charing Cross	3 LT	3 LT	-	Barking
296	Leyton Garage – Waterloo Station	2 LT	2 LT	-	Leyton
297	Turnham Green – Liverpool Street Station	2 LT	2 LT	-	Hammersmith
298	Hornchurch Garage – Charing Cross	5 LT	5 LT	4 LT	Seven Kings
-	Inter-Station Route	1 C or ST	1 C or ST	1 C or ST	Old Kent Road
Bus Total		**25**	**27**	**7**	
TRAM, TROLLEYBUS AND BUS GRAND TOTAL		**48**	**50**	**7**	

A new threat to Londoners was posed from June 1944 by German V1 flying bombs which were followed from September 1944 by the more powerful V2 rockets. Overall, though, the tide of war ran in favour of the Allied Forces. D-Day on 6 June 1944 heralded the Allied invasion of Europe which finally culminated with the surrender of the German Army on 8 May 1945. A ferocious struggle against the Japanese continued in the Far East until, as a consequence of American atomic-bomb raids against Hiroshima and Nagasaki, Japan formally surrendered on 15 August 1945, so marking the end of the Second World War.

The special Inter Station fleetname on the side of one of the blue and cream STs devoted to the service. *Alan B. Cross*

CHAPTER 5
AFTER THE WAR

This is the only photograph traced by the author of a wartime utility bus displaying an all-night bus route number. Tottenham garage allocated G 49, a 1943 Weymann utility-bodied Guy Arab 1, which would have worked to Victoria station on daytime route 76, has had its destination blind set for route 290 for the photographer by an obliging crew. The 290 did not serve the station forecourt, where this shot was taken, but instead called at nearby Wilton Road. The style of the contemporary John Bull advertisement displayed almost certainly dates this view to 1948. *London Trolleybus Preservation Society*

Britain emerged from the Second World War as a victorious but economically weakened nation. Shortages of raw materials and basic commodities persisted as the country entered a period of austerity during which wartime-style rationing continued and even intensified. Bread, unrationed during the War, became rationed for the first time in May 1946. London Transport had to cope with the problems of keeping its vehicles on the road during an era of fuel, labour and spare parts shortages. Not surprisingly, in the prevailing circumstances, minimal changes were made to the all-night road passenger transport network during the five immediate post-war years. One relatively minor, but most interesting, extension to the all-night tram network was effected by the night of 16/17 April 1946 when an additional early morning journey was added to the schedule of the Highgate–Bloomsbury service. The newly-introduced 5.42am departure from Highgate (Archway LT Station) continued in service past the route's normal Bloomsbury terminal point in Theobalds Road, entered the Kingsway Tramway Subway, and then emerged on to Victoria Embankment, where the journey terminated at Westminster Station at 6.16am. The return journey set off at 6.18am bound for Highgate. This journey notionally linked, for the first time ever, London Transport's all-night tram networks serving both north and south London. However, the timing of the journey was such that the last south London all-night tramcar (5.43am ex Westminster Station to Clapham Junction) had already departed from Victoria Embankment over half-an-hour before the Highgate car arrived, although daytime trams would have been running by then.

The North Finchley to Holborn Circus trolleybus route gained an additional early Sunday morning working with effect from 21 April 1946, thus giving two early Sunday morning departures at 4.11am and 4.51am from North Finchley to Holborn Circus on route 621 with corresponding return journeys from Holborn Circus at 5.04am and 5.44am.

From Tuesday night/Wednesday morning 18/19 June 1946 the all-night tram and trolleybus network adopted the use of route numbers, having previously worked most of its routes as unnumbered services. Two of the all-night tram routes, 26 and 35, as well as all the all-night trolleybus routes took up the use of identical route numbers as used by their extant counterpart daytime services whose routeing they covered either in part or in entirety. The remaining four all-night tram routes were given new route numbers.

From the night of 13/14 May 1946 the Monday-Saturday night Special Night Journey on route 29 from Palmers Green Garage to Charing Cross (Trafalgar Square) was back projected to start from Hadley Woods at 11.59pm, although the 1.13am return journey from Charing Cross continued, as previously, to terminate at Palmers Green Garage. Route 9 gained an additional Saturday nights only Special Night Journey between Mortlake Garage and Ludgate Circus from 29/30 June 1946. Two minor enhancements to scarce early Sunday morning journeys on all-night services were also introduced in 1946. The schedule of the Saturday night/Sunday morning service over route 298 was reorganised with effect from 25/26 May 1946. This enabled three early Sunday morning journeys to be projected beyond Aldgate to Holborn Circus whence return journeys bound for Hornchurch Garage

All-Night Tram and Trolleybus Network Route Numbering Introduced 18/19 June 1946

Route No.	Route
	All-Night Tram Routes
1	Tooting Broadway – Victoria Embankment loop via Kennington
	(route number 1 used for service in both directions)
3	Battersea – Victoria Embankment (Blackfriars)
5	Downham – Victoria Embankment (Savoy Street) via Old Kent Road
7	New Cross Gate – Victoria Embankment (Savoy Street) via Camberwell
26	Clapham Junction – London Bridge, Borough
35	Highgate – Westminster Station
	All-Night Trolleybus Routes
513/613	Hampstead Heath – Holborn Circus
	(513 inwards via Grays Inn Road, 613 inwards via Farringdon Road)
521/621	North Finchley – Holborn Circus
	(521 inwards via Grays Inn Road, 621 inwards via Farringdon Road)
543/643	Stamford Hill – Holborn Circus
	(543 inwards via Grays Inn Road, 643 inwards via Farringdon Road)
612	Mitcham – Battersea
628	Hammersmith – Clapham Junction
665	Poplar – Bloomsbury

A fares increase from February 1947 made it necessary for all tram and trolleybus tickets to be reprinted. The new tickets issued for Clapham depot and combined-use tickets for both Streatham and Thornton Heath depots had 'I All N' added to a number of daytime tram routes. By this time numbered fare stages had replaced named ones. *David Seddon Collection*

departed at 3.58am, 5.10am and 6am. On Sunday morning 1 September 1946 a single early Sunday morning working over route 294 was introduced, which departed from Cricklewood Garage at 4.52am and returned from Liverpool Street Station at 5.40am. This journey, together with the recent early Sunday morning service improvement to route 298, was intended to benefit Press workers. The fact that London Transport was not able to restore pre-war running times to all-night bus routes until 8/9 October 1946 gave some idea of the operational difficulties faced by the Board in the immediate postwar period.

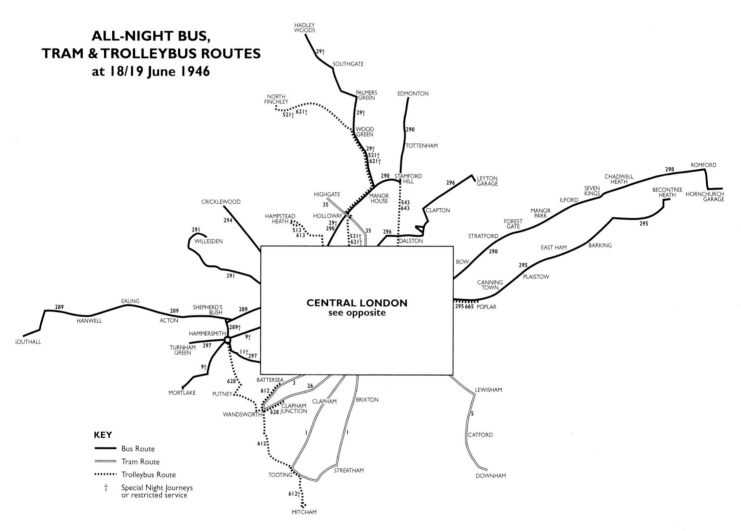

ALL-NIGHT BUS,
TRAM & TROLLEYBUS ROUTES
at 18/19 June 1946

HADLEY
WOODS
29†
SOUTHGATE

NORTH
FINCHLEY
521† 621†

PALMERS
GREEN
29†
EDMONTON

WOOD
GREEN
290

29†
521†
621†

STAMFORD
HILL
290
TOTTENHAM

296 LEYTON
GARAGE

298 ROMFORD

CHADWELL
HEATH
SEVEN
KINGS
BECONTREE
HEATH
HORNCHURCH
GARAGE

CRICKLEWOOD
294

HIGHGATE
35
MANOR
HOUSE
543
643
CLAPTON

ILFORD
MANOR
PARK

HAMPSTEAD
HEATH
513
613
HOLLOWAY
29†
290
521†
621†
35
35
296
DALSTON

FOREST
GATE
295

291
WILLESDEN

STRATFORD
298

EAST HAM
BARKING

291

BOW

CANNING
TOWN
295
PLAISTOW

289 EALING
HANWELL
289 SHEPHERD'S
BUSH
ACTON
289

CENTRAL LONDON
see opposite

295 665 POPLAR

LEWISHAM

SOUTHALL

289†
9†
HAMMERSMITH
297
TURNHAM
GREEN
11† 297

5 CATFORD

9†

MORTLAKE
628
PUTNEY

BATTERSEA
612 3 26
CLAPHAM CLAPHAM
JUNCTION BRIXTON
628

WANDSWORTH

1 1

DOWNHAM

612

TOOTING STREATHAM

612†

MITCHAM

KEY
——— Bus Route
═══ Tram Route
········ Trolleybus Route
† Special Night Journeys
or restricted service

Drawn by Mike Harris

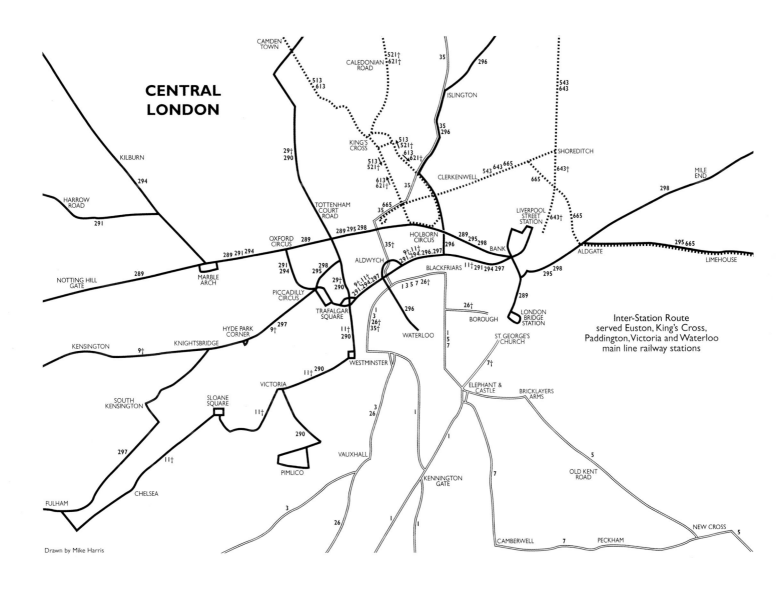

CENTRAL LONDON

Inter-Station Route
served Euston, King's Cross,
Paddington, Victoria and Waterloo
main line railway stations

Drawn by Mike Harris

57

PARLIAMENT LATE NIGHT BUS SERVICES

With effect from Monday night 17 March 1947 London Transport laid on contingency plans to operate special Late Night Bus Routes for Members and Staff of the Houses of Parliament on Monday to Thursday nights, as and when required by late sittings of the House of Commons. Other persons, such as journalists, who had official business at Parliament, could also use the services. Passengers were provided with a book of permits which they exchanged for ordinary tickets issued by the conductor. Official London Transport publicity quoted two fares – 6d for journeys over approximately the first half section of any route and 1 shilling for journeys beyond that point. Individual routes were identified by route letters which were displayed on slip boards on the buses. Each service operated to a fixed route and would set down passengers at any point on the journey. All departures were from Old Palace Yard, Westminster.

Route Letter	Destination	Vehicle Type *	Probable Garage Allocation †
A	Becontree, Bennett's Castle Lane	Double-deck	Barking or Seven Kings
B	Enfield Town Station	Single-deck	Ponders End
C	Highgate, Archway Station	Double-deck	Holloway
D	Queensbury Circle	Double-deck	Edgware or Hendon
E	Harrow-on-the-Hill Station	Double-deck	Harrow Weald
F	Sudbury Town Station	Double-deck	Alperton
G	Isleworth Station	Double-deck	Hounslow
H	Kingston Station	Double-deck	Kingston
I	North Cheam	Double-deck	Sutton
J	Purley Cross	Double-deck	Croydon
K	Sidcup Station	Single-deck	Sidcup

* Source – London Transport Publicity
† Garage Allocation cannot be identified from official LPTB sources. Garages quoted are the author's 'best guess'.

The routes were lengthy and rather convoluted. The Houses of Parliament Special Late Night Buses operated for the first time on Wednesday night 19 March 1947. Unfortunately patronage was most disappointing, as reported by the National Press, 'Forty six people, including fewer than a dozen MPs, travelled home by the special bus service provided for late sittings at the House of Commons, which operated for the first time this morning. The House rose at 1.22am after a long debate on the Navy Estimates. Only a handful of Members then remained. Those who made use of the 11 buses drawn up in the Old Palace Yard were joined by

a number of journalists and officials of the House. None of the buses was filled. Some carried only two passengers. A Highgate bus had a conductress, Miss Dorothy Morris, who was doing extra duty. Like other drivers and conductors, she got no transport home and had to walk two miles from Holloway garage to Crouch End.' *Modern Transport* of 6 June 1947 reported: 'With the reassembly of Parliament after the Whitsun recess, the special late bus services introduced on March 17 were suspended owing to lack of demand. The facility . . . will be available on special demand.' There is no evidence of further operation.

The contemporary Labour Government, elected in 1945 with an unassailable majority, was committed to nationalisation of Britain's key industries, including transport. The Transport Act (1947) led to the formation of the British Transport Commission, which assumed powers from 1 January 1948. London Transport's status changed from public corporation to nationalised industry when, from the BTC's vesting date, it became one of the BTC's Executives and was re-titled as the London Transport Executive.

Wartime specification 'Utility' Guy Arab double-deckers first entered the all-night service duty rota when three G-type buses from Barking garage were allocated to route 295 from 9/10 October 1945, as shown in Table M. Utility Guy Arabs were destined to remain as route 295's allocation for the next 3½ years, but only one other all-night bus route ever received an allocation of Utility-specification buses when route 290 gained a night time allocation of three G-type for nearly 18 months commencing on 4/5 May 1948. The pace of postwar modernisation of all-night bus route vehicle allocations – which, of course, reflected a comparable modernisation of daytime bus routes, from whose workings the all-night allocations were drawn – was spectacular. In just under 18 months, between 4/5 May 1948 and 26/27 October 1949, pre-war LT-types, which up till then had formed the backbone of all-night operations, were swept away, as were STL-types and Utility G-types, by a flood of new AEC Regent RT-type and Leyland Titan PD2-based RTL-type double-deckers. By late October 1949 the 1936-built Leyland Cub allocated to the Inter-Station Route remained the sole prewar vehicle in service on London Transport's all-night bus route network. Starting in November 1949 a batch of 135 RTs and 65 RTLs was fitted with semaphore traffic indicators but also, more significantly, with cab heaters. Many of these buses were allocated specifically to garages which operated all-night bus routes so that they could be used on them to give drivers some extra comfort in the winter months.

INTER-STATION ROUTE BECOMES NIGHT ONLY

With effect from Monday night/Tuesday morning 20/21 November 1950 the Inter-Station Route was completely recast. The entire evening service was withdrawn when the Inter-Station Route was transformed to become solely an all-night service. Most journeys comprised trips between Waterloo, Victoria and Paddington stations or between Waterloo, King's Cross and Euston stations. The service level was enhanced on Sunday nights/Monday mornings when much of the custom comprised National Servicemen returning to barracks after weekend leave. The Inter-Station Route

Table M: All-Night Bus Routes
Vehicle Type and/or Garage Changes
Period: 16 August 1945 – 31 December 1949

Route Number	Garage	Allocation Type			Date Effective/Notes
		M–Fr	Sa	Su	
9	M	1 LT	2 LT	-	29/30 June 1946. Additional Sat night journey.
	M	1 RT	2 RT	-	20/21 Oct 1948 – Type change
11	R	2 RTL	-	2 RTL	26/27 Oct 1949 – Type change
29	AD	1 LT	1 LT	-	26/27 Sept 1945 – Type change
	AD	1 STL	1 STL	-	10/11 Oct 1945 – Type change
	AD	1 LT	1 LT	-	13/14 Feb 1946 – Type change
	WG	1 LT	1 LT	-	By 12/13 Nov 1947 – Garage change
	WG	1 RTL	1 RTL	-	13/14 April 1949 – Type change
289	R	3 RTL	-	3 RTL	12/13 April 1949 – Type change
290	AR	3G	-	3G	4/5 May 1948 – Type change
	AR	3 RTL	-	3RTL	25/26 Oct 1949 – Type change
291	AC	1 RT	-	1 RT	19/20 Oct 1948 – Type change
294	W	2 STL	-	2 STL	25/26 Aug 1946 – Official allocation reduced
	W	2 STL	1 STL	2 STL	31 Aug/1 Sept 1946 – Sunday journey introduced
	W	2 RT	1 RT	2 RT	4/5 May 1948 – Type change
295	BK	3G	-	3G	9/10 Oct 1945 – Type change
	BK	3RTL	-	3 RTL	12/13 April 1949 – Type change
296	T	2RT	-	2 RT	4/5 May 1948 – Type change
297	R	2 RTL	-	2 RTL	12/13 April 1949 – Type change
298	AP	5 LT	3 LT	5 LT	25/26 May 1946. Sat pm/Sun am schedule recast, saving 1 bus
	AP	5 RT	3 RT	5 RT	4/5 May 1948 – Type change
	AP	5 RTL	3 RTL	5 RTL	25/26 Oct 1949 – Type change
Inter-Station	P	1C/ST	1C/ST	1C/ST	9/10 Oct 1946 – Type change
	P	1C	1C	1C	30 April/1 May 1947 – Type change

continued to be worked by Old Kent Road garage but the C-type Leyland Cubs – by then London Transport's last petrol engine buses in public service – were replaced by standard RT-type double deckers – one such being sufficient to cover the service from Monday nights to Saturday nights but with an increased allocation of three being required to work the enhanced Sunday night services. The C-type Leyland Cubs, as well as the dedicated ST-types formerly used on the route, had special provision for luggage space. The RT-types used on the Inter-Station Route were simply standard service buses capable of being deployed on any of Old Kent Road garage's routes. However, their additional seating capacity – 56 seats compared with 40 seats on the ST-type and only 20 on the Cubs – provided ample capacity such that passengers could leave their luggage in the spaces between empty seats.

Above Inter Station Leyland Cub C 110 is seen Waterloo station in 1947. Capacious luggage space was provided beneath the upper half-deck. *DWK Jones/courtesy David Packer*

Right Park Royal-bodied RT 204 was photographed in 1951 at the Inter Station Route's bus stop beside the main entrance to Victoria station. *Alan Cross*

RTL 105, with restricted wartime-style destination blind display, was photographed in the City of London entering King William Street, having just passed Bank, working a route 295 journey bound for Fair Cross (Barking) LT garage. *D A Jones/London Trolleybus Preservation Society*

Tottenham garage-based RTL 276, with restricted wartime-style destination blind display, was photographed in 1950 homeward bound on route 290 at Victoria's Wilton Road bus stop. *Alan Cross*

ALL-NIGHT TRAMS REPLACED BY BUSES

On 15 November 1946 London Transport had announced that its remaining tram routes, by then confined to south London apart from three routes which still penetrated into north London via the Kingsway Subway, would be replaced by buses rather than by trolleybuses. Stage 1 of the South London Tram Conversion programme, which principally involved the conversion of Wandsworth from a tram and trolleybus depot to a bus garage, took effect from Sunday 1 October 1950. All-night tram routes 3 (Battersea, Prince's Head – Blackfriars) and 26 (Clapham Junction – London Bridge, Borough) as well as all-night trolleybus routes 612 (Battersea, Prince's Head – Mitcham) and 628 (Hammersmith – Clapham Junction) operated for the last time on Friday night/Saturday morning 29/30 September 1950. The two former all-night tram routes were replaced by two new all-night bus routes, 168 and 288, which were both extended beyond the former tram routes' outer termini, to operate between common termini at Wandsworth (High Street) and Farringdon Street. The 168, which displayed the same route number as a tram-replacement daytime bus route covering identical routeing, replaced all-night tram route 26 whilst the 288, which adopted the next available route number in the descending all-night bus route numbering series, replaced all-night tram route 3. Since all-night route 168 had two early Sunday morning journeys it became the first of the two new routes to operate when, at 3.54am on Sunday morning 1 October 1950, RT 1869 set off from Wandsworth on new route 168, with London Transport bus chief J. B. Burnell in attendance overseeing the changeover from tram to bus. Author Ken Glazier, who was amongst a group of enthusiasts waiting to travel on it, recalled that RT 1869 stalled in Armoury Way. A long delay ensued before the bus could be restarted, with the result that the inaugural tram replacement bus journey in the SLTC programme ran considerably later than its 3.54am scheduled departure time from Wandsworth, which delay produced some choice language from press workers who had been waiting for it to turn up! RT 1869 was, on its return journey from Farringdon Street

to Wandsworth, the first service bus to run along the westbound reserved tram-track on Victoria Embankment also used by tram replacement bus routes. The first RT-type in service on route 288 set off from Wandsworth that same Sunday evening at 11.27pm. Routes 168 and 288 were unique amongst contemporary all-night bus routes in featuring joint compilation of their duty schedule. Thus the crew starting the night on route 168 took up duty with the 288 bus after their meal break, and vice versa. Wandsworth garage's allocation for both routes 168 and 288 switched from RT-type to RTL-type from 1/2 May 1951. New all-night trolleybus route 630 (Hammersmith Broadway – Tooting Broadway) also started on Sunday night/Monday morning 1/2 October 1950. Between Hammersmith and Wandsworth High Street the 630 simply replaced the all-night service previously provided over route 628 – the remaining section of the 628 beyond Wandsworth to Clapham Junction being covered by all-night bus route 168. Between Wandsworth and Tooting Broadway the 630 replaced former route 612's all-night service. The two remaining sections of the now-dismembered 612 were covered by all-night bus route 288 between Wandsworth and Prince's Head and by early morning journeys between Mitcham and Prince's Head on newly-introduced daytime tram-replacement bus route 44. Route 630 also ran as a high frequency daytime trolleybus service between Harrow Road (Scrubs Lane) and West Croydon. Timetables and allocations for all-night routes 168, 288 and 630 upon inception are to be found in Appendix 6.

Top left This E/1-class tramcar was photographed at Hungerford Bridge on Victoria Embankment at 1.38am on Wednesday 13 April 1949 working hourly-frequency all-night tram route 3 from Blackfriars to Battersea, Prince's Head. *Arthur Packer/courtesy David Packer*

Top right An E/1-class tramcar loads at Hungerford Bridge on Victoria Embankment at 12.40am on Wednesday 13 April 1949. This car, on all-night route 1, would have left the Embankment via Westminster Bridge before heading out to Clapham and Tooting. *Arthur Packer/ courtesy David Packer*

Unconnected with these route changes, but coincidentally occurring at much the same time, was the renaming of Hammersmith garage – which provided the allocation for all-night bus routes 11, 289 and 297 – as Riverside garage on 12 July 1950, from which same date tram and trolleybus depots were given codes. This renaming was in order to clearly differentiate between the former Hammersmith bus garage and Hammersmith trolleybus depot following the merger of London Transport's formerly separate Central Bus and Tram & Trolleybus Departments into a new Central Road Services organisation. Riverside garage's allocation for route 11, which included the early morning Hammersmith – Liverpool Street Station journeys changed from RTL-type to 8ft-wide RTW-type from 10/11 April 1951.

Stage 2 of the SLTC was implemented on Sunday 7 January 1951 and principally involved the conversion of tram routes in the Clapham and Tooting areas to bus operation. Complex all-night tram route 1 was involved and operated for the last time on Friday night/Saturday morning 5/6 January 1951. With effect from Sunday night/Monday morning 7/8 January 1951 tram route 1 was replaced by new all-night bus route 287. Buses on the 287 followed an identical cyclical working pattern between Victoria Embankment and Tooting Broadway to that of the superseded tram route. However, whilst the routeing remained identical, the frequency of bus route 287 was increased to run every 24 minutes (2½ buses per hour) which compared with a 30-minute frequency (two trams per hour) on the former tram route. This was intended to compensate for the reduced capacity of the replacement RT and RTL-type buses (56 seats) compared with, typically, 73 seats on an E/1-class tramcar and thereby maintain the same overall passenger capacity over route 287 as had been provided by all-night tram route 1, which had carried full loads on many journeys. The fact that the replacement buses could achieve faster running times than the trams – a complete 'cycle' of routes 1/287 occupied a tram for exactly three hours whilst a bus could get round in 2 hours 24 minutes, including layover time – meant that, despite the 287's higher frequency, the service could be maintained with the same number of buses as trams; six. Route 287's allocation comprised three RT-type double-deck buses from Brixton garage, the former Streatham (Telford Avenue) tram depot, and 3 RTL-type buses from Clapham garage, the former Clapham tram depot. The 287's schedule maintained the old-established transfer connection between Blackfriars Bridge-direction and Westminster Bridge-direction buses at Kennington Church. The 287 adhered to London Transport's general policy for all-night services in operating 'Saturday Night–Sunday Morning Excepted'.

RT 2034 and RT 3993 behind were photographed at Brixton garage about to take up duties on route 287 which had replaced all-night tram route 1. *G F Ashwell/courtesy Malcolm Papes*

A token Saturday night/Sunday morning service over part of the 287's routeing was provided by a Special Night Journey which worked over a section of daytime bus route 57A – renumbered as route 181 from 17/18 May 1952 and being the embryonic form of what would later become all-night bus route N81 from 2/3 January 1971.

Extract from Timetable Bus Route 57A
Streatham – Victoria via Tooting Broadway
Special Night Journey Introduced 6/7 January 1951
Operated Saturday nights/Sundays mornings only

am				am
1.12	dep	Clapham Common Station	arr	2.03
1.19		Balham Station		1.56
1.26		Tooting Broadway		1.49
1.36	arr	Streatham, St Leonard's Church	dep	1.39

Garage: Clapham. **Allocation:** 1 RTL-type.

The third stage of the SLTC, effected from the night of 7/8 April 1951, principally involved the conversion of lengthy daytime tram routes 16/18 (Purley – Victoria Embankment) to bus operation as route 109 which incorporated a limited all-night service worked by one RT-type bus from Thornton Heath garage. The 109's schedule also featured a number of daily early morning journeys worked by RT-type buses from both Brixton and Thornton Heath garages which started at around 3.50am and certain of which, including journeys to/from Purley, became included in All-Night Bus timetables.

The first tram-replacement bus to enter service in Stage 5 of the SLTC was a Walworth garage-based RTL-type, driven by 68-year-old former tram driver Albert Lee, which worked route 185's 3.04am departure from Camberwell Green to Catford on Sunday 7 October 1951. Daytime bus route 185, which had replaced tram route 58 between Blackwall Tunnel and Victoria, incorporated an irregular-headway all-night service which operated between Catford (St Laurence Church) and Vauxhall Station on all seven nights of the week, utilising one RTL-type bus from Walworth garage.

All-night tram route 7 (New Cross Gate – Embankment (Savoy Street) via Peckham), operated for the last time on the night of 5/6 October 1951. From the night of 7/8 October 1951 tram route 7 was replaced by newly-introduced all-night bus route 286, worked by three RT-type buses based at Peckham garage. Most journeys on the 286 continued to terminate at New Cross Gate, as had predecessor tram route 7, but two journeys on the 286 were projected beyond New Cross Gate to a new terminal point at Brockley Rise. These journeys returned from Brockley Rise at 3.59am and 4.41am and, in common with other through 286 journeys from New Cross Gate, were projected beyond former all-night tram route 7's terminus on Victoria Embankment at Savoy Street to reach a new terminus at Charing Cross (LT Station). From 6/7 January 1952 a third journey was projected to Brockley Rise which returned at 1.06am for Charing Cross. Terminating buses on the 286 then had to complete a lengthy out of service loop working via Northumberland Avenue, Whitehall and

E/1-class car 1846 is seen at the very eastern end of Queens Road in New Cross Gate, having returned from working the return journey on all-night route 7 which deviated from the main line of route at Elephant & Castle to run instead to St George's Church, in Borough High Street, rather than to Charing Cross Underground Station on Victoria Embankment. The conductor had forgotten to change the rear destination blind for the return trip. Having completed that night's last scheduled journey on route 7 at 6.30am at this point, the car would have gone out of service and returned to New Cross depot. *F W Ivey*

Opposite This re-built E/1-class tramcar was photographed at Victoria Embankment's Savoy Street terminus in the early hours of Wednesday 13 April 1949 prior to setting off to Downham on all-night tram route 5. The river Thames is on the far side of the tramcar. *Arthur Packer/courtesy David Packer*

Whitehall Place to change direction ready for their return journeys. Route 286 had a nominal frequency of 30 minutes, the same as tram route 7, but due to a combination of faster running times by the buses and an increased allocation of three buses, compared with two trams, the 286's headway was boosted to approximately every 15 minutes until 12.30am and again from 3.30am, when passengers demand was greater. During the quieter period of the night one bus from the 286's allocation was taken out of service at Peckham garage between 1.21am and 3.38am.

London's penultimate all-night tram route, as well as the last such route to operate south of the River Thames, came to an end in Stage 6 of the SLTC when, at 6.02am on Saturday 5 January 1952, the last tramcar on all-night route 5 (Downham – Embankment) terminated at New Cross Gate. Route 5 laid claim to the distinction of having been London's

Initially, existing stocks of geographical Bell Punch tickets were used up for Early Morning Single issues, such as this 2d ticket for Willesden garage – Liverpool Street route 291 (above left). A fares rise from 2 March 1952 increased the minimum Early Morning Single fare from 2d to 3d. Dedicated Early Morning Single tickets, with numerical fare stages, were printed at this time. *Dennis Cox collection*

longest-surviving all-night tram route to have maintained a continuous service, having originated as London County Council Tramways' New Cross Gate to Blackfriars Road via Old Kent Road all-night horse-tram service inaugurated on the night of 12/13 February 1899. Almost 53 years of all-night tram operation was replaced by new all-night bus route 285 from the night of 6/7 January 1952, worked by four RT-type buses based at London Transport's newly-opened Rye Lane garage in Peckham. The 285 maintained a 30-minute frequency over a substantial section of its route between Catford (LT Garage) and Victoria Embankment. Alternate journeys were projected beyond Catford to give an hourly service to and from the former night tram route 5's terminal point at Downham (Bromley Road). It will be recalled that the cost and labour implications of manning the change-pit between conduit-powered and overhead-powered tramway at Downham Way are thought to have precluded operations by night tram route 5 through the Downham housing estate to Grove Park. This constraint was removed upon conversion to bus operation but, perhaps surprisingly, only two early morning journeys on the 285 were projected along Downham Way to Grove Park, which returned at 3.55am and 4.25am from Grove Park bound for Victoria Embankment. Terminating buses at Charing Cross (LT Station) had to perform an identical out of service loop to the counterparts on route 286 to change direction ready for their return journeys. Also, in similar style to route 286, an increased allocation on route 285 (four buses compared with three trams on route 5), combined with faster bus running times, allowed the 285's nominal 30-minute headway to be boosted up until 12.30am and again from around 4.00am. One bus on the 285's allocation was actually taken out of service for no less then 3½ hours, between 12.27am and 3.57am, during which interval the service was maintained by the remaining three buses.

London's last all-night tram service over route 35 between Highgate (Archway Station) and Bloomsbury, with one early morning journey extended to and from Westminster Station, was withdrawn after operation on Friday night/Saturday morning 4/5 April 1952 in Stage 7 of the SLTC. The all-night tram service from Highgate was something of a London institution, as recorded by the press, 'Early today, the market porters, newspaper vendors and morning chars, the Harrys, Alfs and Berts, had their last ride on the Old Faithful.' Those persons who had acquired an April 1952 issue of London Transport's Central Area Bus Map, to obtain details of new routes introduced following the closure of the Kingsway Subway and related conversion of daytime tram routes 33 and 35 to bus operation as routes 171 and 172 respectively, would have noted that all-night tram route 35 was identified on that map as having been replaced by new all-night bus route 172, described as operating between Highgate (Archway Station) and Bloomsbury. Any such persons who ventured to an appropriate bus stop in anticipation of catching a bus on all-night route 172 might have been bemused by the appearance of an all-night bus displaying route number 292, not 172, and with ultimate destination blind set for Charing Cross (LT Station) and not Bloomsbury. It would seem that London Transport had originally planned to introduce an identical route replacement of all-night tram route 35 as bus route 172 operating between Highgate and Bloomsbury. Apparently at a late stage – certainly too late for the April 1952 Central Area Bus Map to be modified – the proposed operation was reviewed and a decision was made to extend all-night tram route 35's replacement bus route beyond Bloomsbury to Charing Cross (LT Station) as route number 292, which first operated on 6/7 April 1952. Buses on daytime Kingsway Subway tramway replacement routes 170 (converted from tram route 31 on 1 October 1950), 171 and 172 were routed via Kingsway and Aldwych whence they gained access to and from Victoria Embankment via a somewhat convoluted routeing along Arundel Street (southbound) or Norfolk Street (northbound) and Temple Place. In order to form a turning loop, inbound buses on all-night route 292 were routed, after Kingsway, via Aldwych, Strand and Northumberland Avenue to reach their stand on Victoria Embankment at Charing Cross (LT Station). Buses setting off on 292's return journeys to Highgate followed the same routeing as northbound daytime buses on routes 170, 171 and 172, continuing along Victoria Embankment as far as Temple Place and then proceeding via Norfolk Street up to Strand and Aldwych before completing the lengthy two-mile long loop working when turning into Kingsway. An enhanced 30-minute frequency over route 292 represented a distinct improvement on all-night tram route 35's hourly headway. The use of route number 292 was noteworthy since it represented the first instance of London Transport reissuing a vacant route number in the descending all-night bus route number series – at the time numbers 292, 293 and 299 were vacant. With effect from Tuesday night/Wednesday morning 9/10 September 1952 route 292's central London terminal point was changed from Victoria Embankment to Trafalgar Square with 292 buses working between Aldwych and

Trafalgar Square via Strand in both directions of travel. Whilst neither route 292, nor its all-night tram route 35 predecessor, had any long or strong affinity with Victoria Embankment routeing, the 292 could lay claim to having been the first all-night bus route to have been removed from Victoria Embankment.

Unconnected with the tramway conversion programme, route 29 gained an additional Saturday night-only Special Night Journey to Turnpike Lane which departed from Charing Cross at 1.8am, five minutes in advance of the 1.13am departure of route 29's established Monday – Saturday night Special Night Journey.

The eighth, and final, stage of the South London Tram Conversion programme was reached on Saturday 5 July 1952 when daytime tram routes between Victoria Embankment or Southwark Bridge and New Cross, Greenwich, Lewisham, Woolwich and Abbey Wood operated for the last time. Although there were no longer any all-night tram routes left, this conversion introduced what were to prove to be two enduring all-night bus services worked over daytime tram replacement bus routes. These new night services partially replaced untimetabled staff tramcar workings and partially replaced early morning journeys on daytime tram routes.

Extract from Timetable Bus Route 177
Special Night Journeys introduced 5/6 July 1952
Saturday nights/Sunday mornings only

				W		W
		pm	am	am	am
Abbey Wood, LT Garage	dep	-	-	-	-
Plumstead Station		-	1.11	-	-
Greenwich, Ship and Billet		-	1.29	3.01	-
New Cross Gate		11.50	1.44	3.16	4.16
Elephant & Castle		12.06	1.59	-	4.31
Embankment, Savoy Street	arr	-	2.09	-	4.40

			BE	B
		am	am	am
Embankment, Savoy Street	dep	-	2.09	4.40
Elephant & Castle		12.11	2.18	4.49
New Cross Gate		12.27	2.33	5.04
Greenwich, Ship and Billet		12.42	2.48	5.17
Plumstead Station		1.00	-	5.39
Abbey Wood, LT Garage	arr	-	-	5.44

B – via Blackfriars Bridge. W – via Westminster Bridge.
BE – via Blackfriars Bridge. Connected at New Cross Garage with 2.38am route 182 departure to Eltham.
Garage: New Cross (temporarily outstationed at Peckham Garage until 15/16 November 1952). **Allocation:** 1 RT-type.

Also from the night of 5/6 July 1952 a nightly service was introduced on bus route 182, which had replaced daytime tram route 46 between Woolwich and Southwark Bridge, with the 182 bus route being extended to Cannon Street Station. The temporary unavailability of new RT and RTL-type buses

restored the prewar STL-type to all-night bus duties allocated to New Cross garage for route 182. New Cross garage's STLs were temporarily accommodated at Peckham garage whilst the New Cross premises were being converted from tram depot to bus garage and finally took up operation from New

Cross from 12 November 1952. The core all-night service over route 182 operated nightly between New Cross Garage and Woolwich with one weekday early morning return journey projected beyond New Cross to/from Cannon Street Station. The all-night service element of route 182 required a nightly allocation of one STL-type, whilst on weekdays the 182's service was enhanced by additional early morning journeys.

By the high summer of 1952 London Transport's all-night road services had become entirely worked by either buses or trolleybuses. Tramcars, which had inaugurated London's very first all-night public road passenger transport service introduced on 1/2 January 1899 over The North Metropolitan Tramway Company's Stratford–Aldgate route, and which had dominated the provision of London's all-night services for their first thirty years, passed into history.

Route No	Trolleybus Routes	Allocation			Depot/Garage
		Su	M–Fr	Sa	
513/613	Hampstead Heath – Holborn Circus	1	1	-	Highgate
521/621	North Finchley – Holborn Circus	2	2	2	Finchley
543/643	Stamford Hill – Holborn Circus	2	2	-	Stamford Hill
630	Hammersmith – Tooting Broadway	1	1	-	Hammersmith
665	Poplar – Bloomsbury	2	2	-	Poplar
	Trolleybus Total	**8**	**8**	**2**	
	Bus Routes				
9	Ludgate Circus – Mortlake Garage	-	1RT	2RT	Mortlake
11	Hammersmith – Liverpool Street Stn	2RTW	2RTW	-	Riverside
29	Hadley Woods – Charing Cross	-	1RTL	2RTL	West Green
109	Purley – Victoria Embankment	1RT	1RT	-	Thornton Heath
168	Wandsworth – Farringdon Street	1RTL	1RTL	1RTL	Wandsworth
177	Abbey Wood – Victoria Embankment	-	-	1RT	New Cross
181	Clapham Common – Streatham	-	-	1RTL	Clapham
182	Woolwich – Cannon Street Station	1STL	1STL	1STL	New Cross
-	-	-	-	-	(Peckham)
185	Catford – Vauxhall	1RTL	1RTL	1RTL	Walworth
285	Grove Park – Victoria Embankment	4RT	4RT	-	Rye Lane
286	Brockley Rise – Victoria Embankment	3RT	3RT	-	Peckham
287	Tooting Broadway – Victoria Embankment loop	3RT	3RT	-	Brixton
		3RTL	3RTL	-	Clapham
288	Wandsworth – Farringdon Street	1RTL	1RTL	-	Wandsworth
289	Southall – London Bridge Station	3RTL	3RTL	-	Riverside
290	Edmonton – Pimlico	3RTL	3RTL	-	Tottenham
291	Willesden – Liverpool Street Station	1RT	1RT	-	Willesden
292	Highgate(Archway) – Victoria Embankment	2RT	2RT	-	Holloway
294	Cricklewood – Liverpool Street Station	2RT	2RT	1RT	Cricklewood
295	Becontree Heath – Charing Cross	3RTL	3RTL	-	Barking
296	Leyton Garage – Waterloo Station	2RT	2RT	-	Leyton
297	Turnham Green – Liverpool Street Stn	2RTL	2RTL	-	Riverside
298	Romford Garage – Charing Cross	5RTL	5RTL	3RTL	Seven Kings
	Inter-Station Route	3RT	1RT	1RT	Old Kent Road
	Bus Total	**46**	**46**	**14**	
	Trolleybus and Bus Grand Total	**54**	**54**	**16**	

Table N: All-Night Bus and Trolleybus Routes
Vehicle Allocations at 5/6 July 1952

Riverside garage's RTL 241 is seen on the bus stand at London Bridge Station before setting off bound for Hammersmith Broadway on all-night route 289. The bifurcation in service of the night's last two outbound departures on the 289 (later N89) from Shepherds Bush to Hammersmith was a practice which dated back to at least 20/21 April 1943, since the buses were returning to Hammersmith (re-named Riverside from 12 October 1950) garage in any case, but which only became detailed in timetables from 1977 onwards. *A R Packer*

Coronation Year 1953 heralded an end to the austerity of the immediate postwar years. The days of wartime-induced rationing were numbered; sugar rationing ended in September 1953 whilst meat rationing was lifted on 3 July 1954. A spirit of optimism and renewal had seemed to sweep across the nation coincident with Queen Elizabeth II's accession to the Throne. The contemporary wave of modernity seemingly extended even to London Transport's all-night bus network when the last prewar STL-type buses in use on all-night service, on route 182, were progressively replaced, between 4/5 March and 6/7 May 1953, by RT-type buses at New Cross garage. Thereafter the all-night bus network became worked exclusively by LT's highly standardised fleet of RT family double-deck buses.

CORONATION 1953

Her Majesty Queen Elizabeth II was crowned within Westminster Abbey on Tuesday 2 June 1953. The Coronation attracted hordes of spectators, most of whom travelled to and from London, as well as within the metropolis, by public transport. Many such visitors travelled overnight or set off in the early hours of the morning in order to seek good vantage points along the processional route. On Coronation Day vehicular traffic, including London Transport service buses, was excluded from entering a substantial area of central London, which necessitated curtailments and diversions to many Central Bus daytime and all-night bus routes. The all-night route network was augmented on both the night immediately preceding and the night immediately following the Coronation to give, in general, a frequency of four vehicles per hour on each route throughout the night. For the nights of 1/2 June and 2/3 June 1953 the all-night route network's allocation on routes 168, 285-292, 294-298, 513/613, 543/643, 630 and 665 was increased to 129 buses and trolleybuses, which represented a near 300% of the normal

weekday night allocation of 44 buses and trolleybuses on those routes. The all-night service on the Inter-Station Route was also boosted. Many daytime bus routes were also supplemented on Coronation Day and, in some instances, operated a continuous 24-hour service between around 2.30am on 2 June and 2.30am on 3 June. Throughout Coronation Week, starting on Sunday night/Monday morning 31 May/1 June and ending on Saturday night/Sunday morning of 6/7 June, many daytime bus routes operated much later than normal with last departures from the inner area up to around 1.30am.

Above Over the Coronation period all-night route 292 was truncated to terminate at Aldwych whilst that route's allocation was increased to four buses to maintain an enhanced 15 minute frequency service. Holloway garage's RT 2470 is seen at Aldwych in the early hours of Coronation Day itself prior to making a return journey to Highgate, Archway Station. An 'Aldwych' slip-board is displayed in the lower-deck's front window. *Alan Cross*

Left The most extensive all-night bus route diversion over the Coronation period was that which was applied to the 297. Between Fulham Road and Aldwych route 297 buses were diverted via Earls Court, Kensington High Street, Notting Hill Gate, Bayswater Road, Sussex Gardens, Marylebone Road, Euston Road, Woburn Place, Southampton Row and Kingsway. For the duration Riverside garage's allocation to the 297 was increased from two to nine buses in order to maintain a 15 minute frequency over the considerably extended routeing. That garage's RTL 61 passes the Waldorf Hotel in Aldwych on an outbound diversionary journey to Hammersmith Broadway. *Alan Cross*

THE CHAMBERS REPORT

Ironically the general improvement in national prosperity had an adverse effect on London Transport's finances as passenger numbers, and hence revenues, decreased whilst costs, particularly wages, increased. London Transport's finances had veered from a healthy £5.9 million surplus in traffic receipts in 1948 to a deficit of £1.5 million in 1951. There was also a perception that the quality of service was deteriorating, allied with general dissatisfaction amongst passengers. This worrying state of affairs led the then Minister of Transport and Civil Aviation, the Right Hon. A. T. Lennox-Boyd, to appoint a Committee of Inquiry into London Transport on 28 April 1953. That Committee's findings, dubbed the Chambers Report after its Chairman's surname, S. P. Chambers, Chairman of Imperial Chemical Industries Limited, were published in January 1955. Many facets of London Transport's road and rail passenger transport operations were commented upon and included:

NIGHT SERVICES

(Paragraph 119)

'The cost of travel in certain circumstances may be substantially higher than the average cost owing to those circumstances and it may be that the provision of a service can be justified only if a special charge is made. For example, in Birmingham, Glasgow and Manchester all-night services are operated but higher fares are charged. London Transport provides a few all-night bus and trolleybus services but in no cases is any fare charged above the standard (daytime) fare. The demand for services in the night is probably as great in London as in other cities in this country, or it may be greater, but we were informed that the provision of more night services would be uneconomic at the standard fares. The objections to the introduction of extra late services at higher fares do not appear to us to be very strong. It is true that some of the users may be workers on night duty, but at least one provincial city gives special vouchers to night workers enabling them to use the night services at daytime fares. We recommend that this matter of providing more bus services at night should be examined.'

(Paragraph 120)

'One important factor, which must be borne in mind, is that the provision of an adequate public transport service at night by discouraging the use of private cars for night journeys might encourage the use of public transport in the daytime as well. In their competition with the private car London Transport must be at a disadvantage if their services stop at an inconvenient time and this disadvantage will affect their competitive power during the day. We suggest that this subject should be re-examined to ascertain whether the provision of extra services at night, coupled with an increase in the fares for all-night services, i.e. all services operating after some fixed time, might be justifiable (subject to any concession for night workers which might be deemed necessary) – (a) financially; (b) as part of the duty to provide an integrated system of public transport throughout the area, and (c) as part of a campaign to encourage the use of public transport instead of private transport.'

The Chambers Report *(Para 410)* recommended that:

'Consideration should be given to the provision of better all-night services and to the charging of higher fares for night services, as is the practice in certain provincial undertakings.'

The Chambers Report's recommendation that all-night services should be improved was not taken up by London Transport. On the contrary, for more than three years following publication of the Report, almost nothing in the way of change occurred to either the all-night route network itself or to the vehicle types that operated upon it.

From 4/5 May 1955 Mortlake garage's allocation for route 9 changed from RT to RTL-type, affecting that route's Special Night Journeys. London Transport's timetable of All-Night Routes published in December 1955 detailed, for the first time, 'Special Morning Journeys starting between 12.30 and 5am' on daytime bus and trolleybus routes. 100 listed routes incorporated such journeys, many of which could be traced back to tramway origins. From Tuesday night/Wednesday morning 1/2 May 1956 Willesden garage's allocation for all-night route 291 changed from RT to RTL-type in conjunction with the latter type being allocated to that garage's turns on daytime routes 52 and 176. From the night of 15/16 October 1957 Turnham Green garage re-entered the all-night bus garage rota when it took over responsibility for route 297 from Riverside garage, bringing an associated change to RT-type buses on the 297.

On Saturday night/Sunday morning 30 November/ 1 December 1957 the extant single return Special Night Journey on route 181 was extended beyond Clapham Common to Kennington Church at the request of London Transport staff living in the Kennington area for whom no other facilities existed. That section of this Special Night Journey beyond Stockwell Station along Clapham Road to Kennington deviated from the line of route of the daytime service on the 181, which proceeded via South Lambeth Road and Vauxhall to Victoria. From 3/4 December 1955, route 181's Special Night Journey's southern terminal point had been extended in Streatham from St Leonard's Church to the LT Garage.

Extract from Timetable Bus Route 181
Special Night Journey from 30 November/1 December 1957
Operated Saturday night/Sunday morning only

am	am				am
-	2.20	dep	Kennington, Church	arr	2.18
1.12	2.31		Clapham Common Station		2.08
1.19	-		Balham Station		2.01
1.26	-		Tooting Broadway		1.54
1.38	-	arr	Streatham, LT Garage	dep	1.42

With effect from 7/8 January 1958 route 290 (Pimlico – Edmonton) was diverted away from Hampstead Road, between Warren Street and Mornington Crescent LT stations, to travel instead via Euston Road and Eversholt Street, thereby introducing an all-night bus facility to Euston Station.

The Inter-Station Route's 2.30am departure from King's Cross Station was diverted to serve Holborn Viaduct Station at 2.35am on Sunday nights/Monday mornings only, with effect from 27/28 July 1958.

THE 1958 BUS STRIKE AND ITS CONSEQUENCES

On Monday 5 May 1958 all London Transport road passenger services were suspended as a result of a strike by crews. The dispute centred on the refusal of London Transport to award an 8s 6d a week pay increase already agreed for Central Bus staff to their colleagues in the Country Bus and Coach Department. Support for the strike amongst crews was total and no London Transport bus, coach or trolleybus ran in service until a return to work was agreed for 21 June 1958. The majority of all-night services ceased to operate after Friday night/Saturday morning 2/3 May 1958 until resumption of service on Sunday night/Monday morning 22/23 June 1958, although such routes with a Saturday night/Sunday morning service last operated on 3/4 May 1958 and resumed service on 21/22 June 1958. London Transport attributed passenger loss as a consequence of the strike as its reason for implementing a severe package of operational economies in two tranches on 20 August and 26 November 1958. Some daytime Central Bus routes were withdrawn whilst others suffered truncation and/or frequency reduction. The all-night bus route network survived intact but was subjected to garage and vehicle-type allocation changes. As part of LT's economies three Central Bus garages – Clapham, Old Kent Road and Putney Bridge – were closed, the first two of which had participated in the all-night bus route network.

With effect from 25/26 November 1958, Clapham garage's Sunday to Friday night allocation of three RTL-types to route 287 was tranfered to Stockwell garage, although the shared portion of the 287's allocation from Brixton garage with three RT-types remained unchanged. Stockwell garage also assumed responsibility for the early Sunday morning allocation on route 168 from Clapham garage and for which it created a single RTL-type-operated combined duty rota incorporating the Special Night Journeys on route 181, which latter journeys were revised to enter and leave service at Stockwell Station. Wandsworth garage's Sunday-Friday nights allocation of one RTL-type to the 168's all-night service remained unchanged. The Inter-Station Route was re-allocated from Old Kent Road to New Cross garage with retention of RT-type operation. London Transport also took the opportunity to cull the RTL-type bus from its fleet with around 300 of them being withdrawn from passenger service, considerably reducing that vehicle-type's presence on both daytime and all-night routes, as witnessed by a change from RTL-type to RT-type in respect of both Barking garage's allocation to route 295 and Seven Kings garage's allocation to route 298 from the same date.

THE FIRST ROUTEMASTERS ON ALL-NIGHT SERVICE

The first Routemaster buses to see service on London Transport's all-night route network might well have operated on route 11's early morning journeys between Hammersmith Broadway and Liverpool Street Station. London Transport's official Allocation Book recorded that from 13/14 March 1959, route 11's RTW-type allocation from Riverside garage was enhanced to include 6 RM-type buses. This change was in anticipation of London Transport's plan to allocate batches of six Routemasters to each of six Central Bus garages for trial

operation of production Routemasters. In practice the trial use of Routemasters on route 11 did not get under way until the summer of 1959, as it was not until July 1959 that sufficient numbers – RM 14, 19, 32, 33, 34 and 37 – were allocated to Riverside garage. RM 52 followed in September 1959 but the trial of Routemasters on route 11 had ended by 25/26 November 1959 when Riverside garage's allocation to the route reverted to all RTW-type. The RTW-type itself was a great rarity on all-night service since it was never allocated to any of the mainstream 2xx route numbered Nighters. The only other all-night bus route to experience RTW operation was the 185 (Catford – Vauxhall) when, for one year between 13/14 May 1959 and 10/11 May 1960, Walworth garage's allocation became mixed RTL and RTW-types on weekday early mornings and solely RTW-type on Sunday early mornings before reverting back to an all RTL-type allocation on 11/12 May 1960.

The first production Routemasters were intended to replace London Transport's trolleybuses but, due to production delays, the first three stages of the trolleybus replacement programme, which started on 4 March 1959, utilised existing fleet RT and RTL-types. The fourth stage, in which buses replaced trolleybuses on routes along Commercial Road, was the first to deploy Routemasters and included the conversion of all-night trolleybus route 665 to bus operation. From Tuesday night/Wednesday morning 10/11 November 1959 the all-night trolleybus service over route 665 (Poplar–Bloomsbury) was superseded by Routemaster operated all-night bus route 284, the route number selected being the next available number in the descending all-night bus route numbering series. The irregulary-timed core service on route 284 continued to operate from Poplar but five journeys were projected beyond the 665's western terminal point at Bloomsbury via Shaftesbury Avenue and Piccadilly Circus to

Poplar garage's RM 111 is seen emerging from Old North Street into Theobalds Road having just departed from Bloomsbury's Red Lion Square at 6.10am on a summer's morning in 1960. Routes 284 and 299 were the only two numerically-descending 2xx series Nighters to have been worked by Routemasters. *A R Packer*

Tottenham garage's RTL 1060, on route 290, pauses outside the National Gallery in Trafalgar Square. Judging by the strong daylight, this view was taken around Midsummer when the bus was working the last outbound 290 journey, scheduled in Trafalgar Square at 6.38am. *A R Packer*

terminate at Charing Cross, Trafalgar Square. A single early morning return journey on route 284 between Bloomsbury, Red Lion Square and Barking Broadway replaced a 'Special Early Journey', which had previously operated as an element of the daytime schedule of trolleybus route 665. The 284, which operated on Sunday to Friday nights, had an allocation of two RM-type Routemasters from Poplar garage.

The sixth stage of the trolleybus replacement programme, implemented on 27 April 1960, involved the conversion to motor bus operation of those remaining daytime trolleybus routes operated by Walthamstow and West Ham depots, which premises were adapted to become bus garages. This stage of the conversion also saw the introduction of a new

all-night bus route when, from Tuesday night/ Wednesday morning 26/27 April 1960, route 299 commenced service between Chingford Mount and Victoria & Albert Docks. The irregularly-scheduled 299, which operated nightly, replaced former un-timetabled staff trolleybus journeys. Its importance as a crucial LT staff link, which served three large bus garages *en route* – Leyton, Walthamstow and West Ham, at which latter garage the single RM-type Routemaster allocated nightly to the 299 was based, – justified the 299's elevation to the official all-night route network. Route 299, the number having lain dormant since 1941, was unique in the numerically-descending 2xx sequence of all-night bus routes in operating entirely outside Central London.

RT 3314 is seen outside Broad Street station, in Liverpool Street, on a wet morning about to return to Cricklewood garage on route 294's 5.39am scheduled departure. *A R Packer*

The seventh stage of the trolleybus replacement programme included the conversion of those trolleybus routes operated by Hammersmith depot to motor bus operation, whilst the depot premises were adapted for a new role housing the fleet of airport coaches operated by London Transport on behalf of British European Airways. The five return journey all night trolleybus service over route 630 (Hammersmith Broadway – Tooting Broadway, Longmead Road) was reduced to become little more than a late night service upon replacement by bus route 220 from 19/20 July 1960. The two Special Night Journeys provided over route 220 on Sunday to Friday nights went into service at Harrow Road, College Park at 11.24pm and 12.31am, since the journeys utilised two Shepherds Bush

garage-based RM-type buses which finished day turns off route 220 at that point. The corresponding return journeys from Tooting, BR Station terminated at Shepherds Bush Green. Some link with past LCC Tramways route 26 between Hammersmith and Vauxhall was maintained on the two southbound 220 journeys, which were timed to connect at Wandsworth with town-bound all-night 168 departures.

Circa 1960 rebuilding work in the Farringdon area resulted in the demolition of Farringdon Avenue. The terminus for all-night routes 168 and 288 was removed to Stonecutter Street with terminating buses following a loop terminal working from and to Farringdon Street via St Bride Street and Stonecutter Street.

INTRODUCTION OF N-PREFIXED BUS ROUTE NUMBERING

The conversion of London Transport's daytime trolleybus routes to motor bus operation, combined with network expansion, had created a demand for additional bus route numbers. London Transport's policy continued to require all Central Bus routes to be numbered between 1 and 299, although that element of the original intention of LPTB's route numbering of 3 October 1934 to distinguish single-deck bus operated routes in an ascending number series from 200 upwards had become blurred from 1942 onwards, from which date progressively increasing numbers of 2xx series routes had become worked by double-deck buses.

With the introduction of daytime route 278 (Victoria & Albert Docks – Chingford Mount) as a result of stage six of the trolleybus replacement programme on 27 April 1960, daytime bus route numbers had moved very close to 284, the lowest-ranked all-night bus route number then in use. In order to make additional 2xx route numbers available for use by daytime services, London Transport made the decision to renumber the high-ranking 2xx series all-night bus routes with effect from Tuesday night/Wednesday morning 11/12 October 1960. All such route numbers had 200 subtracted

from them and an 'N' prefix added. Thus route numbers 299-294, 292-284 became route numbers N99-N94, N92-N84 respectively. The principle of maintaining a decreasing numerical sequence for all-night bus routes remained inherent in the revised numbering system with such route numbers now descending from N99. The logistics of implementing this renumbering were extensive since it involved alterations to destination blind displays, E-plates on bus stop flags and publicity material. Special Night Journeys or all-night services, which operated over part or all of daytime bus routes 9, 11, 29, 109, 168, 177, 181, 182, 185 and 220, as well as the Inter-Station Route, were unaffected by the renumbering and maintained their original identities. The first reuse of a former all-night 2xx series route number occurred on 11 October 1961 with the introduction of new daytime bus route 286 between Belmont and Raynes Park Station although, ironically, this route had no connection with the trolleybus replacement programme. In practice immediately following the final conversion of trolleybus routes in the Kingston-upon-Thames area on 9 May 1962, only three further former all-night bus 2xx series route numbers – 285, 292 and 293 (this latter dormant since 1941) – had been brought back into use as daytime bus route numbers.

The driver sits in the cab of Turnham Green garage's RT 658 outside Broad Street station in Liverpool Street waiting departure time for this early morning route N97 journey to Turnham Green. *A R Packer*

Wandsworth garage's RTL 1152 (above) and RTL 570 (left) are seen in Stonecutter Street before and after route 288 was renumbered N88. Construction work which obliterated Farringdon Avenue, site of the former bus stand for the Wandsworth all-night bus routes and certain daytime services, is evident behind the buses. Both buses were working the scheduled 5.39am last outbound departure of the night which went out of service at Wandsworth garage and so did not follow the route's full length to Armoury Way.
Both A. R. Packer

Riverside garage's RTL 942 on one of that night's last two route N89 departures from London Bridge station which formed a bifurcation from its normal line of route at Shepherd's Bush to run to Hammersmith Broadway. *Alan Mortimer*

FINAL ALL-NIGHT TROLLEYBUS ROUTES REPLACED BY ROUTEMASTER BUSES

With effect from the Tuesday night/Wednesday morning of 31 January/1 February 1961 new all-night bus route N93 replaced the previous all-night trolleybus service over routes 513/613 from Hampstead Heath. Route N93 enjoyed the distinction of having been the first London Transport all-night bus route to have been introduced with an N-prefixed route number whilst the adoption of this number meant that there were no longer any gaps in the numerically descending all-night bus route number sequence from N99 to N84. Instead of following the former 513/613 trolleybus workings around the Holborn loop the N93 was routed, after King's Cross, via Farringdon Road and Farringdon Street to Ludgate Circus where half the route's journeys terminated. Three journeys were projected beyond Ludgate Circus via Fleet Street and Strand to terminate at Charing Cross, Trafalgar

Square. One RM-type from Highgate garage, where the crew took their relief-break, comprised the irregularly-scheduled route N93's allocation on Sunday to Friday nights.

It will be recalled that traffic congestion, an abiding problem in London, had led to the introduction of the capital's first gyratory traffic flow systems in 1926, such as that around Trafalgar Square. By the early 1960s increased private car ownership had exacerbated traffic problems to such an extent that larger scale gyratory flows were planned. The replacement of London Transport's trolleybuses by motor buses and, more specifically the discontinuance of fixed overhead power-supply wires upon which the trolleybuses were dependent, assisted in the implementation of a rash of 'one-way' traffic systems across the metropolis. The tenth stage of London Transport's trolleybus replacement programme, implemented on 26 April 1961, included the removal of daytime trolleybus routes 627 and 629 from terminal workings at Maple Street and the northernmost end of Tottenham Court Road. This 'cleared the wires' to allow the introduction, from 1 May 1961, of a significant one-way scheme under which Tottenham Court Road became northbound only with southbound traffic between Euston Road and New Oxford Street re-routed via Gower Street and Bloomsbury Street. This new one-way system affected all-night route N90 as well as the Special Night Journeys on route 29. Coincident with this change a further one-way system involved southbound Special Night Journeys on route 29 and all-night routes N84, N90, N95 and N98 being re-routed via Shaftesbury Avenue to Cambridge Circus. Northbound journeys on these routes travelled via Charing Cross Road to Tottenham Court Road Station.

A particularly noteworthy one-way scheme introduced on Sunday 26 November 1961 involved the upper reaches of Piccadilly between St James Street and Piccadilly Circus becoming restricted to eastbound traffic only. Westbound Special Night Journeys on route 9 and all-night route N97, as well as various daytime bus routes, were re-routed via Pall Mall and St James Street. Another significant gyratory traffic flow introduced on 13 November 1961 impacted the Elephant & Castle and St George's Circus areas whilst on March 24 1962, a major one-way system was introduced in the Holborn area.

London's last trolleybus routes with a full all-night service were the 543/643 between Stamford Hill and Holborn Circus which operated for the last time on Monday night/Tuesday morning 17/18 July 1961. The next night, in stage 11 of the trolleybus replacement programme, these services were replaced by new all-night bus route N83 from Stamford Hill. Route N83, which had taken up the next available number in the numerically descending N-prefixed all-night series, followed the pattern set by recently introduced route N93 in being diverted away from the former trolleybus routes 543/643 terminal workings around the Holborn loop, instead being routed via Farringdon Road, Farringdon Street, Ludgate Circus, Fleet Street and Strand to a new terminus at Charing Cross, Trafalgar Square. One journey on the N83 was projected northwards beyond Stamford Hill to Tottenham, Swan in order to facilitate a relief break for the crew at Tottenham garage. The all-night schedule on trolleybus routes 543/643 had been worked by two trolleybuses which had maintained a 30-minute frequency – a level of service which had prevailed since at least the night of 31 December 1922/1 January 1923 when London County Council Tramways had replaced the First World War emergency alternate 25-minute and 50-minute headway over the tram-operated all-night route between Stamford Hill and Holborn with an even 30-minute headway. On its introduction route N83 was scheduled to be worked by a single RM-type Routemaster from Stamford Hill garage, which resulted in a much-reduced level of service combined with an irregular headway. The N83 did offer one improvement over the 543/643 in becoming one of the then rare all-night routes to provide a service on Saturday nights/Sunday mornings. The first half of the N83's Sunday morning service, from 12.14am, appeared innovatory although it is likely that it absorbed elements of former un-timetabled staff trolleybus journeys. The second half of

the N83's early Sunday morning service replaced former Special Early Journeys between Stamford Hill and Holborn which had formerly been scheduled from 3.59am onwards as daytime workings over trolleybus route 543.

Coincident with stage 11 of the trolleybus replacement programme, Edmonton-bound journeys on existing all-night bus route N90 were extended from Park Road to terminate at Lower Edmonton Station from 18/19 July 1961. One journey on the N90 was projected even further northwards to and from Tramway Avenue to replace a former late night journey on daytime trolleybus route 649. A sequence of Saturday night/Sunday morning Special Night Journeys, between Lower Edmonton, Stamford Hill and Waltham Cross was also introduced on bus route 149, which had replaced the 649 trolleybus, but since similarly timed journeys were absent from the 649's timetable, these journeys appear to have replaced former un-timetabled trolleybus staff journeys.

Following the conversion of routes 543/643 to motor bus operation London Transport's sole surviving all-night trolleybus facilities were the two Special Early Journeys provided over routes 521/621 between North Finchley and Holborn, which operated for the last time on Tuesday morning 7 November 1961, being replaced from the following morning by similarly timed Routemaster-operated journeys on replacement bus route 221. The 221 abandoned use of the former trolleybus terminal workings around the Holborn Loop and instead was routed after King's Cross via Farringdon Road to thence follow a loop terminal working via Charterhouse Street, St Andrews Street and Shoe Lane to the route's terminus in Stonecutter Street, which it shared with all-night routes 168 and N88 from Wandsworth. Northbound 221 buses proceeded via Farringdon Street to regain line of route in Farringdon Road.

For the first time in more than 58 years, since the introduction by London County Council Tramways of an electrically-powered all-night tram service between Clapham and Blackfriars Road via Elephant & Castle on 15/16 May 1903, electrically-powered vehicles no longer played any role in the provision of the capital's all-night public road passenger transport services which, from 7/8 November 1961, had become entirely operated by diesel-engine motor buses.

Those remaining vestiges of London Transport's daytime trolleybus network lingered on into 1962. Coincident with the thirteenth, and penultimate, stage of the trolleybus replacement programme, carried out during Arctic-like weather conditions, when Colindale, Finchley and Stonebridge depots were cleared of trolleybuses after operation on 2 January 1962, West Green bus garage was closed with the bulk of its allocation transferred to Wood Green, by then converted from trolleybus depot to bus garage. This affected the Special Night Journeys which operated over daytime bus route 29 and resulted in an allocation change from RTL to RT-type buses as well as a revised schedule.

The total of 55 buses allocated to all-night routes and Special Night Journeys from Sunday to Friday nights at 8/9 May 1962, as shown in Table P, immediately following the final stage in the trolleybus conversion programme, had remained virtually static compared with 54 buses and trolleybuses similarly allocated almost 10 years earlier on

5/6 July 1952, immediately following the tramway conversion programme. The allocation of 18 buses to all-night services on Saturday nights/Sunday mornings was numerically impressive given that then, in general, London Transport's All Night Routes operated 'Saturday Night-Sunday Morning Excepted.' It must be borne in mind that eight of these buses were working either late Saturday night Special Night Journeys or early Sunday morning 'Press journeys' over routes 9, 29, 149, 221 and N94. The actual number of buses which could reasonably have been considered to have worked right through a Saturday night/Sunday morning was just ten. These comprised one turn on routes 168/181 combined, one turn on route 177, one on route 182, one on route 185, one on route N83, three on route N98, one on route N99 and one turn on the Inter-Station Route.

It was noteworthy that the regular headways on former trolleybus routes 513/613, 543/643 and 665 had been sacrificed upon their conversion to bus routes N93, N83 and N84 respectively. In fact by 8/9 May 1962 the all-night bus route network was characterised by irregularly-timed schedules. The only routes which still retained regular headways were

N85 (ex tram 5), N86 (ex tram 7) and N92 (ex tram 35), each with a 30-minute service interval as well as route N87 (ex tram 1) over which a 24-minute headway prevailed. A clear divergence in operating patterns had also developed between former tram and/or trolleybus routes in north London converted to bus operation and routes with similar origins in south London. North London routes, with the exception of the Special Night Journeys on route 221, had elements of their service projected beyond the former tram and/or trolleybus terminal points in Bloomsbury or Holborn to reach Charing Cross, Trafalgar Square where seven all-night routes or Special Night Journeys now terminated compared with only three such routes ten years earlier. South London's all-night bus routes remained embedded in the long established tramway-originated routeing along Victoria Embankment.

The all-night bus route network was served entirely by crew-operated double decker buses. RT-family bus types dominated vehicle allocations, as they had ten years earlier, but the Routemaster had by now made its debut with a presence on seven trolleybus replacement all-night bus routes or Special Night Journeys.

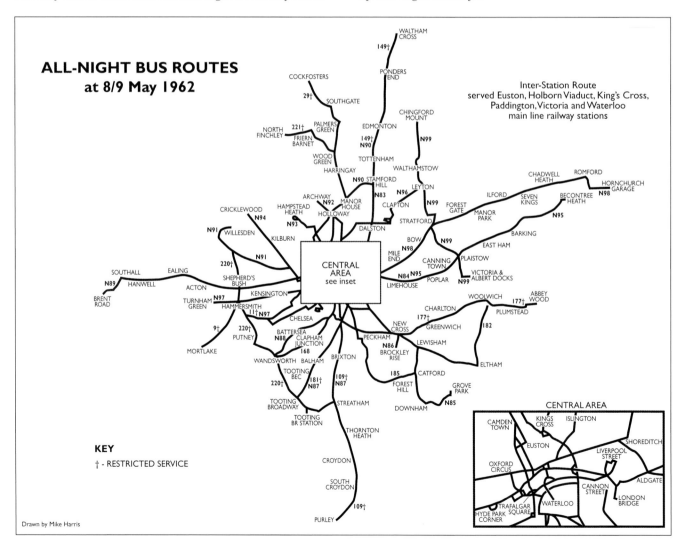

ALL-NIGHT BUS ROUTES
at 8/9 May 1962

Inter-Station Route
served Euston, Holborn Viaduct, King's Cross,
Paddington, Victoria and Waterloo
main line railway stations

KEY
† - RESTRICTED SERVICE

Drawn by Mike Harris

Table P: All-Night Bus Routes
Vehicle Allocations from 8/9 May 1962

Route No	Bus Routes	Bus Allocation			Garage
		Su	M–Fr	Sa	
9	Ludgate Circus – Mortlake Garage	-	1 RTL	2 RTL	Mortlake
11	Hammersmith – Liverpool St Stn	2 RTW	2 RTW	-	Riverside
29	Cockfosters – Charing Cross	-	1 RT	2 RT	Wood Green
109	Purley – Victoria Embankment	1 RT	1 RT	-	Thornton Heath
149	Stamford Hill – Waltham Cross	-	-	1 RM	Edmonton
168	Wandsworth – Farringdon Street	1 RTL	1 RTL	1 ex 181	Wandsworth
177	Abbey Wood – Victoria Embankment	-	-	1 RT	New Cross
181	Streatham – Kennington	-	-	1 RTL	Stockwell
182	Woolwich – Cannon Street Station	1 RT	1 RT	1 RT	New Cross
185	Catford – Vauxhall Station	1 RTL	1 RTL	1 RTL	Walworth
220	College Park – Tooting Station	2 RM	2 RM	-	Shepherds Bush
221	North Finchley – Farringdon Street	2 RM	2 RM	2 RM	Finchley
N83	Tottenham – Charing Cross	1 RM	1 RM	1 RM	Stamford Hill
N84	Barking – Charing Cross	2 RM	2 RM	-	Poplar
N85	Grove Park – Victoria Embankment	4 RT	4 RT	-	Rye Lane
N86	Brockley Rise – Victoria Embankment	3 RT	3 RT	-	Peckham
N87	Tooting Broadway – Embankment loop	3 RT 3 RTL	3 RT 3 RTL	- -	Brixton Stockwell
N88	Wandsworth – Farringdon Street	1 RTL	1 RTL	-	Wandsworth
N89	Southall – London Bridge Station	3 RTL	3 RTL	-	Riverside
N90	Lower Edmonton – Pimlico	3 RTL	3 RTL	-	Tottenham
N91	Willesden – Liverpool St Station	1 RTL	1 RTL	-	Willesden
N92	Highgate – Charing Cross	2 RT	2 RT	-	Holloway
N93	Hampstead Heath – Charing Cross	1 RM	1 RM	-	Highgate
N94	Cricklewood – Liverpool St Station	2 RT	2 RT	1 RT	Cricklewood
N95	Becontree Heath – Charing Cross	3 RT	3 RT	-	Barking
N96	Leyton Green – Waterloo Station	2 RT	2 RT	-	Leyton
N97	Turnham Green – Liverpool St Stn	2 RT	2 RT	-	Turnham Green
N98	Hornchurch Garage – Charing Cross	5 RT	5 RT	3 RT	Seven Kings
N99	Chingford Mount – V & A Docks	1 RM	1 RM	1 RM	West Ham
-	Inter-Station Route	3 RT	1 RT	1 RT	New Cross
	Bus Total	**55**	**55**	**18**	

Last journeys on all-night bus routes were often of importance to early morning workers. Barking garage's RM 1859 moves off to rejoin the heavy traffic flow along Barking Road having just set down passengers at Canning Town station at 07.01 on a summer's morning in 1966. Traction poles, which once supported overhead wiring for the trolleybus system, are visible in the background, adapted for road lighting. *Capital Transport*

The progressive expansion of Routemaster operation to further daytime bus routes allowed the allocation of that vehicle type to be extended to additional all-night bus routes from December 1962 onwards. A notice, dated 26 November 1962, concerning all-night routes, issued by Central Buses Traffic Office, advised staff that 'as heaters are fitted, it is to the advantage of staff to have RM buses where this type of bus is allocated to the same garage for other (daytime) routes'. The table below charts the RM-type's increased dominance of all-night bus route vehicle allocations achieved between 11/12 December 1962 and 9/10 July 1966. By the latter date Routemaster buses had become allocated to 19 of London Transport's all-night bus routes or Special Night Journeys. AEC Regent 111-based RT-type buses had become confined to all-night routes 109, 177, 182, 185, N96, N97 and N98 whilst Leyland Titan PD2-based RTL types were only to be found allocated to Wandsworth garage's turns on routes 168 and N88 along with Stockwell garage's Saturday night/Sunday morning split duty rota on routes 181 and 168.

Table R: All-Night Bus Routes and Special Night Journeys
Dates of Conversion to Routemaster Operation
Period 11/12 December 1962 – 9/10 July 1966

Effective Date	Route No.	Garage	Type change to:		
			Su	M–Fr	Sa
11/12 Dec 1962	N90	Tottenham	3RM	3RM	-
23/24 Dec 1962	N94	Cricklewood	2RM	2RM	1RM
14/15 Jan 1963	N85	Rye Lane	4RM	4RM	-
17/18 Feb 1963	N86	Peckham	3RM	3RM	-
8/9 May 1963	9	Mortlake	-	1RM	2RM
28/29 Jan 1964	N92	Holloway	2RM	2RM	-
28/29 Jan 1964	I-S	New Cross	3RM	1RM	1RM
30 Jun/1 Jul 1964	N95	Barking	2RM	2RM	-
3/4 Oct 1965	N91	Willesden	1RM	1RM	-
23/24 Jan 1966	N89	Riverside	3RM	3RM	-
1/2 Feb 1966	11	Riverside	2RM	2RM	-
9/10 Jul 1966	N87	Brixton	3RM	3RM	-
		Stockwell	3RM	3RM	

Note:
Brixton garage's allocation for route N87 changed from RT to RTL-type from 17/18 November 1964 and reverted back to RT-type from 23/24 January 1966

RM-types were allocated to the Sunday daytime schedule of route 185 between 22/23 January 1966 and 17/18 December 1966, so it is likely that an RM-type worked the second part of that route's Saturday night/Sunday morning service, commencing with the 03.28 departure from Lewisham to Vauxhall, during that period. Other night journeys were worked by RTL-type until converted to RT-type from 9/10 July 1966. From 30/31 December 1966 an RT-type operated the entire all-night service on route 185, including the complete Saturday night/Sunday morning service.

The Transport Act 1962 provided for the dissolution of the British Transport Commission and the Executives under its control. From 1 January 1963 the London Transport Board assumed responsibility for London's public road passenger transport and Underground railway systems. The creation of the Board restored London Transport to the status of a public corporation with a legal position similar to that of the LPTB.

Only one very minor change occurred to London Transport's all-night network in 1963 when, from 11/12 May 1963, the scope of route 149's Saturday night/Sunday morning Special Night Journey was extended to include an 11.34pm departure from Liverpool Street Station to Waltham Cross. The corresponding 12.41am return journey from Waltham Cross picked up, at Lower Edmonton, that route's SNJ cycle established on 22/23 July 1961.

THE BREAKING POINT
Generally speaking, London Transport had scheduled relief-breaks for all-night bus crews at each route's home garage. Exceptions to this practice existed, such as the provision of facilities at London Bridge station for route N89 crews whilst two buses on route N95 ran out of service between Charing Cross and Victoria garage for crew relief-breaks. By 1964 night time canteen facilities had to be provided at 18 garages or locations. A shortage of catering staff had made it increasingly difficult to maintain such broad coverage and, on occasions, absence of catering staff had forced the temporary closure of some canteens. London Transport decided to alleviate such difficulties by concentrating crew relief-break points at three locations – Liverpool Street, New Cross garage and Victoria garage – in respect of the majority of all-night routes which entered central London. Certain all-night routes' rotas included straight duties, which did not involve a crew relief-break, and, in general, such schedules were left unchanged. The changes to crew relief-break points were implemented on Wednesday night/Thursday morning 1/2 July 1964. Many all-night bus routes had to be re-scheduled to accommodate the revised arrangements. Buses which relieved off line of route at Liverpool Street or Victoria garage canteens operated out of service to and from these locations. Full details are in Appendix 7.

Five all-night bus routes were subjected to further significant route and/or scheduling alterations coincident with the crew-relief-break change date. Additionally the infrequent all-night service on route 185 was extended from Catford to Lewisham, now passed through *en route* by buses seeking the 185's revised crew relief-break point at New Cross garage.

ROUTE 11
This route's long-established Monday to Saturday Special Morning Journeys at 04.00 and 04.23 from Hammersmith to Liverpool Street Station, with corresponding return journeys at 04.58 and 05.24, were supplemented from 1/2 July 1964 with 00.58 and 01.13 journeys from Hammersmith to Victoria. After crew relief-break at Victoria garage the two Riverside garage-based RM-type Routemasters allocated to what had developed into a Sunday to Friday nights all-night service over route 11 departed from Victoria at 03.27 and 03.50 respectively back to Hammersmith.

ROUTES N84 AND N95

All-night bus services along the Commercial Road and Barking Road corridor were significantly reduced. Prior to the changes introduced on 1/2 July 1964 routes N84 and N95 combined had provided a total of 15 journeys in each direction of travel along Commercial Road on each night of operation. This reduced to nine such journeys under the revised schedules (See Appendix 8). Route N84, in particular, was decimated and that route's allocation was reduced to just one Routemaster which had to cope with the lengthy projection of one journey beyond Poplar via Barking to Becontree Heath, to compensate for a withdrawn N95 journey. The number of all-night departures from Becontree Heath was reduced from eight on route N95 prior to the changes to just four on routes N84/N95 combined. Two all-night bus duties were saved as a result of these changes but such savings were partially offset by an increase of one duty on daytime bus route 23 which gained a compensatory enhanced early morning schedule. The allocation of RM-type buses to Barking garage for route 23 enabled the N95 to be converted from RT to RM operation coincident with the schedule changes of 1/2 July 1964.

ROUTE N98

Prior to the changes of 1/2 July 1964 crew relief-breaks for route N98 had been taken on line of route in the N98's home garage at Seven Kings. A considerable penalty, in term of both the route's length and level of service over its eastern section was incurred in order to switch the crew relief-break points to Victoria garage on Sunday to Friday nights despite the route's allocation remaining constant at five RT-type buses on those nights. Under the revised arrangements buses ran out of service between Charing Cross and Victoria on Sunday to Friday nights and between Bank and Liverpool Street on Saturday nights. The easternmost section of route N98, between Hornchurch Garage and Romford Station, was withdrawn after operation on Tuesday night/Wednesday morning 30 June/1 July 1964 and thereafter the N98 was truncated to operate between Romford Station and Charing Cross.

However the number of journeys over the revised easternmost section of the route, between Romford Station and Chadwell Heath, was cut from six to three on Sunday to Friday nights and was even more drastically pruned from ten to just two such journeys on Saturday nights. Effectively the core N98 service became that section of route between Chadwell Heath and Charing Cross over which more or less the same level of frequency was maintained. Since no compensatory late night or early morning journeys were added to daytime route 86, which operated parallel to the N98 between Stratford and Hornchurch Garage, it would seem that the eastern end of route N98 had been poorly patronised.

ROUTE N97

West London route N97, between Turnham Green and Liverpool Street Station, had been enjoying a boom in patronage and, in pleasant contrast to the cuts imposed upon east London routes N84, N95 and N98, the N97's allocation was increased from two to three RT-type buses at Turnham Green garage from 1/2 July 1964. This enabled the N97's Sunday to Friday nights frequency to be increased to every 30 minutes for much of the night, although a number of journeys were shortened to operate between Hammersmith Broadway and Liverpool Street Station.

One consequence of the cutbacks in service at the eastern end of route N98 from 1/2 July 1964 was that the 00.24 Sunday to Friday night journey from Charing Cross to Hornchurch Garage was truncated to operate only as far as Stratford Broadway. Seven Kings garage's RT 2330 is seen outside the National Gallery in Trafalgar Square awaiting departure time for such a journey.
Capital Transport

OFF THE RAILS

Cutbacks effected by British Railways to elements of its London area all-night train services in 1963 and 1965 led to the introduction of a new all-night coach service provided by operators other than London Transport as well as to compensatory route extensions to four London Transport all-night bus routes.

As a consequence of the withdrawal of the all-night train service between Holborn Viaduct and Orpington after operation on 14/15 June 1963, Samuelson New Transport Co Ltd, a subsidiary of London Coastal Coaches and jointly controlled by the state-owned Transport Holding Company and Stock Market quoted British Electric Traction, which were then the country's two largest groupings of provincial bus and coach operators, introduced an all-night coach service between Blackfriars Station and Orpington Station. As this route ran entirely within London Transport's 'Special Area' it required LT's consent to operate. The route was introduced on Sunday night/Monday morning 16/17 June 1963 under an eight-week short period licence and operated on six nights of the week, the exception being Saturday nights/Sunday mornings. Departures from Blackfriars were at 1.22am, 1.53am, 2.20am and 3.17am. The route only served British Railways stations which, between terminal points, comprised Elephant & Castle, Herne Hill, West Dulwich, Penge West, Penge East, Kent House, Beckenham Junction, Shortlands, Bromley South, Bickley and Petts Wood. The withdrawn train service and the replacement coach service had both been intended primarily to serve newspaper workers. However, the former train service had been available for use by the general public whilst use of the coach service was restricted to newspaper employees. The coach service appears to have operated in an outbound direction only from Blackfriars Station so passengers had first to reach town by Southern Electric train. Railway season tickets were not accepted on the coach service over which a three shilling single fare applied.

There appears to have been a hiatus in the provision of the coach service after operation on 9/10 August 1963 when Samuelson's short period licence expired. From Sunday night/Monday morning 22/23 September 1963, a similar all-night coach service was reinstated by independent operator R. W. Bird (registered office: 263 Chipperfield, St Paul's Cray, Kent). Bird's service differed from Samuelson's in comprising just two departures at 1.20am and 1.51am which left from Holborn Viaduct Station, the original terminus of the all-night train service, rather than Blackfriars Station. Routeing was identical to that of the Samuelson service apart from a short extra section from Holborn Viaduct Station via Holborn Circus, St Bride Street, Ludgate Circus and New Bridge Street to Blackfriars Station. Bird's service was recorded in London Transport's consent records as being nightly although this entry might have been erroneous in view of the 'Saturday Nights Excepted' nature of the predecessor Samuelson service. The subsequent fate of Bird's service is unknown other than that the licence was formally surrendered in November 1966.

Early morning trains to the South Coast used by newspaper workers were revised to start from Victoria station, instead of London Bridge station, from Monday 14 June 1965.

Under local arrangements from 15/16 June 1965, and formally from 29/30 June 1965, the two journeys on route N95 which had previously operated out of service between Charing Cross and Victoria for crew relief-break purposes were amended to run in service from Charing Cross via Whitehall and Victoria Street to Victoria. In a complementary move the five route N98 journeys which had also run out-of-service from Charing Cross to Victoria for crew-relief break purposes were revised to operate to Victoria in service from 24/25 August 1965. This gave newspaper workers a choice of seven Sunday-Friday night departures from Holborn Circus to Victoria between 01.29 and 03.54 on routes N95 and N98 combined. Route N95 thus became extended to operate between Becontree Heath and Victoria, Wilton Road although only the 04.04 and 04.48 departures from Victoria covered the full length of route between termini. Route N98 in entirety now operated between Romford Station and Victoria, Wilton Road although, due to many intermediate short workings, only two inbound journeys, (01.17 and 02.50 ex Romford) and one outbound journey (03.11 ex Victoria) covered the full length of route N98 on Sunday to Friday nights.

British Railways Eastern Region thinned out the frequency of its all-night train service between Liverpool Street and Chingford from 14 June 1965. This prompted London Transport to divert the 02.13 departure from Waterloo Station on route N96 at Leyton, Bakers Arms to travel to Highams Park Station via Wood Street Station, returning at 03.15 to Leyton Garage. The 03.20 Sunday-Friday night departure from West Ham Garage on route N99 was projected beyond Chingford Mount to terminate at Chingford Station at 04.00, returning from there at 04.15 bound for Victoria & Albert Docks. Both these route extensions were introduced on Tuesday night/ Wednesday morning 24/25 August 1965.

The fortunes of the railway-related Inter-Station Route had always been closely linked to the scale of movements of military personnel between London's main line railway termini. A severe reduction in patronage on the Inter-Station Route during the early 1960's was largely attributable to the ending of male conscription into the armed forces after 31 December 1960. National Servicemen travelling between homes and barracks, particularly at weekends, had comprised a significant element of the Inter-Station Route's custom. London Transport's decision to withdraw the Inter-Station Route entirely after operation on Friday night/Saturday morning 4/5 September 1964 provoked an outcry from those remaining passengers still dependent upon the service. This led London Transport to do some quick back-pedalling, which resulted in the restoration of a much reduced Inter-Station Route on Sunday night/Monday morning 13/14 September 1964. The hastily revised Inter-Station Route operated on Sunday nights/Monday mornings only to a reduced schedule worked by two Routemaster buses from New Cross garage. Holborn Viaduct and St Pancras stations were no longer served. A summer seasonal Friday night and Saturday night service was restored to the route between 18/19 June and 14/15 September 1965 with an allocation one Routemaster on each of those nights. This summer seasonal service restored some journeys to St Pancras station, which continued to be without a service on Sunday nights/Mondays mornings. The schedule of the Sunday night/Monday morning service was further reduced from 23/24 January 1966 to a level which could be worked by just one Routemaster. Summer seasonal operation of the Inter-Station Route on Friday and Saturday nights was reintroduced in 1966 and repeated in successive years up to and including 1979.

Inter-Station Bus Route Timetable from 23/24 January 1966 Sunday nights/Monday mornings only				
Waterloo	dep	23.35	00.49	-
Victoria	arr	23.45	00.59	-
Victoria	dep	23.48	01.01	02.40
Paddington	arr	00.01	01.14	02.53
Paddington	dep	00.06	01.17	02.55
Euston	arr	00.16	-	-
Euston	dep	00.21	-	-
Kings Cross	arr	00.25	01.29	03.07
Kings Cross	dep	00.30	-	03.10
Waterloo	arr	00.44	-	03.24
Waterloo	dep	-	03.27	04.18
Kings Cross	arr	-	03.41	04.32
Kings Cross	dep	01.32	03.44	04.34
Paddington	arr	-	-	04.46
Paddington	dep	-	-	04.48
Victoria	arr	01.53	-	05.01
Victoria	dep	-	-	05.03
Waterloo	arr	-	03.58	05.13

Garage: New Cross
Allocation: 1 RM type

OTHER ROUTE DIVERSIONS AND EXTENSIONS 1964 – JUNE 1968

Mention has been made in the previous chapter of the rash of gyratory traffic flows started in the early 1960s. Such schemes increased in both number and scale from that decade onwards to the extent that it would be too exhaustive to detail all such new one-way systems in this volume. One scheme that does merit description, since it affected an old-established location for all-night services dating back to London County Council Tramways days, was the construction and commissioning of the Blackfriars Underpass. During construction work from 6 September 1964 all eastbound buses, except for route 168, were temporarily diverted off Victoria Embankment to travel via John Carpenter Street, Tudor Street and New Bridge Street to regain their line of route on Blackfriars Bridge. It took almost three years to complete the underpass, which links Victoria Embankment with Upper Thames Street. The Blackfriars Underpass was the first in central London to be used by scheduled bus routes after its opening on Wednesday

26 July 1967. From that date eastbound buses on all-night routes N85, N86 and N87, as well as Special Night Journeys (and daytime services) on routes 109, 155 and 177 travelled through the underpass before turning left into Puddle Dock and Queen Victoria Street to gain access to Blackfriars Bridge.

From Wednesday 27 January 1965 the daytime service on route 168 was diverted to cross the River Thames via Lambeth Bridge rather than Westminster Bridge as previously used. This change of routeing was allied to the withdrawal of daytime bus route 156 (Parliament Hill Fields – Wandsworth) with the daytime 168 intended to replace the southern section of the 156 between Whitehall and Wandsworth. The all-night service on route 168 followed the revised routeing of its daytime counterpart from the night of 26/27 January 1965 and was re-routed off Albert Embankment to give the first ever all-night bus service across Lambeth Bridge and along Millbank. From Parliament Square the 168 travelled halfway up Whitehall before proceeding via Horse Guards Avenue, Whitehall Court and Whitehall Place to regain its original line of route at Charing Cross, LT Station on Victoria Embankment. From 2/3 October 1965 this rather obscure Whitehall routeing, which skirted the perimeter of the War Office, was replaced by a mainstream routeing under which 168 buses travelled the full length of Whitehall, around Trafalgar Square and along Northumberland Avenue to reach Victoria Embankment.

The weekday nights Special Night Journeys over route 9, the sole survivors from the 1921-originated 'Ludgate Circus' Special Night Journeys, made the last use of Ludgate Circus as a terminal point on 26/27 February 1965. From the following night these journeys were projected up Ludgate Hill to terminate at St Paul's Churchyard. This route extension may well have been implemented in order to avoid terminating buses arriving down Fleet Street having to perform a 'U-turn' around Ludgate Circus – although shortworking journeys on routes N83 and N93 which approached Ludgate Circus via Farringdon Street, continued to execute such a manoeuvre at the Circus. St Paul's Churchyard ceased to be used as a terminal point from 11/12 November 1967 when the Special Night Journeys on route 9 were projected even further eastwards to terminate at Mansion House Station.

In early 1966 a wages dispute led to Central Bus crews imposing a ban on working voluntary overtime and on rest days. London Transport implemented a package of route economies from Sunday 23 January 1966 included amongst which was the withdrawal of the Sunday service on route 109, apart from a few Special Early Morning Journeys. The weekday mornings all-night service between Thornton Heath Garage and Streatham, St Leonard's Church survived, as did daily Special Early Morning journeys to both Victoria Embankment and Purley which were included in public all-night bus timetables. From Sunday night/Monday morning 12/13 June 1966 route N91 was re-routed between Harrow Road and Edgware Road via Praed Street in order to serve Paddington station.

Earls Court had gained a reputation for the cosmopolitan nature of its community which, by the late 1960s, notably included many Australians. This burgeoning expatriated

Nighters which terminated at Trafalgar Square set down passengers outside the National Gallery and then pulled across to the offside kerb for layover, with passengers for outbound journeys having to board from the roadway. RM 783 and 1975 have pulled across the road from the National Gallery to the Nighters' traditional unmarked bus stand. RM 783, with seated passengers visible in the lower deck, still retains an old style intermediate blind display with upper case lettering. Both views date from 1969. *Eddie Shirras*

colonial community sought a social life beyond the constraints of then-prevailing English licensing laws, which generally required licensed premises to close by 23.00. A network of all-night coffee bars and restaurants developed around Earls Court. London Transport, to its credit, spotted this changing social pattern as an opportunity to develop the all-night bus network. From Sunday night/Monday morning 1/2 January 1967 route N97 was re-routed at South Kensington via Cromwell Road – along which it served the West London Air Terminal – and Earls Court Road (return via Warwick Road) before regaining its original line of route in Fulham Road.

On 1/2 January 1967 two journeys on route N90 were projected beyond Lower Edmonton to Waltham Cross whilst a third journey was projected to terminate at Ponders End, Enfield garage. In entirety the N90 now operated between Waltham Cross and Pimlico, although only two inbound departures at 00.17 and 00.53 from Waltham Cross covered the full route length to Pimlico. With effect from 11/12 November 1967 route 185's all-night service was revised to operate between Victoria and Lewisham.

Revisions to daytime bus routes in south-east London effected on Saturday 15 June 1968 included the withdrawal of heavy loss making route 182. However, the core all-night service on route 182, between New Cross Gate and Woolwich, had been carrying sufficient passengers to justify its retention. Accordingly the all-night service on route 182 was renumbered as route N82 from 14/15 June 1968 and became worked by one Routemaster bus from New Cross garage on a nightly basis. Journeys which had previously worked through to Cannon Street Station, as elements of the 182's all-night service, were replaced by early morning journeys on daytime route 21.

RMLs . . . AND A FAREWELL TO RTLs

Larger capacity 72-seat versions of the Routemaster bus – type code RML – had first entered service in November 1961 on trolleybus replacement daytime bus route 104. The first uses of the RML-type on all-night service occurred on Sunday night/Monday morning 1/2 January 1967 when Stockwell garage's allocation for route N87, Willesden garage's allocation for route N91, Highgate garage's for route N93, Leyton garage's for route N96, and West Ham garage's for route N99 were converted to RML-type. Brixton garage's allocation for route N87 remained standard RM-type as did West Ham garage's to the N99 on Saturday nights/Sunday mornings only.

By the beginning of 1967 the only remaining Leyland Titan PD2-based RTL-type buses to be found on all-night duties were Wandsworth garage's allocation of one RTL to route 168 and one RTL to route N88 on Sunday to Friday nights along with Stockwell garage's single RTL allocated to work the split-day rota over routes 181 and 168 on Saturday nights/Sunday mornings. Both routes must have been converted to RT-type bus operation by 28 February/1March 1967, since Wandsworth garage's last RTL-types were withdrawn after service on 28 February 1967. The distinction of operating the last RTL-type bus on all-night service appears to have fallen to Stockwell garage with its Saturday night/Sunday morning only split duty rota on routes 181 and 168. Stockwell garage's RTL-types were rapidly displaced during the summer of 1967 by both RM and RT-types at such a pace that by Saturday night/Sunday morning 5/6 August 1967 the 181/168 split duty rota had been converted to RT-type. By this latter date the entire all-night bus network was operated by either Routemasters or RTs.

The bus stand for the Nighters at Liverpool Street was outside Broad Street station to allow departing buses to turn into Old Broad Street. RML 2569 awaits departure here for its N91 journey. *Eddie Shirras*

The importance of last journeys on all-night bus routes for early morning workers is well illustrated in this view of RM 1642 on route N89 loading passengers at London Bridge station, many of whom were probably bound for places of work in the City. *Eddie Shirras*

RM 1365 is seen at the Charing Cross station bus stop in Strand on an outbound N94 journey in 1969. *Eddie Shirras*

Wandsworth garage's allocation to all-night routes 168 and N88 had comprised RTL-type for most of the routes' existence until changed to RT-type in 1967. Here ageing 1947-built RT 184 crosses Westminster Bridge against the backdrop of the Houses of Parliament, on that night's last journey which will go out of service at Wandsworth garage. *Eddie Shirras*

Below left RM 1273 awaits departure time at Charing Cross, LT Station on Vitoria Embankment, for an 'end of shift' outbound route N85 journey to New Cross Gate where the bus will go out of service. *Eddie Shirras*

Below right Route N82 operated between New Cross Gate and Woolwich. RM 470 is seen at Shooters Hill. *Eddie Shirras*

Tottenham garage's RM 1269 was photographed on route N90's terminus bus stand beside the King William IV public house in Pimlico's Grosvenor Road. *Eddie Shirras*

Below left RM 16 is seen in Crownfield Road, Leytonstone on a last N99 journey of the night to the southern terminus of Victoria & Albert Docks. This early Routemaster spent some time as an Aldenham Works float vehicle in connection with the Routemaster overhaul programme. *J G S Smith*

Below right Red Lion Square, former terminus for all-night (and daytime) trolleybus route 665, became a terminus for just two short working early morning journeys on replacement bus route 284/N84. RM 136 is seen ready for an 06.09 departure to Poplar, Blackwall Tunnel where, on arrival, the bus will go out of service and return to Poplar garage. *Eddie Shirras*

THE BUS RESHAPING PLAN

London Transport's Bus Reshaping Plan, published in 1966, set out that Board's strategies to combat the debilitating effects that traffic congestion, declining bus usage and shortage of operating staff were having upon its bus services. The Plan had four essential points: Shortening of routes; extension of one-man operation throughout the fleet; provision of more standing accommodation on short routes; new methods to speed up fare collection.

The publicly issued document 'Reshaping London's Bus Services' contained no specific reference to the all-night route network other than its implicit inclusion within the overall aspirations of the Plan.

The first stage of the Bus Reshaping Plan was launched on Saturday 7 September 1968 with significant expansion of the standee bus Red Arrow network within central London and the introduction of a network of daytime suburban flat-fare bus routes centred around Wood Green. A minimal impact on the all-night network was the conversion of Wood Green garage's Special Night Journeys on route 29 from RT to RM-type operation from the night 7/8 September 1968.

The first section of the new Victoria Line Underground railway, between Walthamstow and Highbury, opened to traffic on Sunday September 1 1968. It had been planned to open the newly constructed bus and tube interchange facility at Walthamstow Central Bus station coincident with the first day of the Bus Reshaping Plan on 7 September 1968 but late completion of building work delayed the opening until Sunday 15 September 1968 from the night of which journeys on all-night route N99 were re-routed to and from Hoe Street to serve the new bus station.

A report by consultant Erwin Wasey published on 2 October 1968 revealed that all-night bus services ran roundly 17,000 miles per week on Central Buses. The weekly operating loss (cost of operation less fare revenue) was roughly £1,350. The report concluded:

'The existing pattern of night services is long established and covers the main known traffics to and from night time objectives. An expansion of the network would be bound to be on less heavily trafficked directions. Whilst it may be argued that the loss of £1,350 per week (or a somewhat greater sum if the night network were expanded) is not large, it certainly gives rise to the question of whether the beneficial effect would be worthwhile increasing the loss. In any event there seems to be little evidence that many of the passengers carried on existing night services are of the younger generation.'

THE ZENITH OF ROUTEMASTER OPERATION ON ALL-NIGHT ROUTES

The allocation of four RM-type buses for route N85 was switched from Rye Lane to Peckham garage on 21/22 March 1969 as a consequence of the closure of Rye Lane garage after traffic on 21 March 1969. Route N85, along with route N86, underwent a significant re-routeing from Sunday night/ Monday morning 30 November/1 December 1969. Inbound journeys on each route were re-routed after Blackfriars Bridge via New Bridge Street, Fleet Street, Strand and Northumberland Avenue to their terminus at Charing Cross,

LT Station. Returning buses maintained their original line of route via Victoria Embankment, Puddle Dock and Queen Victoria Street and so back on to Blackfriars Bridge. This re-routeing of routes N85 and N86 was noteworthy in that it represented a partial break away by south of the Thames all-night bus routes from their long established, tramway originated Victoria Embankment terminal workings. It made these two bus routes more easily accessible to West End passengers and also eliminated the previous need for terminating N85 and N86 buses to run out of service along nearby streets to turn around at the Charing Cross terminus.

On 1 January 1970 the London Transport Executive replaced the London Transport Board when control of Central Buses passed to the Greater London Council. The only immediate effect on the all-night bus route network was that route N90 and the Special Night Journeys on route 149 were required to obtain a road service licence for their quarter-mile section of route beyond the GLC boundary to Waltham Cross in Hertfordshire. Route 149's Special Night Journeys were switched to route 279 from 24/25 January 1970 as a consequence of the withdrawal of the daytime 149 from north of Ponders End. Route 279's SNJs operated between Holloway and Waltham Cross.

Routemaster-family buses had progressively replaced yet more RT-type buses on all-night bus routes and Special Night Journeys. These comprised RM-types allocated to route 177 by March 1969 and to route N97 from 23/24 January 1970. RML-types had taken up the allocations for route N92 from 27/28 October 1969 and for route N89 from 23/24 January 1970. Stockwell garage's allocation for the Saturday night/ Sunday morning split duty rota on routes 181 and 168 had become officially RM-type from 19/20 July 1969 but, due to the omission of route 168 details from many of Stockwell's RM destination blinds, an RT-type was habitually still used for the second half of this duty. The allocation of RM-types at Wandsworth garage to both route 168's all-night service and to route N88 from 17/18 April 1970 brought the Routemaster bus to the pinnacle of its domination of allocations across London Transport's all-night bus route network.

Table S: All-Night Bus Routes – Vehicle Allocations from 17/18 April 1970

Route No.	Routes	Bus Allocation			Garage
		Su	M–Fr	Sa	
9	Mansion House Stn – Mortlake Garage	-	1 RM	2 RM	Mortlake
11	Hammersmith – Liverpool Street Station	2 RM	2 RM	-	Riverside
29	Palmers Green – Charing Cross	-	1 RM	2 RM	Wood Green
109	Purley – Victoria Embankment	1 RT	1 RT	-	Thornton Heath
168	Wandsworth – Farringdon Street	1 RM	1 RM	*	Wandsworth
177	Abbey Wood – Victoria Embankment	-	-	1 RM	New Cross
181	Streatham – Kennington	-	-	1 RM	Stockwell
185	Lewisham – Victoria	1 RT	1 RT	1 RT	Walworth
220	College Park – Tooting BR Station	1 RM	2 RM	-	Shepherds Bush
221	North Finchley – Farringdon Street	2 RM	2 RM	2 RM	Finchley
279	Holloway – Waltham Cross	-	-	1 RM	Edmonton
N82	New Cross Gate – Woolwich	1 RM	1 RM	1 RM	New Cross
N83	Tottenham – Charing Cross	1 RM	1 RM	1 RM	Stamford Hill
N84	Becontree Heath – Charing Cross	1 RM	1 RM	-	Poplar
N85	Grove Park – Victoria Embankment	4 RM	4 RM	-	Peckham
N86	Brockley Rise – Victoria Embankment	3 RM	3 RM	-	Peckham
N87	Tooting Broadway – Embankment loop	3 RM	3 RM	-	Brixton
		3 RML	3 RML	-	Stockwell
N88	Wandsworth – Farringdon Street	1 RM	1 RM	-	Wandsworth
N89	Southall – London Bridge Station	3 RML	3 RML	-	Riverside
N90	Waltham Cross – Pimlico	3 RM	3 RM	-	Tottenham
N91	Willesden – Liverpool Street Station	1 RML	1 RML	-	Willesden
N92	Highgate – Charing Cross	2 RML	2 RML	-	Holloway
N93	Hampstead Heath – Charing Cross	1 RM	1 RM	1 RM	Highgate
N94	Cricklewood – Liverpool Street Station	2 RM	2 RM	-	Cricklewood
N95	Becontree Heath – Victoria	2 RM	2 RM	-	Barking
N96	Highams Park Stn – Waterloo Station	2 RML	2 RML	-	Leyton
N97	Turnham Green – Liverpool Street Station	3 RM	3 RM	-	Turnham Green
N98	Romford Station – Victoria	5 RT	5 RT	3 RT	Seven Kings
N99	Chingford Station – V & A Docks	1 RML	1 RML	1 RM	West Ham
I-S	Inter-Station Route	1 RM	†	†	New Cross
	Totals	**51**	**53**	**17**	

* Saturday night/Sunday morning split duty rota routes 168/181 from Stockwell garage
† Additional Allocation: 1 RM-type Friday and Saturday nights only between 12 June and 5 September 1970

Left Larger capacity 72-seater RML-type Routemasters formed the 'original' Holloway garage's allocation to route N92 from 27/28 October 1969. RML 2611 waits departure time outside the National Gallery in Trafalgar Square. *Capital Transport*

Table S demonstrates the Routemaster-family's ascendancy over the all-night bus route network achieved from 17/18 April 1970. From that date only routes 109, 185 and N98 retained RT-type bus allocations along with the habitual, partial use of an RT-type on Stockwell garage's Saturday night/Sunday morning split duty rota on routes 181 and 168. The Table reveals a small decrease in buses allocated to all-night service compared with the previous analysis of 8/9 May 1962 contained in Chapter 6, Table P. This reduction was largely attributable to reduced allocations on routes N84 and the Inter-Station Route, which losses were partially offset by an increased allocation for route N97.

In view of the aspiration contained within the 1966 Bus Reshaping Plan to extend 'one-man operation throughout the fleet' subsequent vehicle-type changes across the all-night route network might have been expected to incorporate timely conversions to one-man operated buses, although such a premise depended entirely upon such vehicle-types becoming allocated to daytime bus routes at appropriate garages from which the all-night route allocations were drawn. In practice vehicle-type changes implemented to route N95 from 19/20 July 1970 and to route N87 from 3/4 January 1971 involved a regression, in terms of vehicle age, from incumbent Routemasters to ageing RT-type buses. In the case of route N95 this happened because Barking garage lost its allocation of Routemasters used on daytime route 23, from which source the two RMs used on the N95 had been drawn. Replacement was by two RTs, a vehicle type previously allocated to route N95 until 30 June/1 July 1964. Brixton garage's allocation of three RMs on the N87 became casualties as a result of that garage's Routemasters being dispersed elsewhere when route 95 became one of the first two London Transport daytime bus routes to be converted to one-man double-deck operation using DMS-type Daimler Fleetlines. From Sunday night/ Monday morning 3/4 January 1971 Brixton garage's allocation for route N87 reverted to three RT buses, a vehicle type previously used by that garage on the N87 until 7/8

February 1966. Stockwell garage, which also worked three turns on the N87, was unaffected and continued to allocate RML-type Routemasters although by November 1971 Stockwell was habitually substituting RMs for its RMLs due to reliability problems with the latter type. The reinstatement of RT-types to the N87 and N95 increased the total of RTs in service on Sunday to Friday nights across the all-night route network to twelve from 3/4 January 1971.

Trams on all-night route 1, the forerunner of all-night bus route 287/N87, had both entered and left each night's service on the line of route at their depot of origin, either Clapham or Streatham. Such neat scheduling was not possible when bus route 287 replaced tram route 1 from 7/8 January 1951 due to significantly faster bus running times. Each turn on route 287/N87 comprised straight duties and in order to enable buses to finish each night's duty on the line of route at their appropriate garage, the entry point of buses into service was phased with Brixton garage buses entering service at Clapham Common and Clapham garage buses, reallocated to Stockwell garage from 25/26 November 1958, entering service at Brixton, Lambeth Town Hall. This arrangement involved buses running off the line of route to reach their starting point. Such journeys were first listed in a timetable as operating in service between Brixton and Clapham Common via Acre Lane from 27/28 July 1973.

Facing page RT 4027 is seen at Holborn in the latter days of RT operation on route N95. *Steve Fennell*

Brixton garage's RT 746 is seen at Kennington Park at around 05.00 on Saturday 22 March 1975 on a short working end of the night route N87 journey which will go out of service at the RT's home garage. *Mike Harris*

EARLY ONE-MAN OPERATED ALL-NIGHT ROUTES

Shepherds Bush garage-worked route 220 was the second of the two daytime bus routes selected to pioneer double-deck one-man operation using DMS-type Daimler Fleetlines. Since route 220's schedule incorporated Special Night Journeys it was appropriate that fleet number DMS 1 inaugurated one-man operation on the all-night route network as well as being the first Londoner (as the DMS-type was briefly dubbed) to enter revenue earning service. DMS 1 left Shepherds Bush garage at about 00.45 on Saturday 2 January 1971 to replace, in service at Shepherds Bush, the final Routemaster to have worked the 00.32 Special Night Journey from College Park bound for Tooting, Mitre. Since route 220's Special Night Journeys were incorporated at the end of each particular day's schedule, full take up of such duties by DMS buses occurred on Sunday night/Monday morning 3/4 January 1971.

The daytime service on route 177 was converted to one-man operation using DMS-type Fleetlines, allocated to New Cross garage, from Saturday 8 January 1972 but the limited Saturday night/Sunday morning service on the 177 retained crewed Routemaster operation from New Cross garage.

The allocation of DMS-type Daimler Fleetlines to Peckham garage for daytime route 78 assembled sufficient one-man operated double-deck buses at that garage to allow the first two N-prefixed Nighters to be converted to one-man operation with effect from Sunday night/Monday morning 14/15 May 1972. The pair of routes comprised the N85 (Grove Park – Charing Cross, LT Station) and the N86 (Brockley Rise – Charing Cross, LT Station) which gained an allocation of four and three DMS-types respectively. Additional running time was incorporated into both routes' schedules, in order to allow longer dwell times at bus stops for fare collection, which increased the average journey time by three minutes on the N85 and two minutes on the N86. Layover time was also increased from a previous two or three minutes to five minutes, which was adopted as standard on future route conversions to one-man operation. Since there had been no increase in the numerical vehicle allocation to either route, the cumulative time loss over a night's schedule was addressed by widening the headway of each route combined with fore-shortening one outbound N85 departure from Charing Cross to terminate at New Cross Gate and one inbound N86 to turn at Elephant & Castle. The number of departures from Charing Cross, LT Station was reduced by one journey on route N85 and by two journeys on route N86.

The effects of one-man operation from the passengers' perspective were longer journey times combined with irregular headways. In marked contrast journey times across the majority of crew-operated all-night routes were reduced from Friday night/Saturday morning 27/28 July 1973 when new timetables were applied to routes 168 (all-night service), N81, N84, N87, N88, N90, N91, N92, N93, N95, N96, N98 and N99 which typically shaved between one and six minutes off through journey times. The time saved on certain of these routes was even more dramatic with reductions of seven/eight minutes off Romford route N98, ten minutes off the Chingford Station – Victoria & Albert Docks trip on route N99 whilst no fewer than 14 minutes were clipped off route N84's Charing Cross to Becontree Heath journey which was revised to take 55 minutes as opposed to 69 minutes previously. Up until that date these by now Routemaster or RT-operated all-night bus routes had continued to work to timetables which had been applied either when then-extant London General all-night routes were converted from operation by NS-type buses to LT or ST-types in late 1932/early 1933 (see Chapter 3) or upon the later introduction of such routes by London Transport. These schedule changes did not alter any route's numerical vehicle allocation.

Brand new Gardner-powered Daimler Fleetline DMS 323 was photographed outside Charing Cross main line railway station in Strand on Monday 15 May 1972, which was the inaugural night of one-man operation on a mainstream Nighter. The driver glances behind to see how alighting passengers, previously used to Routemaster operation on the N85, are coping with the unfamiliar central exit door arrangement on the Fleetline.
Colin Stannard

ONE-MAN AND CREW FLEETLINES ON N ROUTES

On 9 November 1972 London Transport issued a surprise announcement that it intended to halt further conversions to one-man double-deck bus operation after delivery of extant orders for DMS-type Daimler Fleetlines had been completed in 1975. Slower journey times, along with the cumbersome fare collection equipment installed by London Transport on its buses, had not endeared one-man operation to London's public. 1973 saw few conversions to one-man operation so far as the all-night route network was concerned. The pair of special Early Morning Journeys worked by Finchley garage over route 221 were converted from RM-type to one-man operated DMS-type from 24 March 1973 coincident with which the inner terminal point for the 221 became Holborn Circus, Charterhouse Street, rather than Stonecutter Street. Re-routeing to certain other all-night services in the vicinity of Farringdon Street had occurred in 1972 when the long-established U-turn manoeuvre around Ludgate Circus, performed by Routemaster-operated short-workings on Tottenham route N83 and Hampstead Heath route N93, became considered too hazardous due to increased traffic levels. Such journeys were re-routed to terminate in Stonecutter Street.

The all-night and daytime service on route 185 was converted from RT-type to one-man operated DMS-type with effect from Friday night/Saturday morning 11/12 May 1973. The 185's early Sunday morning service had earlier been expanded to incorporate a through journey between Victoria and Blackwall Tunnel, Delta Works from 18/19 September 1971.

London Transport's woes continued to intensify when, in October 1973, the Executive revealed that it was understaffed by 3,000 bus drivers and 1,500 bus conductors as well as being short of engineers and maintenance staff. The bus fleet's new one-man operated AEC Merlin and Swift single deckers and Daimler Fleetline double deckers – the latter had been re-badged as Leyland Fleetline during 1973 – had proved to be more susceptible to breakdowns than older-generation buses such as the Routemaster. All these circumstances conspired to make service unreliability almost a routine expectation for London Transport's bus passengers. In these deteriorating operational conditions, which were destined to persist for some years, garage staff made every effort to ensure that sufficient buses and crews were available to work all-night routes since the infrequent and irregular schedules of many Nighters meant that any cancelled journeys really would cause hardship to passengers.

Evidence of London Transport's change of policy with regard to one-man bus operation became clear with the conversion of daytime bus routes 16 and 134 to DMS-type operation on 15 December 1973. Unlike previous DMS buses these examples had had their fare-collection equipment removed and were operated as crewed-buses, with driver and conductor, and led to Cricklewood garage's allocation to route N94 being converted from two RM-types to two crewed DMS-types from Sunday night/Monday morning 3/4 March 1974. The use of crewed DMS buses on the N94 was but a temporary expedient, pending receipt of new DM-type Leyland Fleetlines designed for crew operation, which replaced the DMS on the N94 from 15/16 September 1974. Operation of the solitary early Sunday morning return 'Press journey' on the N94 (04.54 ex Cricklewood Garage, 05.39 return from Liverpool Street Station) had lapsed since October 1970, with formal withdrawal effective from 30/31 January 1971.

DM 918 clearly demonstrates two person crewed operation of this Leyland Fleetline model variant which was photographed in Strand, outside Charing Cross station, working an outbound route N94 journey on 19 April 1975. *Eamonn Kentell*

During 1974 only one all-night route was converted to one-man operation when, from 4/5 January, route N84's allocation was switched from one RM-type to one DMS-type, a type change made possible by the allocation of DMSs to Poplar garage for daytime route 277.

Daytime bus route 171 (Tottenham Garage – Forest Hill Station) was suspended south of New Cross garage on Sunday evenings in May/June 1974 due to hooliganism problems. Since the 171's schedule incorporated particularly late Sunday night journeys, which were used by regular passengers, additional late Sunday night journeys to/from Brockley Rise were added to route N86. Such N86 journeys were initially worked by driver-operators on an overtime time basis from that route's existing three DMS-type allocation, but the position became formalised with an increased allocation of four one-man operated Fleetlines from Peckham garage to the N86 on Sunday nights/Monday mornings only from 6/7 October 1974.

Route N83 was officially converted from RML to crew-operated DM-type from 1/2 March 1975 but in practice, habitual operation of a Routemaster on the N83 continued due to the regular crew's preference for that bus type.

A significant all-night route conversion to one-man operation occurred from the night of 19/20 September 1975 when route N97 (Turnham Green – Liverpool Street Station) had its Turnham Green garage allocation on Sunday to Friday nights switched from three Routemasters to three DMS-types. The revised N97 timetable matched most journey times reasonably closely to timings which had applied prior to

one-man conversion despite increased running times of two or three minutes. Route N97, along with the Special Night Journeys on route 9, had benefited earlier from the opening of Piccadilly's westbound contra-flow bus lane on 13 May 1973. The 'Charing Cross' Special Night Journeys on route 29 operated by Wood Green garage were converted from RM to crew-operated DM-type from 15/16 December 1975, but reverted back to RM-type operation from 19/20 March 1977, from which date the 29's inbound SNJ on Monday to Saturday nights was projected to start from Enfield Town, although the corresponding return journey from Charing Cross only went as far as Winchmore Hill.

Route N96 was converted from RML to one-man operated DMS-type Fleetline operation out of Leyton garage from 18/19 March 1977. Coincident with this type change the solitary Highams Park Station journey was extended to Chingford Mount, due to turning difficulties for Fleetlines at Highams Park.

Poplar Garage's RM 175 is seen at Trafalgar Square on Saturday 15 December 1973 before setting off on that night's sole Becontree Heath route N84 journey at 00.54. Behind stands RML 2709 on route N83. Despite increased traffic levels and the imposition of a double yellow line 24-hour parking restriction, terminating Nighters continued to use this unmarked offside lane bus stand at the Square until this late date. Photographic evidence shows that this old established practice ended shortly afterwards, probably from 4/5 January 1974 when route N84 was converted to one-man operation. Thereafter terminating Nighters used a bus stand against the Square's nearside kerb close to the National Gallery. *Mike Harris*

RT 2542 is seen parked outside the Greyhound public house on Streatham Common in the early hours of Sunday morning 13 October 1974. Although route N81's outbound journey from Stockwell station terminated at Streatham garage, it was impossible to turn the bus inside that garage during the night due to other parked buses and so the N81 vehicle continued for some distance beyond the garage to take its short layover period at the top of Greyhound Lane.
Mike Harris

ROUTE N81 – LONDON TRANSPORT'S MOST INFREQUENT ALL-NIGHT BUS ROUTE

The N81 incorporated complexities of operation which belied the simple timetable of a route which deployed one bus on scheduled service for barely 75 minutes on just one night of the week. Route N81's origins had lain in a return early Sunday morning Special Night Journey between Clapham Common and Streatham over a section of daytime bus route 57A which had been introduced on 6/7 January 1951 in Stage Two of the South London Tram Conversion programme. The 57A became re-numbered route 181 from 14 May 1952 and its Special Night Journey extended beyond Clapham Common to Kennington from 30 November/1 December 1957. The daytime service over route 181 (Streatham – Victoria) was converted from crewed double-deck to one-man single-deck AEC Swift SMS-type operation from Saturday 2 January 1971 but the early Sunday morning Special Night Journey retained crewed double-deck bus operation and was renumbered as route N81 from 2/3 January 1971. Operation of route N81 comprised a split duty rota with the crew completing their shift by working the early Sunday morning service over route 168 (Wandsworth – Farringdon Street). Because of the infrequent nature of route N81 only a handful of Stockwell garage's RT or RM buses were fitted with N81 destination blind displays whilst initially none of that garage's Routemasters was equipped with destination blind displays for route 168, despite the fact that a Routemaster comprised the official allocation for N81/168. This meant that the split duty rota on routes N81/168 was often worked by a RT since use of a Routemaster on the N81 meant that the crew had to switch buses to RT-type half way through the night for the 168 element of their duty.

The Kennington Park (Post Office) – Stockwell Station journey on route N81 was back-projected to start from Windmill Row with official effect from 28/29 July 1973 although, in practice, this journey had worked in passenger service from Windmill Row since at least November 1971 under local arrangements made by Stockwell garage. This back-projection was probably introduced simply to form a turning circle for the bus. Apocryphal accounts have indicated that operation of the Windmill Row – Stockwell journey

on route N81 was 'more honoured in the breach than the observance' since on arrival at Kennington Park from Streatham crews often chose to run out-of-service to Victoria garage where the attraction of hot canteen meals overcame any possible lingering concerns about theoretical, but possibly non-existent, passengers who might have wanted to travel between Windmill Row and Stockwell in the early hours of a 1970s Sunday morning.

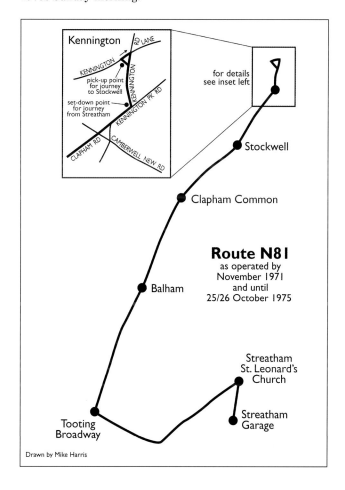

Route N81
as operated by
November 1971
and until
25/26 October 1975

Drawn by Mike Harris

Night Buses

TIMETABLES & DIAGRAM OF ROUTES

LONDON TRANSPORT
55 BROADWAY, S.W.1
01-222 1234

from July 27, 1973

The re-routeing of the all-night service on route 168 via Strand and Fleet Street, with its associated re-numbering as route N68, from 25/26 April 1975 did nothing to ease vehicle-type allocation difficulties in the early Sunday morning split duty rota on routes N81 and N68. Route N68 destination blind sets were fitted to only a handful of Stockwell garage's RT-types and, initially, not to any of its RM-types. This led to the continued habitual use of an RT-type bus on the N81/N68 split duty rota. The shortage of compatible N81 and N68 destination blind sets was related to management's anticipation of the conversion of routes N68 and N81 to crewed DM-type Fleetline operation from 20/21 September 1975. Operation of route N81 was rationalised with effect from 1/2 November 1975 when the unofficial practice of running out of service from Kennington Park to Victoria for crew relief-break was addressed by formally re-routeing the northbound N81 journey at Kennington Oval to continue in service via Vauxhall Bridge to terminate at Victoria, Wilton Road. The corresponding N68 journey to Wandsworth was modified to enter service at Victoria, Vauxhall Bridge Road.

SERVING CAMDEN TOWN AND KENTISH TOWN AT NIGHT

Apart from the diversion of southbound journeys via Camden Street as part of a one- way traffic flow system introduced on 1 September 1963, all-night route N93 (Hampstead Heath – Charing Cross) had maintained identical routeing through Camden Town and Kentish Town to that established by the pioneering North Metropolitan Tramway Company's all-night horse-tram route between Hampstead Heath and Holborn Circus introduced in January 1899. The N93 was re-routed twice between 15/16 September 1972 and 27/28 June 1975, as described in the caption accompanying the photograph of DM 1767 on the route (page 104).

Highgate garage (HT), which operated route N93, was renamed Holloway garage from 3/4 September 1971 upon the closure of the 'original' Holloway garage (J). RM 466 on route N93 was the first bus to run in service out of the renamed Holloway garage – although officially allocated one RML-type, in practice a standard length Routemaster was habitually used on the N93. Coincident with the closure of J garage route N92 (Highgate, Archway Station – Charing Cross) was re-allocated to HT garage. Both routes N92 and N93 were officially converted to crewed DM-type Fleetline operation from 26/27 January 1975.

Route N90 (Waltham Cross – Pimlico), which also served Camden Town, had its Friday night/Saturday morning allocation from Tottenham garage converted from RM to RML-type from 5/6 January 1973. Conversion to the larger capacity bus was only possible on that night of the week since on other nights insufficient RMLs were available due to the requirement for their use on daytime route 243.

Bus 185

BLACKWALL TUNNEL - GREENWICH - LEWISHAM - CAMBERWELL - VAUXHALL - VICTORIA

This service is operated by Pay As You Enter buses. Please have your exact fare ready to pay as you board.

Sunday night/Monday morning

Blackwall Tunnel *Delta Works*	....	....	0312	....	....
Lewisham *Odeon*					
Catford *Lewisham Town Hall*	0012	....	0323	....	....
Forest Hill Station	0021	0053‡	0333	....	0456§
Camberwell Green	0038	0101	0350	0443†	0516
Vauxhall Station	0048	——	0401	0452	0527
Victoria *Wilton Road*	0054	....	0407	0458	0533

Victoria *Vauxhall Bridge Road*	2356	0024	0106	....	0412	....
Vauxhall Station	0001	0029	0111		0418	
Camberwell Green	0011	0039	0121	0409†	0431	0441†
Forest Hill Station	0028	0047§	0138	0430	0451§	0502
Catford *Lewisham Town Hall*	0036	——	0146	0439	——	0511
Lewisham *Odeon*	....	....	0154	0447	....	0519
Blackwall Tunnel *Delta Works*			0503		0535	

Mon. night/Tues. morning to Thurs. night/Fri. morning

Blackwall Tunnel *Delta Works*	....	....	....	0312	....	....
Lewisham *Odeon*				0323		
Catford *Lewisham Town Hall*						
Forest Hill Station	0016§	0030§	0053‡	0333	....	0456§
Camberwell Green	0036	0050	0101	0350	0443	0516
Vauxhall Station	0047	——		0401	0452	0527
Victoria *Wilton Road*	0053	....		0407	0458	0533

Victoria *Vauxhall Bridge Road*	2356	0020	0058	....	0412	....
Vauxhall Station	0002	0026	0104		0418	
Camberwell Green	0015	0039	0117	0409†	0431	0441†
Forest Hill Station	0033	0047‡	0135	0430	0451§	0502
Catford *Lewisham Town Hall*	0042	——	0144	0439	——	0511
Lewisham *Odeon*			0152	0447		0519
Blackwall Tunnel *Delta Works*			——	0503	....	0535

Friday night/Saturday morning

Blackwall Tunnel *Delta Works*	....	....	....	0316	....	....
Lewisham *Odeon*				0326		
Catford *Lewisham Town Hall*						
Forest Hill Station	0016§	0030§	0053‡	0335	....	0457§
Camberwell Green	0036	0050	0101	0353	0441†	0517
Vauxhall Station	0047	——		0404	0450	0528
Victoria *Wilton Road*	0053			0410	0456	0534

Victoria *Vauxhall Bridge Road*	2356	0020	0058	0415	....	....
Vauxhall Station	0002	0026	0104	0421		
Camberwell Green	0015	0039	0117	0432	0438†	0457†
Forest Hill Station	0033	0047‡	0135	0452§	0458	0517
Catford *Lewisham Town Hall*	0042	——	0144		0507	0526
Lewisham *Odeon*	....	....	0152	....	0515	0534
Blackwall Tunnel *Delta Works*					0529	0548

Saturday night/Sunday morning

Blackwall Tunnel *Delta Works*	....	....	....	0334
Lewisham *Odeon*				0343
Catford *Lewisham Town Hall*	0003			
Forest Hill Station	0012	0034§	0053‡	0352
Camberwell Green	0030	0054	0101	0409
Vauxhall Station	0041	——		0419
Victoria *Wilton Road*	0047			0425

Victoria *Vauxhall Bridge Road*	0022	0055	0430
Vauxhall Station	0028	0101	0435
Camberwell Green	0039	0112	0445
Forest Hill Station	0047‡	0130	0502
Catford *Lewisham Town Hall*	....	0139	0510
Lewisham *Odeon*	....	0147	0518
Blackwall Tunnel *Delta Works*	....	——	0532

†—Time at Camberwell *Walworth Garage*.   ‡—Time at East Dulwich *Goose Green*.   §—Time at Forest Hill *Railway Telegraph*.   6

Bus N81

KENNINGTON - CLAPHAM - TOOTING - STREATHAM

Saturday night/Sunday morning only

Kennington *Windmill Row*	....	0223
Stockwell Station	0113	0229
Clapham Common Station	0117	——
Balham Station	0123	....
Tooting Broadway	0128	....
Streatham *St. Leonards Church*	0136	....
Streatham Garage	0138	....

Streatham Garage	....	0150
Streatham *St. Leonards Church*		0153
Tooting Broadway		0200
Balham Station		0205
Clapham Common Station		0211
Stockwell Station		0215
Kennington Park *Post Office*....		0220

Bus N82

NEW CROSS - ELTHAM - WOOLWICH

Saturday night/Sunday morning excepted

	SO	MF				
New Cross Gate	2304	2328	0037	0226	....	....
Lewisham *Odeon*	2311	2335	0044	0233	0417‡	....
Lee Green *Tigers Head*	2316	2340	0049	0238	0423	
Eltham Church	2323	2347	0056	0245	0430	0512
Eltham Well Hall Station	2325	2349	0058	0247	0432	0514
Shooters Hill *Herbert Hospital*	2328		——	0250	0450	0517
Woolwich Arsenal Station	2333	....	——	0255	0440	0522

	SO					
Woolwich Arsenal Station	2353	....	....	0347	0456	0530
Shooters Hill *Herbert Hospital*	2358	MF	....	0352	0501	0535
Eltham Well Hall Station	0001	0001	0107	0355	0504	0538
Eltham Church	0003	0003	0109	0357	0506	0540
Lee Green *Tigers Head*	0010	0010	0116	0403	....	0547
Lewisham *Odeon*	0015	0015	0121	0409‡	....	0552
New Cross Gate	0022	0022	0128	——	....	0559

Saturday night/Sunday morning only

New Cross Gate	0032	0236	0424	....	....
Lewisham *Odeon*	0039	0243	0431	0535‡	....
Lee Green *Tigers Head*	0044	0248	0436	0541	0626†
Eltham Church	0051	0255	0443	0548	0631
Eltham Well Hall Station	0053	0257	0445	0550	0633
Shooters Hill *Herbert Hospital*	0056	——	0448	0553	0636
Woolwich Arsenal Station	0101	....	0453	0558	0641

Woolwich Arsenal Station	0136	....	0504	0607	0647
Shooters Hill *Herbert Hospital*	0141	....	0509	0612	0652
Eltham Well Hall Station	0144	0308	0512	0615	0655
Eltham Church	0146	0310	0514	0617	0657
Lee Green *Tigers Head*	0153	0317	0521	0620†	0704
Lewisham *Odeon*	0158	0322	0526‡	....	0709
New Cross Gate	0205	0329	....		0716

†—Time at Eltham *Yorkshire Grey*.   MF—Monday to Friday night/Tuesday to Saturday morning only.
SO—Sunday night/Monday morning only.   ‡—Time at Lewisham *Rennell Street*.

7

IMPROVED SERVICE TO MAIN LINE STATIONS

During the 1970s London Transport modified elements of the all-night bus route network to make it more accessible to passengers using London's main line railway stations. The nation's holiday and travel aspirations had become increasingly ambitious, whilst the spread of higher education had led to the emergence of a new generation of student back-packers in succession to an earlier generation of National Servicemen, for whom the term 'back-pack' held a profoundly different connotation. The Inter-Station Route, once the prime all-night link between many of London's main line railway stations, had contracted from 13/14 September 1964 to become a restricted Sunday night/Monday morning facility enhanced with a summer seasonal Friday night and Saturday night service, as detailed in Chapter 7.

PADDINGTON STATION

Paddington station was already served by route N91 (Willesden Garage – Liverpool Street Station) as well as by the Inter-Station Route. With effect from Sunday night/Monday morning 19/20 September 1971 route N89 (Southall, Brent Road – London Bridge Station) was diverted away from Bayswater Road between Marble Arch and Lancaster Gate and re-routed in order to serve Paddington station. The level of service to Southall on route N89 was improved from the same date with four journeys extended across Southall to Brent Road as opposed to two such journeys previously.

WATERLOO STATION

Waterloo station was served by both route N96 (Highams Park Station – Waterloo Station) and the Inter-Station Route. The N96 terminated remotely from the station in Waterloo Road whilst the Inter-Station Route bus used private railway-owned roads to reach its terminal point on the station's forecourt, close to the main passenger entrance. With effect from Friday night/Saturday morning 10/11 March 1972 route N96 journeys arriving in Waterloo Road were projected in service via railway-owned roads to gain access to the station forecourt. Unfortunately drivers of Leyton garage's longer RML variant Routemasters used on the N96 often experienced difficulty in negotiating the private station roads, due to obstruction by parked cars and delivery vehicles. As a result of such problems this attempt to improve road/rail passenger interchange at Waterloo station was abandoned after a couple of months when N96 buses reverted to terminating in Waterloo Road from 19/20 May 1972. The Inter-Station Route, operated by a standard length RM, continued to terminate at the station forecourt and still did so following conversion to longer RML-type operation from 3/4 June 1977.

LIVERPOOL STREET STATION

By the standards of the time Liverpool Street station was well served by all-night bus routes with, by January 1972, 21 nightly departures on routes 11, N91, N94 and N97 combined on each night of the week except Saturdays. All-night bus links with Liverpool Street were long established since the all-night service on routes N94 to Cricklewood and N91 to Willesden had originated with the London General Omnibus Company's first two all-night motor bus routes 94 and 94A respectively, introduced in 1913. The established high level of all-night bus services from Liverpool Street station probably explained why that significant main line railhead to East Anglia had been excluded from the Inter-Station Route's all-night service introduced on 20/21 December 1943.

As noted in Chapter 7, the canteen at Liverpool Street – located on Underground station premises – was used for relief-break purposes by crews of most all-night bus routes which terminated at Liverpool Street Station as well as by crews from a further six all-night bus routes which ran out of service to reach Liverpool Street. During 1972 and 1976 appropriate journeys from this latter category of routes were revised to operate to Liverpool Street in public service. The first such revision was triggered when London Transport officially sanctioned an unofficial act of kindness by the regular crew on route N83. Mike Harris's article in *London Bus Magazine 23* revealed that LT officials had discovered that a member of the public was being carried regularly to Liverpool Street Station on the 02.20 southbound N83 journey from Tottenham which officially went out of service at Old Street Station at 02.40 whence the Stamford Hill garage based RML was scheduled to run light to Liverpool Street Station for the crew's relief-break. It transpired that this passenger sought a connection with the 02.49 route N97 departure from Liverpool Street Station. With effect from 7/8 April 1972 this N83 journey was revised to continue in public service between Old Street Station and Liverpool Street Station. The corresponding return journey continued to run out of service between Liverpool Street and Ludgate Circus where the bus took up the 03.32 northbound N83 departure journey bound for Stamford Hill.

London Transport decided to revise almost all other Liverpool Street station out of service crew relief-break journeys to operate in passenger-carrying service with effect from Friday night/Saturday morning 5/6 March 1976. The logic was that since mileage costs were already being accrued by buses running light to Liverpool Street Station, such journeys might as well be activated for public use in case anyone wanted to use them. From that date single return journeys on routes N68, N84, N88 and N93 were projected to/from Liverpool Street Station, in addition to which the crew relief-break return journey on route N83 was activated to operate in public service between Liverpool Street Station and Ludgate Circus via Bank. Since the N83 operated on all seven nights of the week this journey introduced an isolated 03.27 Sunday morning journey between Liverpool Street and Ludgate Circus via Bank along routeing previously without any all-night service on Saturday nights/Sunday mornings. The most extensive alteration affected three journeys on route N89 which, on arrival at London Bridge Station, were revised to continue in service back across London Bridge and via Bank to Liverpool Street Station. After crew relief-breaks these three N89 buses returned in service via Bank to London Bridge Station whence they took up westbound N89 journeys to Southall or Hammersmith Broadway, thus crossing and re-crossing London Bridge four times. Saturday night/Sunday morning crew relief-break journeys on route N98 continued to run out of service between Bank and Liverpool Street until

revised to operate in service between Bank and Liverpool Street Station from 9/10 October 1976, coincident with garage and vehicle type changes to the N98 which are detailed later in this chapter. From 17/18 October 1976 buses on daytime route 11, along with its related all-night service, were re-routed to approach Liverpool Street Station via Eldon Street rather than via London Wall as previously used.

The convergence of buses from ten all-night routes did lead to a degree of bus parking congestion in Liverpool Street at certain times. The bus total reached its peak between 02.49 and 02.53 on Monday to Friday mornings when eight buses from seven different all-night routes were scheduled to be in Liverpool Street. These comprised: routes N68 = 1 DM, N83 = 1 RML, N84 = 1 DMS, N88 = 1 DM, N93 = 1 RM, N94 = 1 DM, N97 = 2 DMS.

KING'S CROSS STATION
This railhead was served by route N93 (Hampstead Heath – Charing Cross) as well as by the Special Early Morning Journeys on route 221 and the restricted-service Inter-Station Route. From 10/11 October 1975 route N90 (Waltham Cross – Pimlico) was subjected to a significant re-routeing south of Camden High Street to travel via Pancras Road to King's Cross Station, in parallel with route N93, after which the N90 travelled along Euston Road to regain its original line of route at Euston Station.

VICTORIA STATION
The problem at Victoria was that most bus stops used by all-night bus routes were located remotely away from the main line station. This particularly applied to the Vauxhall Bridge Road bus stop from which point passengers might well have had difficulty in finding the main line station, unless familiar with the area. With effect from Friday night/Saturday morning 10/11 October 1975 southbound N90, N95 and N98 journeys were re-routed away from Vauxhall Bridge Road to allow passengers to use the Victoria Street bus stop much closer to the main line station. From 30/31 January 1976 the sole Trafalgar Square journey on route N84 was projected to and from Victoria Station along identical routeing to the N95 and N98. The opening of a contra-flow bus lane along Buckingham Palace Road from 12 September 1976 allowed eastbound route 11 buses to travel direct to the station's bus stop in Terminus Place and so discontinue the circuitous routeing via Ebury Street. All the while the restricted-service Inter-Station Route continued to terminate on the main line station's forecourt.

Road-Rail Interchange has never been bettered than when London Transport's Inter-Station Route served Paddington station! New Cross Garage's RML 2284 had used a service road to gain access to the station's main concourse where the Routemaster awaits departure time on Sunday morning 26 June 1977. *Mike Harris*

RM 1335 had gained a full set of route N81 blinds by the time this view was taken outside Streatham Common's Greyhound public house on Sunday morning 17 August 1975. *Mike Harris*

Here is hard photographic evidence that the last-ever scheduled Windmill Row route N81 journey did indeed start there! The conductor stands beside the driver of Stockwell garage's DM 1077 in Windmill Row in the early hours of Sunday 26 October 1975. *Bob Turner*

RML 2651 is seen on a short working of route N89 back to its home garage of Riverside one night in mid-1974. The full route from London Bridge Station to Southall had a journey time of one hour and five minutes. *Steve Fennell*

With a scheduled arrival time of 03.14 on Saturday 29 October 1977 Leyton garage's DMS 456 was photographed arriving at Chingford Mount on that night's sole route N96 journey to that destination. *Mike Harris*

Route N93 was re-routed via Camden High Street (outbound) or Bayham Street (inbound) and Chalk Farm Road from 15/16 September 1972 and no longer served Kentish Town Road. This improved the service to Camden Town residents at the expense of those living in Kentish Town. A permanent re-routeing from 27/28 June 1975, suggested by the N93's regular driver, effected a compromise by restoring the N93's service to Prince of Wales Road and Kentish Town Road. This photo was taken in June 1975. *Capital Transport*

Willesden garage's RML 2750 is seen outside Broad Street station in August 1978. A night bus map and route listing is displayed on the station's facade to the right of the Routemaster. The neglected-looking Broad Street station would be closed in 1986 to make way for a new large commercial development including a bus station. *David Bowker*

New Cross garage's RM 1117 stands outside King's Cross station on Sunday morning 23 June 1974. The prospective lady passenger seems to be waiting for the appearance of the Routemaster's conductor for advice on where to stow her suitcases. *Derek Persson*

Tottenham garage's RML 2536 stands in Waltham Cross in the very early hours of Saturday 29 October 1977 awaiting departure time for one of the only two journeys (both inbound) on each night of operation which covered the N90's entire route length between Waltham Cross and Pimlico with a through journey time of 1 hour 13 minutes. *Mike Harris*

BREAKING LINKS TO VICTORIA EMBANKMENT

Victoria Embankment had been a long-time terminus for south London's all-night road passenger transport services. Electrification of the tramway across Westminster Bridge had enabled the Clapham all-night tram service to become London County Council Tramways' first such route to serve Victoria Embankment when it adopted Charing Cross District Line Station as its terminus in December 1906. The opening of the rebuilt Blackfriars Bridge enabled a further three all-night tram routes from New Cross and Brixton to be extended beyond Blackfriars Road to reach a new terminus at John Carpenter Street on Victoria Embankment from 14/15 September 1909. The Earlsfield route became the first all-night tram service to traverse the full length of Victoria Embankment upon its introduction on 7/8 March 1909. Dual-direction circular terminal working between Kennington Gate and Victoria Embankment via Blackfriars Bridge and Westminster Bridge had been initiated by London County Council Tramways from 31 January/1 February 1922 in respect of its Brixton and Tooting all-night tram services. This established Victoria Embankment terminal routeing for south London all-night services was maintained upon the routes' conversion from tram to bus operation between 1950 and 1952 and so Victoria Embankment continued in its role as an important thoroughfare used by south London's all-night bus services until Thursday night/Friday morning 24/25 April 1975 when all-night routes 168, N87 and N88 made their final journeys along it.

With effect from Friday night/Saturday morning 25/26 April 1975 routes N87 and N88 were re-routed away from Victoria Embankment to travel instead via Whitehall, Trafalgar Square, Strand, Fleet Street and Ludgate Circus to Stonecutter Street. From the same night the all-night service on route 168 was re-numbered N68 and re-routed at Trafalgar Square to follow identical routeing to the N87 and N88 to Stonecutter Street where both the N68 and N88 terminated. The use of route number N68 broke with London Transport's previous convention of numbering all-night bus routes in a numerically descending series from N99 since, at the time, N81 was the lowest ranking route number in use. Evidently the use of route number N68 was intended to retain numerical affinity with the daytime service on route 168 (Putney Heath – Farringdon Street, Stonecutter Street) which maintained its routeing along Victoria Embankment. A ban on right-hand turns from Fleet Street into New Bridge Street had necessitated outbound N87's loop working via Stonecutter Street, which involved buses passing through Ludgate Circus twice before gaining their original line of route on Blackfriars Bridge. Coincident with this date of re-routeing, Brixton garage's allocation to route N87 was changed from three RT-type buses to three crew-operated DM-type Fleetlines. Due to a misunderstanding at that garage, RT4633 was allocated in error to the 23.51 departure from Streatham, Telford Avenue on 25 April 1975 and completed a circuit of the re-routed N87 via Fleet Street before being substituted by DM 1809 when passing Brixton garage at 01.11 on 26 April. Stockwell garage maintained its allocation of three RML-type Routemasters on the N87 for a while longer until that garage's allocation was brought into line with Brixton's from 2/3

November 1975 with three DM-types. The ban on right-hand turns from Fleet Street into New Bridge Street was subsequently rescinded, which allowed outbound N87s to discontinue the loop working via Stonecutter Street from 23/24 November 1975. Routes N68 and N88 were officially converted to crewed DM-type Fleetline operation from 19/20 September 1975 in respect of the Sunday to Friday night allocation of one bus to each route from Wandsworth garage as well as Stockwell garage's early Sunday morning allocation on route N68, although full type conversion at Wandsworth was not achieved until 24/25 October 1975.

The re-routeing of all night routes 168/N68, N87 and N88 away from Victoria Embankment removed three routes from the constraints of an Edwardian era tramway-originated routeing peripheral to central London and replaced it with a revised routeing, which made these services more easily accessible to potential passengers from both the West End and Fleet Street. This severance left the very restricted all-night service on routes 109 and 177 as the sole element of the all-night bus route network to maintain circular terminal workings along the full length of Victoria Embankment although a number of daytime bus routes continued to follow this routeing too. All the routes in this latter category incorporated early morning journeys, with tramway origins, which complemented the official all-night network and certain of which were, or later became, detailed in all-night bus time tables. At 25/26 April 1975 these comprised route numbers 109, 131, 155, 177 and 184.

Outbound journeys on routes N85 and N86 continued to serve that section of Victoria Embankment between Charing Cross, LT Station and Blackfriars whilst two short-working inbound N68 journeys from Wandsworth continue to access Victoria Embankment from Bridge Street to gain their terminal point in Horse Guards Avenue until such journeys were revised to travel along the full length of Whitehall and terminate at Trafalgar Square from 15/16 April 1977. With effect from Saturday night/Sunday morning 22/23 April 1978, route 177 disappeared from Victoria Embankment when that route's daily early morning and Saturday/Sunday all-night Embankment journeys were re-routed to follow a unidirectional loop working identical to that of eastbound N87 buses between Westminster Bridge and Blackfriars Bridge via Whitehall, Trafalgar Square, Strand and Fleet Street.

Having almost denuded Victoria Embankment of all-night bus services, it seemed as if London Transport wished to expunge any remaining links with that Embankment's tramway associations by renaming and relocating termini. The renaming of the Underground's Circle and District Lines Charing Cross Station as Embankment Station precipitated a similar change in terminal point designations for routes N85 and N86, first detailed in London Transport's timetable dated 19 March 1977. This change severed over seventy years use of 'Charing Cross Station' or derivatives 'Charing Cross, District Railway Station' and 'Charing Cross, LT Station' as a terminus for all-night services on Victoria Embankment. That designation had originated in December 1906 when London County Council's all-night tram service between Clapham (The Plough) and Westminster Bridge Road had been extended along the newly opened tramway across

RM 2024 is seen on Victoria Embankment, near Charing Cross LT station, on 22 March 1975 displaying blinds set for the N87's outbound routeing across Blackfriars Bridge and onward to Tooting via Streatham. Unusually, the N prefix in the route number blind aligns with the top of the figures. *Mike Harris*

Westminster Bridge to terminate on Victoria Embankment at Charing Cross, District Railway Station. The following year the time-honoured terminal point of 'Embankment, Savoy Street', which itself had replaced the previously used nomenclature 'Waterloo Bridge' in London County Council Tramways timetables by 1918, was dropped in favour of retiming appropriate routes at Embankment Station.

Immediately prior to this latter change, which became fully implemented and detailed in the London Transport Staff Timetable dated 22 April 1978, the only all-night service to have retained 'Embankment, Savoy Street' timings was route 109 but this move also affected the early morning journeys, as well as daytime and peak hour services, where appropriate, on routes 109, 131, 155 and 184.

RT 2293 is seen at the same location as RM 2024, but on the river side of the road, with blinds set for an outbound N87 journey across Westminster Bridge and on to Tooting which will return via Streatham. This view was taken in the early hours of Friday 25 April 1975, the last night of RT-type operation on route N87. *Mike Harris*

DM 1057 was photographed outside the National Gallery on route N87's revised routeing via Trafalgar Square. This view was taken in the dawn light of Midsummer Day 21 June 1975 when the Leyland CRL6-variant Fleetline was working an end of the night journey as far as Brixton garage. *Colin Stannard*

DM 1128 heads on to Westminster Bridge at around 05.50 bound for Wandsworth garage on the last route N88 journey of a July night in the very hot summer of 1976. *John Smith*

Early Sunday morning Victoria Embankment loop journeys on route 131 were complementary to route N87's weekday service along the Tooting-Clapham-Embankment route corridor. DMS 629 is seen working route 131 in Blackfriars Road on Sunday morning 17 June 1973. This journey, which originated at Merton Garage, would cross Blackfriars Bridge to reach Victoria Embankment, leave it via Westminster Bridge and continue to Wimbledon station, or Kingston station if this was the last journey. Other such 131 journeys traversed the Embankment loop in the opposite direction.
Colin Stannard

Route 177 ran daily Victoria Embankment early morning journeys in addition to its dedicated Saturday night/Sunday morning all-night service. Unlike route 131, all the 177's early morning journeys reached the Embankment via Westminster Bridge and left across Blackfriars Bridge. DMS 281 (NX 4) is seen on Victoria Embankment, at Westminster LT station, on Sunday morning 17 June 1973. *Colin Stannard*

New Cross garage's RM 1546 stands at Eltham, Yorkshire Grey, prior to its 06.26 departure to Woolwich Arsenal station on a short working route N82 journey on Sunday morning 8 June 1975. The Routemaster was later scheduled to depart from Woolwich Arsenal station at 06.47 on its final N82 journey of that night, due to arrive at New Cross garage at 07.16. *Mike Harris*

ALL-NIGHT ALLOCATIONS FOR DAYTIME ROUTES

Prior to 15 May 1976 the only post-Second World War daytime bus routes with a formal all-night allocation had been the all-night service on route 168 (re-numbered N68 from 25/26 April 1975), the Saturday night/Sunday morning element over route 182 (re-numbered N82 from 14/15 June 1968) and the Sunday night/Monday morning journeys on route 109 – all-night journeys on both the 109 and 182 on other nights of the week had been covered from the appropriate route's daytime vehicle allocation. The Routemaster operated Saturday night/Sunday morning Victoria Embankment journey route 177 had earlier been listed in the All-Night Services section of London Transport's Official Allocation of Scheduled Buses from the issue dated 8 January 1972. With

effect from Saturday 15 May 1976 a formal all-night vehicle allocation was also applied to routes 11 (Sunday to Friday nights), 109 (Monday to Friday nights additionally to the established Sunday night allocation), 177 (existing Saturday night only allocation retained), 185 (nightly), 220 (Sunday to Friday nights) and 221 (Sunday to Friday nights). Most of these services had been detailed in London Transport All-Night Services timetables for many years prior to their gaining a formal all-night vehicle allocation and, in the interests of chronicling service continuity, such operations have been recorded in earlier chapters.

Special Night Journeys on routes 9, 29 and 279, as well as the later of the pair of Early Morning Journeys on 221, continued to be worked as part of daytime vehicle allocations.

West Ham garage's RM 1872 is seen at the bleak Victoria & Albert Docks terminus on 20 November 1976 whilst working one of route N99's thrice nightly journeys to that destination. *Mike Harris*

EAST LONDON ROUTE N99

The vehicle allocation to isolated nightly route N99 (Chingford Station – Victoria & Albert Docks) became one West Ham garage-based RML-type Routemaster on all nights of the week from 18/19 July 1970 but changed back to one standard RM-type from 30 June/1 July 1972.

With effect from 7/8 April 1973 the 23.59 departure from Plaistow to Victoria & Albert Docks was re-routed to operate a spur return journey to Canning Town, following observations by the regular N99 driver of potential passenger demand after the last journey on daytime route 69 had departed. West Ham garage's allocation to route N99 switched back to RML-type from 15/16 January 1977.

THE SECOND RT RESURGENCE

This chapter opened with details of a then unexpected increase in the number of RT-type buses allocated to the all-night bus route network in 1970 and 1971 and will be closed with the account of an even more unexpected surge of RTs allocated to the network in October 1976.

By early 1976 it looked as if the demise of the ageing RTs from all-night duties was imminent. Only east London routes N95 and N98, worked by Barking and Seven Kings garages respectively, and the limited all-night service on south London route 109, worked by Thornton Heath garage, retained RT-type operation. The allocation of standard length Routemasters to Seven Kings garage, for the conversion of daytime route 86 from RT to RM-type operation, enabled route N98's allocation to be converted to RM-type from Friday night/Saturday morning 27/28 February 1976 in what was destined to be the last conversion of an N-prefixed all-night bus route to Routemaster operation. The progressive conversion of Thornton Heath garage's allocation on route 109 from RT to RM-type, which had started on 19/20 September 1976, made it seem likely that route N95 would be the last Nighter with RT operation, an expectation that was destined to be changed by events at Seven Kings garage.

Centre Barking garage's RT 2370 is seen in London Road, Barking working a route N95 journey on 20 November 1976. *Mike Harris*

Right RT 1561 is seen on layover outside Romford station between route N98 journeys in the early hours of Saturday morning 29 October 1977. *Mike Harris*

Seven Kings garage's operation of Routemasters on route N98 lasted for barely seven months. RM 2019's driver glances at his nearside mirror watching the progress of two late passengers running for his waiting bus on 19 June 1976. Night bus crews recognised the importance to potential passengers of the then-limited frequency service on London's all-night bus routes and generally did all that they could to accommodate them. *Colin Stannard*

Mike Harris's article in *London Bus Magazine 23* revealed that Seven Kings garage had sought, over a number of years, to get operation of route N98 transferred to another garage. Seven Kings' dislike of operating the N98 was related to unruly passenger behaviour, which had included assaults on platform staff, with Saturday nights singled out as the most troublesome. London Transport's management had resisted Seven Kings' requests because it was doubtful whether another garage would be willing to take over responsibility for the N98. Following discussion it emerged that Barking garage would be prepared to assume operation of route N98 provided that a regular panel of night crews could operate it. The required number of volunteers was forthcoming and route N98 was re-allocated from Seven Kings to Barking garage from Friday night/Saturday morning 8/9 October 1976. Barking garage's allocation at this time comprised a majority of one-man operated DMS-type Fleetlines as well as RTs used on daytime routes 62 and 87. It is probable that the past record of passenger behavioural problems on the N98 influenced a decision to retain crewed-operation with the result that Seven Kings garage's Routemasters were replaced, after less than eight months' service on the N98, by elderly RTs from Barking garage with a resultant increased allocation of seven RT-types on Sunday to Friday nights (two on route N95, five on route N98) and three RT-types on Saturday nights (route N98) from that garage. Route N98's timetable remained essentially unchanged upon Barking garage's adoption of the route although the remoteness of Barking garage, at 1¾ miles distant by road from the nearest main axis points

of the N98, meant that lengthy in-service garage journeys, between the garage and either Goodmayes or Ilford, were added to the timetable. Although certain Saturday night/ Sunday morning 298/N98 'Press journeys' had terminated at Holborn Circus since 29 October 1944, it emerged that no official bus stand had ever been designated at that location. This omission was addressed from Saturday night/Sunday morning 9/10 October 1976 when certain N98 journeys were projected beyond Holborn Circus to terminate at Holborn LT Station and to re-enter service from Bloomsbury.

The swan song of the RT-type bus on London Transport's all-night bus route network lasted just over nineteen months. Allocation changes to daytime bus routes effected on Saturday 22 April 1978 had reduced the daytime pvr to just 103 RTs in service on five routes which included Barking garage-worked routes 62 and 87, from which source the allocations to all-night routes N95 and N98 were drawn. Barking's RTs soldiered on with their night-time duties until Thursday night/Friday morning 25/26 May 1978 when RTs worked the N95 and N98 for the last time, to be replaced from the following night by crew-operated DMS-type Fleetlines.

The RT-type bus had given continuous service on elements of the all-night bus route network for just over 30 years, after having first entered all-night service on routes 290, 294, 296 and 298 from 4/5 May 1948. The RT's longevity on London's all-night bus duties set a vehicle-type record which, at the date of writing this book, has not been exceeded by any other vehicle-type.

RT 3410 was waiting for its 06.02 departure time on 26 May 1978 for the last RT-type operated route N98 journey to Barking garage via Goodmayes Road when it was passed in Trafalgar Square by Tottenham garage's RM 1753 on route N90. *Mike Harris*

Just over 30 years of continuous service by RT-type buses on London Transport's all-night bus routes came to an end with RT 2816's scheduled 07.24 arrival on 26 May 1978 at Barking garage on the N95. A smiling crew pose with their bus outside the garage. *Mike Harris*

Operation of all-night services on Saturday nights/Sunday mornings had been rare ever since the inception of London's public all-night road passenger transport services. The most notable exception to this institutionalised restriction in service provision was the Saturday night/Sunday morning service provided over route N98 between Romford and Holborn which had originated in 1930 with independent Fleet Coaches' Romford to Aldgate service. By the beginning of 1978 just nine London Transport buses were scheduled to work a full rota on Saturday nights/Sunday mornings – one bus on each of routes 177, 185, N68/N81 combined rota, N82, N83 and N99 respectively along with three buses needed for the N98.

Regular-frequency Saturday night/Sunday morning all-night bus services first served the West End with effect from 27/28 January 1978 when extant route N97 was upgraded to provide an enhanced 30-minute clockface frequency on each night of the week over a significantly extended route revised to operate between Heathrow Airport and Liverpool Street Station. The N97's nightly allocation became eight one-man operated DMS-type buses from Turnham Green garage which represented the highest allocation to the-then contemporary Nighters. The significant projection of the N97 route beyond its outer terminal point at Turnham Green to Heathrow Airport was allied to the opening on 16 December 1977 of London Underground's Piccadilly Line extension to Heathrow Central with the all-night service on route N97 intended to complement the daytime and evening Tube service and, between modes of transport, provide 24-hour public transport access to Heathrow Airport. In fact Heathrow Airport had enjoyed an all-night service linking it with London since at least 16 July 1947, when London Transport had assumed the contract to operate British European Airways' London terminal passenger coach services relating to which a Traffic Circular, dated 29 October 1947 included an allocation of one coach to work all-night services between 'Victoria (Airways Terminal) and Croydon, Heathrow and Northolt Airports.' This airline service remained a London Transport responsibility at the time of route N97's extension to Heathrow Airport, by which date it was operated under contract to British Airways (European Division), utilised double-deck AEC Routemasters which towed luggage trailers and ran non-stop between Heathrow Airport (Terminals 1 and 2) and the West London Air Terminal for the conveyance of airline passengers. Route N97 offered a stage carriage service between Heathrow Airport and central London which included a stop en route outside the West London Air Terminal in Cromwell Road. The advent of the Piccadilly Line Underground's and all-night route N97's extensions to Heathrow Airport abstracted traffic from the British Airways-sponsored coach service, which latterly had a nightly all-night service allocation of two Routemasters, and led to the withdrawal of the airline service after operation on 30 March 1979.

Route N98 became London's second West End-serving all-night bus route to gain a regular clock face 30-minute frequency on all seven nights of the week when, in association with schedule changes introduced on 14/15 July 1978, the N98's pre-existing irregular headway Saturday night/Sunday

morning service was aligned with that route's service pattern on other nights of the week and extended beyond Holborn to Victoria via the West End. Barking garage's allocation to the N98 increased to become five crew-operated DMS-type Fleetlines on all nights of the week.

The advent in 1978 of regular-frequency Saturday night/Sunday morning all-night bus services through the West End on routes N97 and N98 represented a significant milestone in the development of London's all-night bus network. Prior to that time the West End had been almost devoid of Saturday night/Sunday morning all-night bus facilities with only isolated journeys on routes 177, N68 and N83 whose very existence would scarcely have been known of at all beyond a small coterie of regular passengers, some LT staff and timetable-reading bus enthusiasts.

Route N95 was revised to operate exclusively between Barking Garage and Victoria from 3/4 November 1978 as a consequence of the withdrawal of the sole Becontree Heath journey.

Facing page The first deployment of Leyland Titans to all-night service duties occurred from the night of 16/17 May 1980 coincident with route N98's change in garage allocation from Barking to Romford, North Street. T 46 waits departure time in Trafalgar Square for an end of the night outbound journey that will run to the Titan's home garage on Friday morning 25 June 1982. *Mike Harris*

Route N97 was the first Nighter to gain an official allocation of the Metrobus-type from 18/19 December 1979. Turnham Green garage's M 134 is seen in Chiswick High Road on Monday 4 February 1980, about three months before the N97's allocation was transferred to Stamford Brook garage upon the closure of Turnham Green garage. *Colin Stannard*

Table T: Changes to Allocations and Vehicle-Types on All-Night Bus Routes
Period: 27/28 October 1978 – 1/2 November 1981

Route Number	Effective Date	Garage/Commentary	Su	M–Fr	Sa
109	27/28 Oct 1978	Thornton Heath: Completion of progressive type change.	1DM	2DM	-
177	14/15 April 1979	New Cross: Type change.	-	-	1 DMS
221	1/2 Feb 1980	Finchley: Start of progressive type change.	2M	2M	2M
279	20/21 Sep 1980	Edmonton: Last night of operation of Saturday night Special Night Journeys which became incorporated into new Saturday night service on route N90 from 27/28 September 1980.	-	-	-
N68	14/15 Dec 1980	Wandsworth: Type change.	1RM	1 RM	-
	20/21 Dec 1980	Stockwell: Type change.	-	-	1RM
N81	20/21 Dec1980	Stockwell: Type change.	-	-	1RM
N82	2/3 Nov 1979	New Cross: Type change.	1MD	1MD	1MD
	30/31 Jan 1981	New Cross: Type change.	1DM	1DM	1DM
N83	26/27 Sep 1980	Stamford Hill: Official allocation change to DMS-type but RM or RCL-types habitually used.	1RM	1RM	1RM
	c. June 1981	Stamford Hill: Type change.	1M	1M	1M
N85	24/25 Feb 1980	Peckham: Type change.	4MD	4MD	-
	1/2 Nov 1981	Peckham: Type change.	4LS	4LS	-
N86	24/25 Feb 1980	Peckham: Type change.	4MD	3MD	-
	1/2 Nov 1981	Peckham: Type change.	4LS	3LS	-
N87	14/15 Dec 1980	Brixton: Allocation unchanged.	3DM	3DM	-
		Stockwell: Type change.	3RM	3RM	-
	15/16 Aug 81	Brixton: Official allocation changed to DMS-type but DM-type habitually allocated until at least December 1981.	3DM	3DM	-
		Stockwell: Allocation unchanged.	3RM	3RM	
N88	14/15 Dec 1980	Wandsworth: Type change.	1RM	1RM	-
N89	27/28 Oct 1978	Riverside: Type change.	3RM	3RM	-
N90	27/28 Oct 1978	Tottenham: Friday night allocation switched from RML to RM-type as on other nights of operation.	3RM	3RM	-
	27/28 Sep 1980	Saturday night service and allocation introduced.	3RM	3RM	3RM
	25/26 Apr 1981	Official allocation became RML-type on all nights but continued to be habitually worked by RM-type.	3RM	3RM	3RM

Route Number	Effective Date	Garage/Commentary	Su	M–Fr	Sa
N91	29/30 March 1981	Willesden: Type change.	1M	1M	-
N92	29/30 Apr 1981	Holloway: Type change.	2RML	2RML	-
N93	29/30 Apr 1981	Holloway: Type change.	1RML	1RML	-
N94	9/10 Feb 1979	Cricklewood: Official allocation remained DM-type but often worked by M 1-3 giving the first appearance of Metrobus on all-night duties.	2DM	2DM	-
	25/26 May 80	Cricklewood: Official type change to DMS but in practice worked exclusively by Metrobuses M1-5.	2M	2M	-
	June/July 1980	Cricklewood: Official type change to Metrobus.	2M	2M	-
N95	June 1980	Barking: Type change	2T	2T	-
N96	30/31 Jan 1981	Leyton: Type change.	2LS	2LS	-
N97	18/19 Dec 1979	Turnham Green: Type change.	8M	8M	8M
	10/11 May 1980	Turnham Green Garage closed, allocation transferred to Stamford Brook Garage and increased nightly.	9M	9M	9M
N98	16/17 May 1980	Allocation transferred from Barking Garage to Romford (North Street) Garage. Associated type change introduced the T-type Leyland Titan to all-night duties.	5T	5T	5T
N99	27/28 Oct 1978	West Ham: Official allocation remained RML-type but habitually used crewed DM-type.	1DM	1DM	1DM
Inter-Station Route	11/12 Nov 1979	New Cross: Type change.	1MD	-	-
	16/17 May 80	New Cross: Friday and Saturday night service reintroduced.	1MD	1MD+	1MD
	4/5 Oct 1980	New Cross: Friday night service discontinued after 26/27 Sept 1980. Saturday night service revised to operate all year round.	1MD	-	1MD
	30/31 Jan 1981	New Cross: Type change.	1DM	-	1DM

Key: + Friday nights only

Note: By 25 April 1981 Stockwell Garage often substituted crew-operated DM-types in Round London Sightseeing Tour livery for RM-types on routes N68, N81 and N87.

Clearly other road traffic was light enough at 07.19 on Sunday morning 18 June 1978 to allow the driver of New Cross garage's RML 2270 to execute this 'U-turn' manoeuvre in front of King's Cross Station! The Inter-Station Route bus was bound for Euston Station and then Waterloo Station. *Mike Harris*

Opposite above Holloway garage's crew-operated Leyland CRL6 Fleetline DM 1771 is seen in Pancras Road, King's Cross, at around 01.30 on Tuesday 31 July 1979 working that night's sole N93 journey which would continue in service beyond Trafalgar Square to Victoria Garage, where the crew's relief-break would be taken. The contemporary public timetable and bus map showed the N93 as routed between Camden Town and King's Cross via Euston Station but due to a delay caused by road works such re-routeing was not achieved until over one year later. *Mike Harris*

Opposite below Route N93 was included amongst those Nighters which regained a Routemaster allocation in 1980/1981. The N93's official allocation from Holloway garage became one RML-type but in practice standard RM-type Routemasters were habitually used as exemplified by RM 115 seen in Euston Bus Station on a southbound N93 journey during 1981. *David Bowker*

MORE RAILWAY CONNECTIONS

London Transport continued with its policy of re-routeing all-night bus routes to better serve mainline railway stations when route N96 (Chingford Mount – Waterloo Station) was subjected to a substantial 1½-mile long re-routeing between Angel, Islington and Mount Pleasant from 29/30 June 1979, in order to serve King's Cross station.

The timetable of Hampstead Heath route N93 was simplified from Friday night/Saturday morning 27/28 July 1979 when previous short working journeys between Hampstead Heath and Stonecutter Street, as well as the crew relief-break journey to Liverpool Street Station, were withdrawn in favour of the introduction of a clock face hourly-frequency service worked between Hampstead Heath and Trafalgar Square by all journeys bar one which was projected beyond Trafalgar Square to Victoria for crew-relief break purposes. London Transport had wanted to re-route the N93 to serve Euston station but the contemporary timetable advised that: 'Buses will run via Euston Station, instead of direct via Pancras Road, upon completion of local road works'. Those local roadworks must have been quite extensive since it was not until 15/16 August 1980 that the N93 was able to take up its revised Euston station routeing. Only southbound N93s entered Euston Bus Station, as had eastbound N90 journeys and the Inter-Station Route since the bus station's opening on 7 October 1979.

The Inter-Station Route, which since 23/24 January 1966 had declined into a rather marginal irregular-frequency facility which operated on Sunday nights/Monday mornings only, supplemented by a summer seasonal Friday night and Saturday night service, was revitalised with effect from Friday night/Saturday morning 16/17 May 1980 to provide a clock face hourly-frequency service on Friday, Saturday and Sunday nights. All journeys followed an identical clockwise circular routeing which started at Waterloo Station and ran via Victoria, Paddington, Euston and St Pancras Stations to King's Cross Station. Buses returned from King's Cross via St Pancras and Euston Stations and thence directly back to Waterloo Station. The crew relief-break continued to be taken at Victoria with a resultant two-hour gap in service interval. Although the Friday night service was withdrawn after oper-

ation on 26/27 September 1980 and not seasonally reinstated in subsequent years, Saturday night operation was retained and so the Inter-Station Route became a Saturday night and Sunday night feature throughout the year.

VEHICLE CRISIS

London Transport's vehicle procurement programmes of the late 1960s and early 1970s proved to be both financially and operationally disastrous. In November 1976 LT had declared the single-deck AEC Swift classes to have been 'a failure' whilst by the time the last double-deck Leyland Fleetlines were delivered in 1978, significant numbers of that vehicle type were already laid up out of service due to technical problems. 164 MCW Metropolitan Scania MD-type double-deckers were bought 'off the peg' by LT between 1975 and 1977 in an effort to alleviate immediate vehicle shortages whilst long term Fleetline replacement plans were heralded when the first MCW Metrobus M-type and Leyland Titan T-type double deckers joined the fleet in 1978. The MD-type was fated to have but a transient presence on London's all-night bus routes of just two years but the M and T-types, which first entered all-night service in 1979 and 1980 respectively, were destined to achieve longevity on such duties. In early 1980 a programme of adaptation was begun for vehicles of the DM, DMS, M, MD and T-types to make them operable on both crew and one-man operated services. DM-type buses so treated were re-classified as D-type. The operational life of the Routemaster family was extended and, in 1980/1981, some all-night routes reverted back to Routemaster operation as a consequence of Fleetline withdrawals.

Table T (p. 116–117) highlights the plethora of allocation type changes which the all-night bus route network experienced over the three years between 27/28 October 1978 and 1/2 November 1981. Unquestionably the most unexpected change occurred from the night of 30/31 January 1981 when two one-man operated single-deck LS-type Leyland Nationals were allocated to route N96 in replacement of double-deck Fleetlines. That allocation change represented the first ever deployment of single-deck buses to an N-prefixed (or preceding 2xx series) all-night bus route. LS-types subsequently were allocated to routes N85 and N86 too.

LS 419 is seen at Embankment Station in 1982 on an end of the night N86 journey which would go out of service at Peckham garage. Leyland National LS-type operation of Peckham garage-allocated routes N 85 and N 86 lasted for just ten months, between 1/2 November 1981 and 2/3 September 1982. *John Smith*

MANAGERIAL CRISIS

London Transport's service delivery had deteriorated progressively throughout the 1970s due to factors both within and outside its control. Staff shortages, bus fleet unreliability and increased traffic congestion had combined with political interference in such key matters as fares policy to have a debilitating effect upon the level and quality of service. In 1978 the Bus Plan had been launched which had been intended to match daytime services more closely to staff and buses' availability, but failed to meet its objectives. A management consultancy report published in April 1980 was critical of the London Transport Executive and acted as the catalyst for a purge of that Executive's members by the Conservative-controlled Greater London Council, which culminated with the summary dismissal of London Transport's Chairman, Ralph Bennett, on 24 July 1980.

The turn of events at London Transport was symptomatic of a fundamental shift in the economic direction of the nation as a whole. The 'Winter of Discontent' in January and February 1979, which saw widespread strike action and uncollected rubbish piling up on the streets, precipitated the fall of the Labour Government and the election of the Conservatives, led by Margaret Thatcher, in May 1979. The Conservatives instituted tough economic policies in support of an enterprise culture, and the previously accepted Keynesian primacy of public spending, the power of the unions and the corporation of the welfare state were all blamed for contributing to economic decline. Other nationalised industries and many businesses, in addition to London Transport, were to go through fundamental changes.

London Transport's parlous financial situation, allied with accusations of extravagance and waste, led to reviews of certain of that Executive's functions including the all-night bus route network. Whilst certain all-night bus journeys did carry heavy passenger loadings, such as the first outbound N89 and N91 departures, particularly on Friday nights, and the last inbound N83 bus on Monday to Friday mornings, certain other journeys were essentially providing a bespoke service for, at best, a handful of passengers. An apocryphal account related that there existed elements amongst the management at 55 Broadway who advocated abandonment of the entire all-night bus route network. In the event during 1980 London Transport commissioned a team of consultants from the Transport Studies Unit of Oxford University to examine the structure and demand pattern of the extant all-night bus route network and make recommendations for its improvement. The outcome of this investigation and London Transport's response are detailed in Volume 2.

ROUTE CHANGES 1981-1983

The only recorded alteration to London's all-night bus route network during 1981 occurred with effect from Friday night/Saturday morning 24/25 April 1981 when Liverpool Street Station terminating journeys on routes N68, N83, N88, N89, N91, N94 and N97 were re-routed away from London Wall to make their easterly approach to Liverpool Street Station via South Place and Eldon Street, as route 11 had done since 17/18 October 1976. Return journeys towards Bank maintained their established routeing via Old Broad Street.

A link was broken with the trolleybus past of all-night route N84 when the former trolleybus stand on the north side of Red Lion Square, Bloomsbury was used for the last time by short-working N84 journeys on Friday night/Saturday morning 5/6 February 1982. In fact, use of Red Lion Square as a terminus had declined immediately upon the former all-night trolleybus route 665's conversion to Routemaster-type operation as route 284 with effect from 10/11 November 1959, when the main service had been projected beyond Bloomsbury to Charing Cross, Trafalgar Square and Red Lion Square had become the terminal point for just two short-working journeys, latterly a 04.34 departure for Barking, Blakes Corner and a 06.12 departure for Poplar, Iron Bridge Tavern. These N84 journeys were projected to Holborn Station and the stand moved to New Oxford Street, with the N84 bus returning via Bloomsbury Way and Vernon Place.

It will be recalled that daytime route 29 had a long established Monday – Saturday night Special Night Journey, with origins traceable back to 11/12 December 1940 (see Chapter 4), and which latterly departed from Trafalgar Square at 01.18 bound for Winchmore Hill. With effect from Friday night/Saturday morning 26/27 February 1982 new all-night route N29 absorbed this Special Night Journey into an expanded two-hourly frequency service. This operated between Enfield Town and Trafalgar Square on all nights of the week with an allocation of one crew-operated M-type from Wood Green garage, where the crew relief-break was taken. Daytime route 29 journeys operated directly between Trafalgar Square and Cambridge Circus via Charing Cross Road but route N29 was routed via Piccadilly Circus and Shaftesbury Avenue better to serve the West End. Following the N29's introduction certain journeys on daytime route 29 continued to be listed in the contemporary Night Buses timetable as giving a complementary service between Trafalgar Square and Manor House to all-night route N90. Route number N29 was the second N-prefixed route number to have been brought into use which did not conform to LT's policy of numbering all-night bus routes in a numerically-descending series from route number N99. Clearly, in a similar vein to when the all-night service on route 168 had been re-numbered as route N68 on 25/26 April 1975, the use of route number N29 was intended to give numerical affinity with daytime bus route 29. The early Sunday morning 04.30 Victoria–Blackwall Tunnel, Delta Works route 185 journey was truncated to operate between Victoria and Lewisham from 1 August 1982.

The closure of two small bus garages in west London impacted three long-established all-night bus services.

In anticipation of the imminent closure of Riverside garage the allocation for route N89 (Southall, Brent Road – London Bridge Station) was switched to Hanwell garage with effect from Friday night/Saturday morning 3/4 September 1982. Coincident with this change of garage, route N89 became enhanced with a Saturday night/Sunday morning service and was converted from crewed Routemaster to one-man operation, with a nightly allocation of three Metrobuses. The timetable for route N89 remained comparable to that which had applied before the garage change, although the number of journeys which worked right through Southall to Brent Road was reduced from four to three on each night, and former garage journeys between Hammersmith Broadway and Shepherds Bush Green were no longer operated. Following the loss of route N89, Riverside garage still retained a presence on the all-night route network since its allocation to daytime route 11 included responsibility for that route's all-night service. As if in a final flourish by Riverside garage, the all-night Routemaster operated service on route 11 was enhanced from 24/25 April 1983 when all journeys were extended to operate between Hammersmith, Brook Green Hotel and Liverpool Street Station with an hourly all-night frequency (apart from a two hour gap for crew relief-break at Liverpool Street Station). Closure of Riverside garage after service on Friday 24 June 1983 led to the allocation for route 11's all-night service, as well as an element of its daytime service, being transferred to Victoria garage from 24/25 June 1983 with continued use of RM-types. At this date the route was withdrawn between Brook Green and the Broadway at Hammersmith, but this section was reinstated on 29 October 1983.

Mortlake garage, which at the time had the smallest allocation of buses of any LT garage, also closed after traffic on Friday 24 June 1983, although the last bus to run out of service into that garage, at 01.45 hours on Saturday 25 June 1983, was the Routemaster-operated Special Night Journey on route 9 from Mansion House Station. Mortlake had maintained operation of the sole surviving 'Ludgate Circus' Special Night Journey on route 9 ever since its introduction on 6/7 November 1921. Latterly this Special Night Journey had been extended beyond Ludgate Circus to St Paul's Churchyard (from 27/28 February 1965), to Mansion House Station (from 11/12 November 1967) and, on Saturday nights only, to Liverpool Street Station (from 31 January/1 February 1981). A second Saturday night only Special Night Journey on route 9 had been introduced from 29/30 June 1946. Stamford Brook garage assumed operation of route 9's Special Night Journeys from Saturday night/Sunday morning 25/26 June 1983.

New route N80 was introduced on Friday night/Saturday morning 24/25 June 1983 and extended the all-night bus route network to a new northern extremity at Potters Bar garage in Hertfordshire. The N80 replaced previous privately-operated staff bus journeys and linked Potters Bar garage with Finchley garage via rather convoluted alternative route-ings outlined in the caption accompanying the picture of M 691 on route N80 on page 127. Certain N80 journeys connected at Finchley, Tally Ho Corner, with northbound and southbound route 221 journeys. The N80 operated on all seven nights of the week with a allocation of one one-man operated Metrobus from Potters Bar garage. Use of route number N80 reverted to the logic of using the next available route number in the descending all-night bus route numbering series. As later events will reveal, the four-month period between 24/25 June and 22/23 October 1983 was the only time that the complete sequence of numerically descending all-night bus route numbers between N99 and N80 was in simultaneous use.

The paucity of London's public road passenger transport operations on Saturday nights and Sunday mornings has been commented upon in previous chapters. In more recent years this deficiency in weekend service had been slightly ameliorated by the expansion of Saturday night/Sunday morning operation to include routes N89, N90 and N97 from 1978 onwards as well as by the introduction of new nightly services on routes N29 and N80. Nevertheless large sections of the all-night bus route network remained devoid of Saturday night and Sunday morning services. This deficiency was addressed with effect from Saturday night/Sunday morning 29/30 October 1983 when Saturday night and Sunday morning operation was extended to encompass all routes except the 220.

Routes 177, 185, N68, N80, N81, N82, N83, N89, N90, N97, N98, N99 and the Inter-Station route, along with the Special Night Journeys on routes 9 and 221, already had a Saturday night/Sunday morning service. From 29/30 October 1983 Saturday night/Sunday morning operation was expanded to include also routes 11, 109, N84, N85, N86, N87, N88, N91, N92, N93, N94, N95 and N96. In most cases the Saturday night timetables introduced on these routes were identical to those that applied on Sunday to Friday nights.

The advent of a Saturday night 24-minute frequency service on route N87 (Tooting Broadway to Victoria Embankment loop) obviated the need for the somewhat intriguing and infrequent route N81 (Streatham Garage – Victoria Station via Tooting Broadway, Clapham and Stockwell) which last operated the previous weekend, in the early hours of Sunday 23 October. With the N81's demise Stockwell garage lost its Saturday night/Sunday morning split duty rota on routes N81 and N68 in favour of Wandsworth garage which assumed operation of the N68 to an identical timetable on all nights of the week. This meant that the N68's former Sunday morning crew relief-break at Victoria garage was switched to Liverpool Street Station, as used by N68 crews on other nights of the week, and that the short single direction Sunday morning only spur section of route N68 between Victoria and Vauxhall Station was also withdrawn.

Special Night Journeys Route 9 Timetable with effect from 25/26 June 1983				
		M–Fr	Sa	
Mortlake, Avondale Road	dep	0014	0007	0038
Hammersmith Broadway		0025	0016	0047
Trafalgar Square		0052	0043	0114
Ludgate Circus		0057	0048	0119
Mansion House Station	arr	0100	0051	0122
Liverpool Street Station	arr	-	0056	-
Liverpool Street Station	dep	-	0058	-
Mansion House Station	dep	0103	0103	0129
Ludgate Circus		0106	0106	0132
Trafalgar Square		0111	0111	0137
Hammersmith Broadway		0136	0136	0202
Mortlake, Avondale Road	arr	0147	0147	0213

Garage: Stamford Brook.
Allocation: 1 RM-type (Mon–Fri), 2 RM-type (Sa).

Table V: Other Changes to Allocations and Vehicle-types on All-Night Bus Routes
Period: 30/31 July 1982 – 1/2 September 1983

Route No	Effective Date	Garage/Commentary	Su	M–Fr	Sa
109	3/4 Sept 1982	Thornton Heath: Type change	1RM	1RM	-
220	1/2 Sept 1983	Shepherd's Bush: Start of progressive type change	1M	1M	-
N68	Winter 1982	Wandsworth: Habitually worked by DMS-type instead of allocated RM-type	1DMS	1DMS	-
N68	Winter 1982	Stockwell: as Wandsworth	-	-	*
N81	Winter 1982	Stockwell: as Route N68	-	-	1DMS
N83	By 30/31 Oct 1982	Stamford Hill: Habitually worked by RM/RML instead by allocated M-type	1RM	1RM	1RM
N84	18/19 August 1982	Poplar: Type change	1T	1T	-
N85	3/4 Sept 1982	Peckham: Type change	4T	4T	-
N86	3/4 Sept 1982	Peckham: Type change	4T	3T	-
N87	22/23 April 1983	Stockwell: Type change	3DM	3DM	-
N87	22/23 April 1983	Brixton: Unchanged	3DM	3DM	-
N88	Winter 1982	Wandsworth: as route N68	1DMS	1DMS	-
N92	Winter 1982	Holloway: habitually worked by DMS-type instead of allocated RML-type	2DMS	2DMS	-
N93	Winter 1982	Holloway: habitually worked by DMS-type instead of allocated RML-type	1DMS	1DMS	-
N95	5/6 Sept 1982	Barking: converted to one-man operation	2T	2T	-
N98	3/4 Sept 1982	Romford: converted to one-man operation	5T	5T	5T
N99	3/4 Sept 1982	West Ham: converted to one-man operation	1T	1T	1T

Key: * Utilised bus off route N81

Stockwell garage's DMS 2454 is seen loading passengers outside Streatham garage at 01.50 on Sunday morning 23 October 1983 for route N81's last-ever journey. *Paul Davis*

Slimline timetables were introduced from 1 July 1981 and continued in use until November 1989. Examples illustrated are, from left to right: Issue 2 of 28 November 1981, Issue 3 of 29/30 October 1982 (when the Night Owl marketing symbol first appeared) and Issue 5 of 29/30 October 1983 (when Saturday night operation was expanded to cover almost all routes).

Barking Road routes N84 and N95 gained Saturday night/ Sunday morning services with timetables which differed quite significantly from those which applied on Sunday to Friday nights. In the case of route N84 (Becontree Heath – Victoria) two journeys were scheduled to work through to Victoria on early Sunday mornings, as opposed to one such journey on other nights of the week. This was in order to facilitate the crew relief-break at Victoria garage on Sunday mornings rather than Liverpool Street Station, where it continued to be taken on other nights.

Route N95 was scheduled with a particularly late (for an all-night route) 06.55 Sunday morning departure from Victoria with a 07.53 arrival at Barking Garage which made it the latest of the contemporary Nighters to run out of service. Route N95 had earlier, from 29/30 October 1982, regained its former haunt at Becontree Heath (to where it had last operated on 2/3 November 1978) with a Monday to Saturday morning 03.26 departure from Victoria which extended eastwards beyond Barking Garage to Becontree Heath. The return journey at 04.40 from Becontree Heath worked back through to Victoria.

Route 220 (Harlesden, Willesden Junction – Tooting, Mitre) was the sole all-night bus route not to gain a Saturday night/Sunday morning service. Essentially the 220's all-night service comprised a return Special Night Journey over a section of its daytime route. By this date the *Buses, Tubes and Trains for Night Owls* timetable booklet detailed additional late night and/or early morning journeys, which were formed from daytime bus allocations, as being complementary to the all-night service or Special Night Journeys on routes 11, 109, 177, 185, 220 and 221.

The expansion of Saturday night/Sunday morning operation to encompass almost the entire all-night route network from 29/30 October 1983 represented a watershed in the development of London's all-night bus services. Up until that date the capital's all-night bus service schedules had been based largely upon the concept of providing public transport for those persons who needed to get to and from weekday work only. Universal Saturday night operation recognised changing patterns of social behaviour amongst the populace who, in increasing number, pursued activities and sought entertainment well into the late hours at weekends.

The Metropolitan Scania MD-type's allocation to all-night bus route duties spanned just short of two years, between 2/3 November 1979 and 30/31 October 1981. MD 5 is seen at New Cross on an inbound N86 journey during 1980. *John Smith*

The N84 was an elusive route to photograph with just one bus in service on each night of operation working along an axis between Victoria Station and Becontree Heath. John Smith succeeded in locating Poplar garage's T 402 in Barking Road, Canning Town at around 05.00 during summer 1982 working a journey that originated at Bloomsbury Way. *John Smith*

Wood Green garage's crew-operated M 626 was photographed outside the National Gallery in Trafalgar Square on 27 February 1982 during the inaugural night of route N29's operation. *Mike Harris*

Hanwell garage's M 499 is about to leave London Bridge station working the scheduled 01.37 departure time route N89 journey on Monday 26 March 1984 which will run as far as Southall garage. *Paul Davis*

If one had worked out where was the right place to be to take advantage of early morning summer sunshine, then it was once possible to photograph a London Transport all-night bus route in an idyllic rural setting! M 691 is seen at around 07.25 on Sunday 21 August 1983 near South Mimms heading for its home garage on the preceding night's final route N80 journey from North Finchley. Other N80 journeys operated to and from Potters Bar garage more directly along the Great North Road whilst, south of New Barnet station, some N80 journeys ran via Southgate and Friern Barnet and others operated more directly via Whetstone High Road. *Mike Harris*

Stamford Brook garage's MCW Metrobus M 145 is seen outside the derelict-looking facade of Broad Street station in the early morning hours of Monday 26 March 1984. Evidence of construction work, which would transform the appearance of the-then run-down Liverpool Street area, may be seen in the background. *Paul Davis*

The importance of Farringdon Street as a terminus for all-night bus routes would become much diminished following the network's expansion from 13/14 April 1984. RT 1869, working the all-night element of route 168 from Wandsworth on 1 October 1950, had been the first modern Nighter to terminate in the vicinity, at Farringdon Avenue. Over 33 years later Wandsworth garage's M 955, on successor route N68, is seen at Stonecutter Street, the revised terminal point for Farringdon Street routes since circa 1960, in the early morning hours of Saturday 18 February 1984. *Paul Davis*

Route N94 originated from the LGOC's first all-night motor bus route 94, between Cricklewood and Liverpool Street, introduced in July 1913. Over 70 years later the N94's routeing remained unchanged, apart from diversions due to gyratory traffic flow systems, to that of its forerunner and it remained crew-operated. The nature of passengers who used the Nighters was changing though, as evidenced by the group of young people waiting around the bus stop in Duncannon Street, off Trafalgar Square, as Cricklewood garage's MCW Metrobus M 312 prepares to pull away during the early morning hours of Monday 26 March 1984. *Paul Davis*

A few vehicle-type changes occurred in late 1983. On 15/16 November 1983 the introduction of Leyland Titans to New Cross garage led to crewed T-type operation of route N82 and the Inter-Station Route, as well as the Saturday all-night service on route 177. Crew-operated Metrobuses replaced Fleetlines on Wandsworth garage's allocation to routes N68 and N88 from Tuesday night/Wednesday morning 22/23 November 1983. A minor revision to route N86's terminal working at Brockley was effected from 20/21 November 1983.

No further alterations occurred to either routeing or vehicle-type allocation across the all-night route network for nearly five months until London Transport, in its response to the Oxford Report, modified and expanded the network from 13/14 April 1984, as described in Volume 2.

Table W details routes operated and vehicle-type allocations on Thursday night/Friday morning 12/13 April 1984, which was the final night of operation for London Transport's traditional all-night bus route network. Clearly the most striking feature was the dramatic increase up to 61 buses in service on Saturday nights/Sunday mornings which compared with never more than 18 such vehicles in any earlier year. The number of buses in nightly service on Mondays to Fridays had increased to 60, which was attributable to the increased

vehicle allocation necessitated by route N97's extension to Heathrow Airport from 27/28 January 1978 and the introduction of route N80 on 24/25 June 1983. One-man operated buses comprised 58% of the all-night bus route network's vehicle allocation. London Transport's then-most modern double deckers, M-type MCW Metrobus and T-type Leyland Titan, predominated in vehicle-type allocations across the Nighters. The ill-starred DMS-type Fleetline remained in all-night service on routes N87, N92 and N93 whilst the single-deck LS-type Leyland National could be encountered on route N96. The stalwart Routemaster, which had first taken up regular all-night service from Poplar garage from 10/11 November 1959 on trolleybus replacement route 284, still maintained a presence on the all-night bus route network almost 25 years later with allocations on all-night routes 11, 109 and N90 as well as on route 9's Special Night Journeys.

A crew member of New Cross garage's Leyland Titan T 895 approaches the Inter-Station Service bus seen on the otherwise deserted station service road at Waterloo in the early hours of Monday morning 26 March 1984. *Paul Davis*

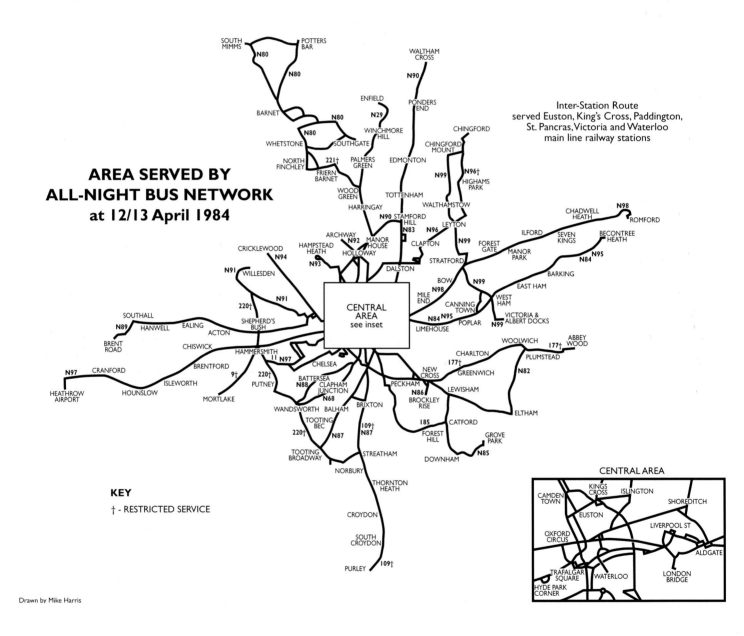

**AREA SERVED BY
ALL-NIGHT BUS NETWORK
at 12/13 April 1984**

Inter-Station Route
served Euston, King's Cross, Paddington,
St. Pancras, Victoria and Waterloo
main line railway stations

KEY

† - RESTRICTED SERVICE

Drawn by Mike Harris

SOUTH
MIMMS
POTTERS
BAR
N80
N80
BARNET
WHETSTONE
N80
N80
NORTH
FINCHLEY
221†
FRIERN
BARNET
WOOD
GREEN
HARRINGAY
SOUTHGATE
PALMERS
GREEN
WINCHMORE
HILL
N29
ENFIELD
PONDERS
END
WALTHAM
CROSS
N90
CHINGFORD
CHINGFORD
MOUNT
N99
N96†
HIGHAMS
PARK
EDMONTON
TOTTENHAM
N90 STAMFORD
HILL
N83
WALTHAMSTOW
LEYTON
N96
CHADWELL
HEATH
N98
ROMFORD
CRICKLEWOOD
N94
ARCHWAY
N92 MANOR
HOUSE
HOLLOWAY
CLAPTON
N99
FOREST
GATE
ILFORD
SEVEN
KINGS
BECONTREE
HEATH
HAMPSTEAD
HEATH
N93
DALSTON
STRATFORD
MANOR
PARK
BARKING
N84 N95
N91
WILLESDEN
BOW
N98
EAST HAM
N91
MILE
END
N99
WEST
HAM
SOUTHALL
220†
N89
HANWELL
EALING
ACTON
SHEPHERD'S
BUSH
CANNING
TOWN
N84 N95
POPLAR
N99
VICTORIA &
ALBERT DOCKS
BRENT
ROAD
CHISWICK
LIMEHOUSE
CENTRAL
AREA
see inset
N97
CRANFORD
BRENTFORD
HAMMERSMITH
11 N97
9†
CHELSEA
WOOLWICH
177†
ABBEY
WOOD
HEATHROW
AIRPORT
HOUNSLOW
ISLEWORTH
MORTLAKE
220†
PUTNEY
BATTERSEA
N88 CLAPHAM
JUNCTION
N68
CHARLTON
177†
NEW
CROSS
GREENWICH
PLUMSTEAD
N82
WANDSWORTH BALHAM
BRIXTON
PECKHAM
N86
BROCKLEY
RISE
LEWISHAM
ELTHAM
TOOTING
BEC
220†
N87
109†
N87
FOREST
HILL
185
CATFORD
GROVE
PARK
N85
TOOTING
BROADWAY
STREATHAM
DOWNHAM
NORBURY
THORNTON
HEATH
CROYDON
SOUTH
CROYDON
PURLEY
109†

CENTRAL AREA
CAMDEN
TOWN
KINGS
CROSS
ISLINGTON
SHOREDITCH
EUSTON
OXFORD
CIRCUS
LIVERPOOL ST
ALDGATE
TRAFALGAR
SQUARE
WATERLOO
LONDON
BRIDGE
HYDE PARK
CORNER

Table W: All-Night Bus Routes. Vehicle Allocations at 12/13 April 1984

Route No	Bus Routes	Bus Allocation			Garage
		Su	M–Fr	Sa	
9	Liverpool Street Station – Mortlake	-	1 RM	2 RM	Stamford Brook
11	Hammersmith – Liverpool Street Station	2 RM	2 RM	2 RM	Victoria
109	Purley – Embankment Station	1 RM	1 RM	1 RM	Thornton Heath
177	Abbey Wood – Trafalgar Square	-	-	1 T	New Cross
185	Lewisham – Victoria	1 T	1 T	1 T	Walworth
220	Harrow Road – Tooting	1 M	1 M	-	Shepherds Bush
221	North Finchley – Holborn Circus	2 M	2 M	2 M	Finchley
N29	Enfield Town – Trafalgar Square	1 M	1 M	1 M	Wood Green
N68	Wandsworth – Farringdon Street	1 M	1 M	1 M	Wandsworth
N80	Potters Bar – North Finchley	1 M	1 M	1 M	Potters Bar
N82	New Cross Gate – Woolwich	1 T	1 T	1 T	New Cross
N83	Tottenham – Trafalgar Square	1 M	1 M	1 M	Stamford Hill
N84	Becontree Heath – Victoria	1 T	1 T	1 T	Poplar
N85	Grove Park – Embankment Station	4 T	4 T	4 T	Peckham
N86	Brockley Rise – Embankment Station	4 T	3 T	3 T	Peckham
N87	Tooting Broadway – Trafalgar Square	6 DMS	6 DMS	6 DMS	Brixton/Stockwell
N88	Wandsworth – Farringdon Street	1 M	1 M	1 M	Wandsworth
N89	Southall – Liverpool Street Station	3 M	3 M	3 M	Hanwell
N90	Waltham Cross – Pimlico	3 RM	3 RM	3 RM	Tottenham
N91	Willesden – Liverpool Street Station	1M	1 M	1 M	Willesden
N92	Archway – Trafalgar Square	2 DMS	2 DMS	2 DMS	Holloway
N93	Hampstead Heath – Victoria	1 DMS	1 DMS	1 DMS	Holloway
N94	Cricklewood – Liverpool Street Station	2 M	2 M	2 M	Cricklewood
N95	Becontree Heath – Victoria	2 T	2 T	2 T	Barking
N96	Chingford Mount – Waterloo	2 LS	2 LS	2 LS	Leyton
N97	Heathrow Airport – Liverpool Street Station	9 M	9 M	9 M	Stamford Brook
N98	Romford Station – Victoria	5 T	5 T	5 T	Romford
N99	Chingford Station – V & A Docks	1 T	1 T	1 T	West Ham
	Inter-Station Route	1 T	-	1 T	New Cross
	Bus Total	**60**	**59**	**61**	

Despite some recent route innovations which had extended the extremities of the all-night bus route network northwards to Enfield Town and Potters Bar, as well as westwards to Heathrow Airport, the route network operated at 12/13 April 1984 was not dissimilar to that of 50 years earlier, apart from diversion routeings due to gyratory traffic flow systems. Route N83 followed identical routeing between Stamford Hill and the junction of Clerkenwell Road with Gray's Inn Road to the North Metropolitan Tramway Company's horse-tram operated all-night service between Stamford Hill and Holborn introduced in January 1899. Routes N91 (Willesden – Liverpool Street Station) and N94 (Cricklewood – Liverpool Street Station) remained virtually identical to London General's first two motorbus-operated all-night bus routes introduced in 1913, as routes 94A and 94 respectively, Route N87 (Tooting Broadway – Trafalgar Square) still maintained a similar cyclical working pattern to that established by London County Council Tramways on 17/18 July 1928 in respect of its all-night tram services from Tooting Broadway via Brixton and via Clapham, although since 25/26 April 1975 the N87 had served Trafalgar Square and Fleet Street rather than Victoria Embankment as previously routed. In fact the most marked contrast between the route network as it existed at 12/13 April 1984 and that of earlier years was the diminution in the number of all-night services along Victoria Embankment and the marked increase in the number of such services routed between Trafalgar Square and Ludgate Circus via Strand and Fleet Street.

Upper left T 934 is seen at Charing Cross on 25/26 March 1984 working one of then-only two nightly route N86 journeys originating in central London which worked the entire route length of the N86 through to Brockley Rise. Three short working Sunday night-only journeys from Camberwell Green (which had replaced late night journeys on daytime route 171 in 1974) and one nightly short working journey from Elephant & Castle also served Brockley Rise. Most other N86 journeys only went as far as New Cross Gate. *Paul Davis*

Lower left Although route N83 had an official allocation of one Metrobus, RCL 2251 was substituted to work that route on its last night of crew-operation. Enthusiasts stand beside the former Green Line coach Routemaster at Trafalgar Square in the early hours of Friday morning 13 April 1984. The Safeway advertisement forms an unwitting but apt link with the N83's ancestry in trolleybus routes 543/643. *Paul Davis*

Below Route N92 had an official allocation of two DMS-types. Holloway garage substituted RML 2266 for one of those Fleetlines on the last night of crewed operation on the N92 and that bus is seen outside the National Gallery, in Trafalgar Square, awaiting departure time on the 30-minute frequency service to Archway station on 13 April 1984. *Mike Harris*

London Transport had introduced initiatives to improve its all-night route network, and so broaden its appeal to a wider public, through some significant routeing innovations, particularly since 1975, and by the adoption of universal Saturday night/Sunday morning operation from 29/30 October 1983. Yet despite these welcome changes an entrancing sense of timelessness pervaded much of London's all-night bus operations, with its preponderance of irregular frequency, and sometimes infrequent, services. That ethereal quality is well illustrated by route N91 on which an 11.56pm (23.56) departure from Liverpool Street Station to Willesden had been scheduled ever since that route's reintroduction after the First World War as London General's route 94A on 17/18 August 1920. That 11.56pm departure time remained unchanged for almost 54 years and had always been worked by a Willesden garage bus, during which period the vehicle-type changed from B-type to K-type, to NS-type, to ST-type, to STL-type, to RT-type, to RTL-type, to RM-type, to RML-type and finally to M-type until the 23.56 N91 journey set off from Liverpool Street Station for the very last time on Thursday night 12 April 1984.

FARE POLICIES

THE NORTH METROPOLITAN TRAMWAYS COMPANY LTD

Upon the inception of London's first all-night public road passenger transport services by Northmet in January and February 1899 Workman's fares of 1d single or 2d for a two journey ticket were charged on all the company's horse-trams departing termini at or after 12 midnight. The two journey ticket, which allowed a second journey in any direction at any time and by any person, was discontinued at an unknown date in 1899 prior to 2 October 1899 when the time at which Workman's fares could be bought on all-night services was revised to become nominally 4am, the same time as that when Workman's fares became available on early morning journeys over daytime routes. Exact times varied according to route and were:

Hampstead to Holborn: 4.20am (inbound), 5.2am (outbound)
Stamford Hill to Holborn: 3.25am (inbound), 4.15am (outbound)
Stratford to Aldgate: 3.55am (inbound), 4.36am (outbound)
Poplar to Aldgate: 4.20am (inbound), 4.51am (outbound)

This change of policy deprived users of Northmet's all-night routes of the benefit of reduced-price Workman's fares. Predictably this produced an outcry from disgruntled passengers, many of whom worked for newspapers, and so the Press added its voice to the protests. All the protestations were of no avail since, as chronicled in Chapter 1, Northmet was incurring losses on the operation of its all-night services which were suspended in 1900. Although the Hampstead and Highgate routes were reinstated during 1902 operation of Northmet's all-night services was not sustained. Northmet's entire tramway was taken over by London County Council Tramways on 1 April 1906.

LONDON COUNTY COUNCIL TRAMWAYS

LCC Tramways all-night horse-tram routes, introduced from February 1899, charged 1d single or 2d return 'All The Way Midnight Car' fares. The complementary all-night horse-bus routes introduced across Blackfriars Bridge and across Westminster Bridge charged a ½d fare. LCC Tramways applied Workman's fares from 1 January 1901, valid between 1.30am and 8am, and which appear to have replaced the 'All The Way Midnight Car' fares. Passengers using the Council's all-night trams prior to 1.30am now had to pay full fare. From 9 May 1904 Workman's fares are recorded as having been ½d and 1d, for any distance single journey beyond those covered by the ½d fare, and 2d, to be paid in advance, for a return or double journey ticket. The 2d ticket was available, on the day of issue only, for a return journey or for a further single journey on any other LCC Tramways route. 2d tickets could not be issued on all-night services until after 1.30am.

When LCC Tramways reinstated the former Northmet-operated all-night tram routes north of the river Thames in early 1907, it maintained Northmet's practice of applying Workman's fares from 4am, thus compelling all-night passengers to pay full fares. This resulted in different fare policies being applied in respect of LCC Tramways all-night services north and south of the Thames. At this time London County Council's Highways Committee seems to have been swayed towards the merits of the former Northmet's policy in respect of all-night tram fares and, because of the unremunerative nature of these services, recommended in June 1907 that, in order to secure uniformity throughout the Council's tramways, both north and south of the Thames, that ordinary fares should be charged up to 3.30am. However, other counsel prevailed and with effect from Monday 22 July 1907 the fares policy already in place south of the Thames was extended to cover its northern tramway which meant that, thereafter, Workman's fares applied across the Council's entire network from 1.30am to 8.0am. By this date fares were 1d single or 2d for a return or double journey ticket.

Privations caused as a result of the First World War included a decision made by London County Council's Highways Committee to charge ordinary fares, from 1 July 1916, on all-night cars scheduled to arrive at or leave the central London termini up to 3.30am after which time Workman's fares became available. The time at which Workman's fares became available was modified to 3am on 16 July 1917 and, from the same date, the issue of Workman's fares on outbound journeys ceased at 7.30am. The 'double journey' element of 2d Workman's fares was also abolished and thereafter a 2d Workman's return became only valid for a return journey over the same section of tramway as that on which it had been issued for the original journey.

A meeting of the Council's Highways Committee held on 23 March 1920 resolved to continue to charge ordinary fares on all-night cars until 3am, because of losses of 6½d per car mile being incurred on all-night services. Thus reduced-price Workman's fares remained only available between 3am and 7.30am on outbound journeys or on inbound Workman's cars from the suburbs timed to reach their London termini by 8am. This fares policy in respect of all-night tram services was maintained by London County Council Tramways until it was absorbed by the London Passenger Transport Board on 1 July 1933.

LONDON GENERAL OMNIBUS COMPANY LTD

The LGOC applied daytime service fare stages to London's first motor bus-operated all-night bus routes 94 (Cricklewood – Liverpool Street Station) and 94A (Willesden – Liverpool Street Station) when introduced in July and November 1913 respectively.

Fares ranged from ½d, for short stages, up to 5d for the journey between either Cricklewood or Willesden and Liverpool Street Station.

The 28 January 1916 issue of *Electric Railway and Tramway Journal* reported that 'owing to the loss incurred in running the (LGOC) night omnibuses from Cricklewood to Liverpool Street it has been decided to increase the fares by approximately 100%. 1d fares, for example, will be doubled and a 5d ticket only increased to 8d'. The Willesden – Liverpool Street route was not mentioned in the piece but was probably also included in this imposition of premium fares to

LGOC's all-night bus routes at that time. LGOC's routes 94 and 94A were suspended, due to wartime exigencies, after operation on 14/15 July 1916.

When routes 94 and 94A were reinstated from 17/18 August 1920 fare stages equivalent to those of daytime services over comparable sections of routeing were applied except that a *minimum fare* of 3d was imposed upon those two all-night bus routes. Just afterwards, in September 1920, LGOC's lowest fare on daytime bus routes was increased from 1d to 1½d. This increase caused a vociferous outcry from passengers which was quickly taken up by the Press, elements of which would have used routes 94 and 94A. This contemporary sustained criticism of its fares policy *may* have influenced LGOC's decision to abandon the 3d minimum fare on routes 94 and 94A from 8 January 1921 when 1½d and 2d fare stages were brought into operation with the result that the fares on the company's all-night services corresponded in every respect with those in force on its daytime services. LGOC's policy of equivalent fares on both daytime and all-night services was applied thereafter to all new all-night bus routes, as introduced, up until the absorption of the company by the London Passenger Transport Board on 1 July 1933.

One interesting outcome of LGOC's *volte-face* on its 1920 lowest fare increase, as a result of which 1d fares were restored to shorter stages of daytime routes from 1 December 1921, was the introduction of half price Child fares from 1 January 1922. Perhaps surprisingly, Child fares were applied to the company's all-night bus routes at this time.

LONDON TRANSPORT

Following its assumption of operating powers from 1 July 1933 the London Passenger Transport Board maintained the respective fares policies on all-night services of the two constituent former operators of such services. Equal fares applied over equivalent stages of route on both daytime and all-night bus routes. Ordinary daytime fares applied to all-night tram routes until 3am after which time reduced price Workman's fares were available up until 7.30am on outbound journeys or on inbound Workman's cars from the suburbs timed to reach their London termini by 8am. Workman's fares, with similar conditions to those of the tramway, were subsequently applied to tram-replacement trolleybus routes.

When the LPTB took over operation of P. Hearn's 'Inter Station Autobus Service' on 1 October 1936 as the (then-daytime) Inter-Station Route, the Board maintained Hearn's policy of charging a one shilling flat fare, which continued to apply when an all-night element was added to the Inter-Station Route from 20/21 December 1943.

A revised fares policy, introduced by the London Transport Executive on 1 October 1950, impacted all-night services' fare structures which had remained unchanged, other than by the adoption of a flat fare on the Inter-Station Route, since just after the First World War. Most cheap fares, transfer tickets and Workman's fares, these latter largely on the tram and trolleybus network, were abolished. These quite fundamental changes were accompanied by a general fares increase as well but, to sweeten the pill, a new Early Morning Single (EMS) ticket was introduced across London Transport's entire bus, tram and trolleybus system. The EMS was issued between 3am and 8am on Mondays to Saturdays. The cheapest EMS fare of 2d, upon introduction, allowed journeys of up to ten miles to be made on any particular route. Bus passengers, for whom Workman's fares had not normally been available, benefited from the introduction of the EMS but tram and trolleybus passengers, who had previously bought Workman's return tickets, were disadvantaged because they now had to pay a full fare for their return journey later in the day. The price of the Early Morning Single ticket was increased over the years and the differential in price between it and ordinary fares was progressively eroded until the EMS was finally abolished from 3 June 1962.

Apparently amongst Night bus conductors the 2d Early Morning Single ticket became dubbed 'Early Morning Sex' since it was not unknown for prostitutes to board Night buses in the vicinity of Piccadilly Circus and use the cheap ticket to travel as far as necessary in attempts to accost a client from amongst the passengers.

Fares for most journeys on London's all-night bus routes were increased to become *double* the daytime fare from Sunday 18 June 1972. This swingeing increase was introduced in an attempt to reduce a then-annual direct operating (staff wages and fuel) loss of £71,000 which was being incurred by the London Transport Executive in running the all-night bus network. Double fares were charged on all journeys between 00.30 and 05.00 and were not only applied to all-night bus routes and Special Night Journeys but also to early or late journeys, which ran between the times specified, on daytime bus routes. In response to public complaints, as well as to overcome difficulties that had arisen with passengers re-booking tickets, the cut-off time for double-priced fares was changed to 04.30 from Sunday 9 July 1972. Some further amelioration was given to passengers from Sunday 10 September 1972 when the maximum fare charged between 00.30 and 04.30 was reduced from 40p (double 20p) to 24p (double 12p, which was the maximum off-peak fare at that time) for journeys made wholly within the Greater London Council area. The unpopular double fares-policy on night journeys was rescinded from Sunday 23 March 1975 when fares equivalent to corresponding stages of daytime bus routes were once again applied throughout the night.

Fare stages had coarsened during the 1970s and from 4 October 1981 a four fare-zones system was applied. The issue of Child fares after 22.00 at night, and thus on the Nighters, was abolished from 21 March 1982, some 60 years after the LGOC had first made them available from 1 January 1922.

Weekly, monthly and annual Travelcards, initially valid for use on LT's bus and Underground railway networks, were introduced from 22 May 1983. Availability extended to use on all-night buses until 03.00 on the day following that of issue. The Travelcard was sold at child rates too and, surprisingly, such tickets were not subject to the 22.00 curfew on night journeys.

CHRISTMAS ALL-NIGHT SERVICES

ALL-NIGHT TRAMS

Documentary evidence relating to 1929 shows that London County Council Tramways operated all-night tram services throughout the nights of Christmas Eve/Christmas Day 24/25 December and Christmas Day/Boxing Day 25/26 December in that year, when Christmas Day fell on a Wednesday. LCC Tramways practice of running all-night tram services on the nights of both Christmas Eve/Christmas Day and Christmas Day/Boxing Day almost certainly had much earlier origins, possibly dating back to the inception of LCC Tramways all-night tram services in 1899. In years when Christmas Day fell on a Sunday or a Saturday all-night services would not have run on the nights of 24/25 December or 25/26 December respectively in maintenance of LCC Tramways established policy of not operating all-night tram services on Saturday nights/Sunday mornings. However, for many years there was a break in service between Christmas daytime and all-night operations on the night of 25/26 December because, from 1917 onwards, all LCC Tramways daytime services were withdrawn after 4pm on Christmas Day. Nevertheless, eight hours later all-night trams would have started running at just after midnight on Boxing Day morning, as long as 26 December was not a Sunday.

Records of the London Passenger Transport Board's activities post 1 July 1933 show that, between Christmas 1933 and Christmas 1944 inclusive, the LPTB maintained former LCC Tramways practice and operated all-night services over the Christmas period in the manner described in the preceding paragraph. As examples, in 1934 Christmas Day fell on a Tuesday so in Christmas week all-night tram services operated on successive nights from Sunday night/Monday morning 23/24 December through to Friday night/Saturday morning 28/29 December whilst in 1938, when Christmas Day fell on a Sunday, all-night tram services operated on Friday night/ Saturday morning 23/24 December and resumed just after midnight on Sunday night/Monday morning 25/26 December.

Commencing with Christmas 1945 the LPTB's all-night trams adopted the then-prevailing all-night motor bus practice of not operating services on 25/26 December, irrespective of the day of the week on which that night fell, whilst also continuing not to operate on any Saturday night/Sunday morning. As an example in 1950, when Christmas Day fell on a Monday, all-night tram services operated on Sunday night/ Monday morning 24/25 December and were resumed on Tuesday night/Wednesday morning 26/27 December.

Timetables of all-night tram and trolleybus routes available for the Christmas holiday in the 1944 to 1951 period show that on some routes, particularly trams 1 and 5, a service was maintained for around two hours longer than normal, in those years in which all-night trams and trolleys ran on the night of 24/25 December, in order to match the later start of the daytime services on Christmas Day. The most extreme example was on tram route 5, where the last tram from Savoy Street to New Cross Gate was at 8am, compared with 5.37am on other nights. Route 1 maintained a service for two extra hours, while other routes were extended for about an hour (3, 7, 543/643, 665) or were un-affected (26, 35, 612, 628, 513/613) but with earlier daytime journeys to compensate in some cases.

Until 1940, for those years in which details can be traced, all-night tram and trolleybus routes ran normal schedules over Christmas, but to compensate there were special early journeys, on both 25 and 26 December, on those daytime routes parallel with all-night services. On other daytime routes the usual later Sunday first times applied. It is not known when the all-night service pattern that applied from 1944 was first introduced, but given the similarity of operation of the years from 1942 to 1944, then 1942 looks a likely date of introduction. London Transport's final all-night tram service, over route 35, last operated on Friday night/Saturday morning 4/5 April 1952.

ALL-NIGHT TROLLEYBUSES

The LPTB's all-night trolleybus routes adhered to a similar operating pattern to its all-night trams routes over the Christmas period, following the inception of all-night trolleybus operation on 12/13 September 1937. That pattern, which had included adoption from Christmas 1945 of the all-night motor bus practice of not operating on 25/26 December, irrespective of the day of the week on which that night fell, was maintained by the London Transport Executive up to and including Christmas 1954. In 1955 no all-night trolleybus routes operated on 24/25 December, due to 25 December being a Sunday, or 25/26 December. Between Christmas 1956 and Christmas 1959 inclusive all-night trolleybus routes fell into line with a fresh practice adopted on all-night motor bus routes of only operating until about 2.30am on 24/25 December and, as previously established, not at all on 25/26 December. Due to Christmas Day 1960 falling on a Sunday the then-surviving all-night trolleybus routes operated on Friday night/ Saturday morning 23/24 December with a resumption of service on Monday night/ Tuesday morning 26/27 December. Those remaining all-night trolleybus routes were all converted to motor bus operation during 1961.

ALL-NIGHT BUSES

It had been the London General Omnibus Company's policy not to operate all-night bus routes on the nights of 24/25 December or 25/26 December, irrespective of the days of the week on which those nights fell. That policy was continued by the London Passenger Transport Board after it assumed operating powers on 1 July 1933 and was maintained, with one exception introduced from Christmas 1934, over successive Christmas periods between 1933 and 1938. The exception, introduced from Christmas 1934, arose after the LPTB's Central Bus Department incorporated the former Fleet Coaches Romford to Aldgate all-night service into all-night bus route 617 from 12/13 June 1934, following a short period of operation of the former Fleet Coaches service by the LPTB's Country Bus Department as part of its route Y. Fleet Coaches had operated its service on all seven nights of the week unlike the LPTB and its LGOC predecessor, which had not operated all-night services on Saturday nights/Sunday mornings. The LPTB maintained Saturday night/Sunday morning operation of the former Fleet Coaches all-night service as part of route 617F (re-numbered 298 from 2/3 October 1934) and also instituted operation of a Saturday night/Sunday morning schedule all-night service over route 298 (only) on 24/25 December from Christmas 1934. The fact that the LPTB had maintained the former Fleet Coaches practice by operating routes 617F/298 on Saturday nights/Sunday mornings adds support to the contention that Fleet Coaches had probably operated their Romford to Aldgate route on the night of 24/25 December, possibly since the origination of their service in 1930. Route 298 remained the LPTB's sole all-night bus route to operate a service, to a Saturday night/Sunday morning schedule, on the night of 24/25 December between Christmas 1934 and Christmas 1938 inclusive.

For a period during the Second World War the London Passenger Transport Board operated the most sustained all-night bus service that London has ever experienced over the Christmas period. That did not apply to the first wartime Christmas, in 1939, when not even route 298 ran on 24/25 December and, in accord with established practice, no all-night bus routes operated on the night of 25/26 December. Under the prevailing State of Emergency Boxing Day was declared to be a normal working day in years 1940 and 1941. Daytime buses operated a full Monday to Friday service and the all-night bus operation responded in a similar vein in support of the War Effort. Although the Nighters did not run on 24/25 December in either 1940 or 1941, all-night bus routes (except route 292) did operate on the night of 25/26 December for the first time ever in 1940 and continued to do so annually up to and including 25/26 December 1944. Bank Holiday status was restored to Boxing Day from 1942 onwards but this slight easing of official restriction did not indicate a diminution of the War Effort, in support of which the LPTB instituted operation of all-night bus routes on the night of Christmas Eve/Christmas Day 24/25 December for the first time ever in 1942. This intensity of all-night bus operations over the Christmas period, when a full service ran over the all-night bus route network on the nights of both 24/25 December and 25/26 December was maintained in each of successive years 1943 and 1944 although, due to 25 December 1943 falling on a Saturday, only the Saturday night/Sunday morning service on route 298 operated on 25/26 December 1943. The bolstering of all-night bus operations over the Christmas periods 1942, 1943 and 1944 resulted in continuous operation of both day and all-night scheduled bus services for 365 days of the year between 25/26 December 1941 and 24/25 December 1945. This was the first and, up to the date of writing, only occurrence of such sustained operation in London's transport history.

An even more impressive record of unbroken service over Christmas can be claimed if the combination of all-night services of the buses, trams and trolleybuses are considered together. This record shows that between Christmas 1934 and Christmas 1944 inclusive there was only a single night (25/26 December 1937) when no all-night services were scheduled to operate. There was also a four week bus strike in May 1937, when there would have been four Saturday

nights without all-night bus services. But, for eight consecutive years, from 26/27 December 1937 until 24/25 December 1945, an all-night service was scheduled to operate 365 days a year, taking the buses, trams and trolleybuses together.

The end of hostilities in 1945 was followed by a partial reversion to a pre-war Christmas period working pattern on the Nighters. All-night bus routes once more did not operate on Christmas night/Boxing Day morning 25/26 December from Christmas period 1945, irrespective of the days of the week on which that night fell. However the wartime-instituted practice of operating all-night bus routes on the night of Christmas Eve/Christmas morning 24/25 December was retained. This immediate post-war operating pattern for the Nighters, with full services running on 24/25 December or to a Saturday night/Sunday morning schedule if Christmas Day fell on a Sunday, but with no service at all on 25/26 December, held sway across the Nighters over the Christmas periods between 1945 and 1955 inclusive. Over Christmas 1954 Farringdon Street – Wandsworth routes 168 and 288 did not operate on 24/25 December, whilst other Nighters did run, and on Saturday night/Sunday morning 25/26 December exceptionally, and in that year only, early Sunday morning 'Press Journeys' were operated on route 294 from Liverpool Street Station (depart 5.39am) to Cricklewood Garage and on route 298 from Holborn (depart 5.10am and 6.0am) to Hornchurch Garage. All-night bus routes which had normally operated a full schedule on 26/27 December, or had run to a Saturday night/ Sunday morning schedule if the 27th fell on a Sunday, did not do so on Monday night/Tuesday morning 26/27 December 1955, with the exception of the Inter-Station Route which did operate.

From the Christmas period 1956 operation of all-night bus services on 24/25 December became curtailed with services nominally ceasing at around 2.30 am and, as established, with no service at all on 25/26 December. This reduced operating pattern was repeated over successive Christmas periods in 1957, 1958 and 1959 and marked the beginning of a deterioration in the level of Christmas all-night bus service operations in London. In practice, the 2.30am curfew on Christmas morning operation was interpreted fairly liberally, as all-night routes retained their journeys leaving central London termini until around 2.30am, with the exception of lengthy Hornchurch route 298 which had a last outbound departure from Charing Cross, Trafalgar Square at 1.15am. The net result was that some last Nighters did not return to their garages until after 3am, with the final such arrival being the Riverside garage RTL-type on route 289 which went out of service at 4.28am, by which time several daytime bus and trolleybus routes had started their Christmas Day service. This overlap with daytime services was maintained until Christmas Day 1960, which fell on a Sunday, when only the Saturday night/Sunday morning service on routes N94 and N98 operated on 24/25 December 1960, with no all-night services at all operating on the nights of both 25/26 and 26/27 December that year. No Nighters, other than the Inter-Station Route, operated on Sunday night/Monday morning 24/25 December 1961 and, as established, no all-night routes at all ran on 25/26 December 1961 although, unlike 1960, the Nighters did run a full service on 26/27 December 1961.

A slow decline in the substantial level of daytime bus services which operated on Christmas Day began from 1961 onwards, which included the withdrawal of the remaining handful of routes which ran a service after 4pm. Christmas period all-night services were also trimmed back, with services on 24/25 December being advertised as operating until about 1am. In practice, the cutbacks were not so severe, with most Nighters finishing after 2am and with the N89 continuing to run until 4.28am. This pattern of operation on 24/25 December prevailed from 1962 to 1965, with the Inter-Station Route also running a full service on that night from 1962 to 1964. Christmas Day 1966 fell on a Sunday so that only the reduced Saturday night/Sunday morning service on routes N83, N98 and N99 operated on 24/25 December 1966 until around 2am when the last-ever Nighters to operate over the immediate Christmas period came off the road.

Post Christmas 1966 no London Transport Board or London Transport Executive all-night bus routes operated on the nights of either Christmas Eve/Christmas Day 24/25 December or Christmas Day/Boxing Day 25/26 December. Additionally all-night bus routes did not operate on 26/27 December in each of the years 1971, 1976, 1977 and 1982.

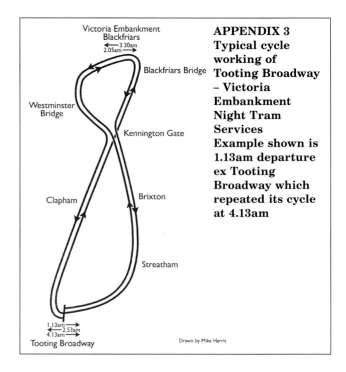

APPENDIX 3
Typical cycle working of Tooting Broadway – Victoria Embankment Night Tram Services
Example shown is 1.13am departure ex Tooting Broadway which repeated its cycle at 4.13am

Drawn by Mike Harris

APPENDIX 4
LGOC All-Night Bus Routes – Allocation Type Changes and Running Time Reductions: Period 1/2 January 1929 – 29/30 June 1933.

Route Number	Garage	Allocation Type Change			Running Time Reduction		
		From	To	Date of Change	From	To	Date of Reduction
4B	J	1 K	1 NSc	2/3 Oct 1930	*	28	By 31 May/1 June 1933
9C	M	1 NSc	1 NSc	No change	*	46	By 31 May/1 June 1933
11D	R	2 NSc	2 ST	27/28 May 1930	*	48	By 30/31 May 1933
			2 LT	6/7 Oct 1930			
13B	AE	1 NSc	†		*	53	By 31 May/1 June 1933
39D	AR	2 NSc	2 LT	17/18 Jan 1933	40	32	17/18 Jan 1933
91	AC	1 NSc	1 ST	30/31 Oct 1932	54	47	17/18 Jan 1933
94	W	2 NSc	2 LT	4/5 Oct 1932	46	40	1/2 Nov 1932
189	V	1 S	1 NSc	1/2 Oct 1930	*	42	By 31 May/1 June 1933
			1 ST	31 May/1 June 1932			
529B	AD	1 NSc	1 NSc	No change	*	20	By 31 May/1 June 1933
601	T	1 NSc	1 LT	4/5 Nov 1930	*	35	By 31 May/1 June 1933
614	V	2 NSc	2 LT	17/18 Jan 1933	55	49	17/18 Jan 1933
615	D	1 NSc	1 LT	24/25 Mar 1932	12	12	No change
616	D	3 NSc	3 LT	24/25 Mar 1932	16	16	No change
617	G	2 NSc	2 LT ◊	17/18 Jan 1933	50	45	17/18 Jan 1933

KEY:
* Not known
† Route 13B types – ranged from mixed K/NSc at 1/2 February 1929 to mixed NSc/ST at 30 November/1 December 1932
◊ Up to 13/14 February 1933. Subsequent allocation type and Garage changes detailed in text

APPENDIX 5
All-Night Trolleybus Route: Tooting Broadway – Battersea (Prince's Head)
All-Night Tram Route: Battersea (Prince's Head) – Victoria Embankment (Blackfriars)
Combined Timetables from 12/13 September 1937: Sunday – Friday nights

		am	am	am	am	am	am	am
Tooting Broadway	dep	-	1.39	-	2.39	-	3.39	-
Princes Head	arr	-	2.01	-	3.01	-	4.01	-
Princes Head	dep	1.01	-	2.03	-	3.03	-	4.03
Blackfriars	arr	1.31	-	2.32	-	3.32	-	4.32
Blackfriars	dep	1.32	-	2.33	-	3.33	4.33	-
Princes Head	arr	2.02	-	3.02	-	4.02	5.02	-
Princes Head	dep	-	2.04	-	3.04	-	-	-
Tooting Broadway	arr	-	2.26	-	3.26	-	-	-

Depot: Wandsworth. **Allocation:** 1 tram, 1 trolleybus.

All-Night Trolleybus Route: Hammersmith Broadway) – Clapham Junction (Grant Road)
All-Night Tram Route: Clapham Junction (Falcon) – Westminster Station
Combined Timetables from 12/13 September 1937: Sunday – Friday nights

		am	am	am	am	am	am	am	am
Hammersmith	dep	12.42	1.34	-	2.24	-	3.20	-	-
Clapham Junction	arr	1.05	1.57	-	2.47	-	3.43	-	-
Clapham Junction	dep	-	-	1.59	-	2.50	-	3.45	4.39
Westminster Station	arr	-	-	2.23	-	3.14	-	4.09	QR
Westminster Station	dep	-	-	2.24	-	3.17	-	4.12	QR
Clapham Junction	arr	-	-	2.48	-	3.41	-	4.36	4.50
Clapham Junction	dep	1.09	1.59	-	2.51	-	3.48	-	-
Hammersmith	arr	1.32	2.22	-	3.14	-	4.11	-	-

Key: QR - to/from Queens Road, arrive 4.44 am, depart 4.45 am
Depots/ Allocation: Hammersmith – 1 trolleybus, Wandsworth – 1 tram

APPENDIX 6
Timetables and allocations for all night bus routes 168, 288 and trolleybus route 630 1 October 1950

All-Night Bus Route 168
Wandsworth (High Street, Armoury Way) – Farringdon Street
via Clapham Junction and Wandsworth Road
Timetable from 30 September/1October 1950: Nightly

		Sun mornings		*Sun-Fri nights*			
		am	*am*	*pm*	*am*	*am*	*am*
Wandsworth High Street	dep	3.54	5.08	11.59	1.01	3.36	4.34
Horse Guards Avenue	arr	4.22	5.36	12.24	1.26	4.01	4.59
Farringdon Street	arr	4.28	5.42	12.30	-	-	5.05
		am	*am*	*am*	*am*	*am*	*am*
Farringdon Street	dep	4.30	5.46	12.32	-	-	5.07
Horse Guards Avenue	arr	4.36	5.52	12.38	1.34	4.03	5.13
Wandsworth High Street	arr	5.04	6.20	1.03	2.02*	4.30	5.39*

* Time at Wandsworth, High Street, Spread Eagle.
Garage: Wandsworth. **Allocation:** 1 RT-type.

All-Night Bus Route 288
Wandsworth (High Street, Armoury Way) – Farringdon Street
via Battersea and Nine Elms
Timetable from 1/2 October 1950: Sunday-Friday nights

		pm	*am*	*am*	*am*	*am*	*am*
Wandsworth, High Street	dep	11.27	12.35	1.41	2.44	3.59	5.07
Farringdon Street	arr	11.57	1.05	2.11	3.14	4.29	5.37
		pm	*am*	*am*	*am*	*am*	*am*
Farringdon Street	dep	11.59	1.07	2.13	3.23	4.31	5.39
Wandsworth, High Street	arr	12.28	1.36	2.42	3.52	5.00	6.06*

* Time at Wandsworth Garage. **Allocation:** 1 RT type.

All-Night Trolleybus Route 630
Hammersmith Broadway –Tooting Broadway (Longmead Road)
Timetable from 1/2 October 1950: Sunday-Friday nights

		pm	*am*	*am*	*am*	*am*
Hammersmith Broadway	dep	11.46*	12.53	2.01	3.09	4.17
Wandsworth, High Street	arr	12.00	1.08	2.16	3.24	4.32
Tooting Broadway	arr	12.13	1.21	2.29	3.37	4.45
		am	*am*	*am*	*am*	*am*
Tooting Broadway	dep	12.16	1.24	2.32	3.40	4.48
Wandsworth High Street	arr	12.30	1.38	2.46	3.54	5.02
Hammersmith Broadway	arr	12.45	1.53	3.01	4.09	5.16*

* Time at Hammersmith LT Bus Garage
Depot: Hammersmith. **Allocation:** 1 trolleybus.

APPENDIX 7 Special Night Journeys and All-Night Bus Routes
Original and Revised Crew Relief-Break Points from 1/2 July 1964

Route No	Garage	Relief Break Point			
		Original	Duties	Revised	Duties
		Sunday nights/Monday mornings – Friday nights/Saturday mornings			
9*	Mortlake	Straight Duty	1	Straight Duty	1
11	Riverside	Straight Duties	2	Victoria	2
29*	Wood Green	Straight Duty	1	Straight Duty	1
109	Thornton Heath	Thornton Heath	1	Thornton Heath	1
168	Wandsworth	Wandsworth	1	Liverpool St	1
182	New Cross	New Cross	1	New Cross	1
185	Walworth	Walworth	1	New Cross	1
220	Shepherds Bush	Straight Duties	2	Straight Duties	2
221	Finchley	Straight Duties	2	Straight Duties	2
N83	Stamford Hill	Tottenham	1	Liverpool St	1
N84	Poplar	Bow	2	Liverpool St	1
N85	Rye Lane	New Cross	4	New Cross	4
N86	Peckham	Peckham	3	New Cross	3
N87	Brixton	Straight Duties	3	Straight Duties	3
	Stockwell	Straight Duties	3	Straight Duties	3
N88	Wandsworth	Wandsworth	1	Liverpool St	1
N89	Riverside	London Bridge	3	Liverpool St	3
N90	Tottenham	Victoria	3	Victoria	3
N91	Willesden	Willesden	1	Liverpool St	1
N92	Holloway	Highgate	2	Highgate	2
N93	Highgate	Chalk Farm	1	Liverpool St	1
N94	Cricklewood	Cricklewood	2	Cricklewood	1
				Liverpool St	1
N95	Barking	Victoria	2	Victoria	2
		Barking	1	-	
N96	Leyton	Leyton	1	Leyton	1
		Straight Duty	1	Straight Duty	1
N97	Turnham Green	Riverside	2	Liverpool St	3
N98	Seven Kings	Seven Kings	4	Victoria	5
		Straight Duty	1	-	
N99	West Ham	West Ham	1	West Ham	1
I-S	New Cross	Victoria	1	Victoria	1
		Saturday nights/Sunday mornings			
9	Mortlake	Straight Duties	2	Straight Duties	2
29	Wood Green	Straight Duties	2	Straight Duties	2
149	Edmonton	Straight Duty	1	Straight Duty	1
168/181	Stockwell	Stockwell	1	Stockwell	1
177	New Cross	New Cross	1	New Cross	1
182	New Cross	New Cross	1	New Cross	1
185	Walworth	Walworth	1	New Cross	1
221	Finchley	Straight Duties	2	Straight Duties	2
N83	Stamford Hill	Tottenham	1	Liverpool St	1
N94	Cricklewood	Straight Duty	1	Straight Duty	1
N98	Seven Kings	Seven Kings	3	Liverpool St	3
N99	West Ham	West Ham	1	West Ham	1
I-S	New Cross	Victoria	1	Victoria	1

Key: * Monday nights/Tuesday mornings – Friday nights/Saturday mornings
Inter Station Route increased to 3 duties on Sunday nights/Monday mornings only
Straight duty comprised a night shift without a relief-break

APPENDIX 8
All-Night Bus Route N84
Becontree Heath – Charing Cross via Bloomsbury
All-Night Bus Route N95
Becontree Heath – Charing Cross via Holborn
Combined Timetable effective 1/ 2 July 1964
Saturday night – Sunday morning Excepted

Route Number		N84	N95	N95	N84	N95	N95	N84	N84	N95	N95
Becontree Heath	dep	-	-	00.49	01.55	-	-	-	-	05.29	06.07
Barking Garage		-	00.18	01.01	02.07	-	-	-	-	05.41	06.19
Barking		-	00.22	01.05	02.11	02.18	03.02	-	05.20	05.45	06.25
Poplar		00.05	00.42	01.25	02.31	02.39	03.23	04.00	05.41	06.05	-
Aldgate		00.18	00.55	01.38	02.44	02.52	03.36	04.13	05.53	06.18	-
Bloomsbury		00.31	-	-	-	-	-	04.27	06.07	-	-
Holborn Station		-	01.06	01.49	-	03.03	03.47	-	-	06.29	-
Charing Cross	arr	00.36	01.13	01.56	-	03.10	03.54	-	-	-	-

Route Number		N95	N84	N95	N95	N84	N95	N84	N95	N84	N95
Charing Cross	dep	-	00.40	01.23	02.07	-	04.08	-	04.52	-	-
Holborn Station		-	-	01.32	02.16	-	04.17	-	05.01	-	06.34
Bloomsbury		-	00.47	-	-	-	-	04.30	-	06.09	-
Aldgate		-	01.00	01.43	02.27	03.39	04.28	04.44	05.12	06.23	06.45
Poplar		-	01.12	01.56	02.40	03.53	04.41	04.56	05.25	06.36	06.58
Barking		00.26	01.32	02.15	02.59	-	05.01	05.15	05.45	-	07.18
Barking Garage		00.30	01.36	-	-	-	05.05	-	05.49	-	07.22
Becontree Heath	arr	00.43	01.49	-	-	-	05.18	-	06.02	-	-

Additional Journeys (Route N95)
00.13 Barking Garage to Barking
06.28 Barking to Barking Garage
Garages and Allocation:
Route N84   Poplar 1 RM-type
Route N95   Barking 2 RM-type

BIBLIOGRAPHY

Barker, T. C, and Robbins, M. *A History of London Transport* (George Allen and Unwin Ltd, 1974)

Blacker, K, Lunn, R, and Westgate, R. *London Buses Volume 2 – Country Independents 1919–1934*

Garbutt, Paul E. *London Transport and the Politicians* (Ian Allan Ltd, 1985)

Harris, M. *The Greater London Night Bus Map 19th March 2011* (M. Harris, 2011)

Kennington. *London County Council Tramways Handbook* (The Tramway and Light Railway Society)

London Historical Research Group. *Motor Omnibus Routes in London*, Volumes 3, 4, 5, 6A, 7A (The Omnibus Society 1991, 2001, 2004, 2009, 2006 respectively)

London Historical Research Group. *London Bus and Underground Timetables* (The Omnibus Society, 1998)

Morris, O. J, et al. *Fares Please* (Ian Allan Ltd, 1953)

Oakley, E. R. *London County Council Tramways*, Volumes 1 and 2 (Author, 1989)

Oakley, E. R, and Willoughby, D. W. *London Transport Tramways Handbook* (Authors, 1972)

Robbins, George. *General Buses of the Twenties* (Images Publishing (Malvern) Ltd, 1996)

Stewart, D. *SUP8: Electric to Diesel 1935–1962* (London Omnibus Traction Society, 1977)

Weinreb, Ben, and Hibbert, Christopher. *The London Encyclopaedia* (Macmillan Reference Books, 1995)

Wilson, Geoffrey *London United Tramways, A History 1894–1933* (George Allen and Unwin Ltd, 1971)

Yelton, Michael *Trams, Trolleybuses & Buses and the Law* (Adam Gordon, 2004)

Chronicle of Britain (Chronicle Communications Ltd, 1992)

London Operators' Route Working Indexes (The PSV Circle, London Omnibus Traction Society, various dates)

London Vehicle Type Histories (Joint The Omnibus Society and The PSV Circle, various dates)

ALL-NIGHT BUS ROUTE NUMBER CHRONOLOGY TO 12/13 APRIL 1984 AND INDEX

London General Omnibus Company, London Passenger Transport Board and London Transport (Executive and Board) all-night motor bus routes and Special Night Journeys which have operated between 14/15 July 1913 and 12/13 April 1984.

The Index is intended to help readers to trace the development of all-night bus services along particular route corridors.

Route Number(s)	First Night of Operation	Last Night of Operation if ceased	Pages
94*,294, N94	14/15 July 1913		15, 16, 18, 19, 22, 23, 24, 25, 28, 29, 31, 37, 38, 41, 42, 43, 44, 46, 47, 49, 50, 53, 55, 59, 67, 69, 74, 78, 79, 81, 91, 95, 100, 101, 112, 117, 121, 122, 131, 134, 135, 137, 138, 141
94A*,91,291, N91	12/13 November 1913		15, 16, 18, 19, 22, 23, 24, 25, 28, 29, 31, 37, 38, 41, 42, 44, 47, 50, 53, 59, 67, 70, 79, 81, 84, 86, 91, 94, 100, 117, 121, 122, 131, 133, 134, 135, 138, 141
94A(Elephant & Castle jnys)	7/8 June 1914	14/15 July 1916	15, 16, 19, 22, 35
95	25/26 August 1915	22/23 August 1916	18, 19, 51
93	2/3 September 1915	22/23 August 1916	18, 19, 51
4,4B,4	6/7 November 1921	10/11 June 1941	23, 24, 25, 28, 30, 31, 37, 38, 41, 43, 46, 47, 49, 50, 138
9,9C,9B,9	6/7 November 1921		23, 24, 25, 28, 29, 30, 31, 37, 38, 39, 41, 43, 46, 47, 48, 49, 50, 52, 53, 55, 59, 67, 70, 74, 77, 78, 79, 81, 84, 91, 96, 110, 122, 129, 131, 138, 141
28	6/7 November 1921	27/28 November 1921	22, 23
29,29D,129A,529B,29C,29	6/7 November 1921	10/11 December 1940	22, 23, 24, 25, 28, 31, 37, 38, 41, 43, 46, 47, 49, 50, 138, 141
63	6/7 November 1921	27/28 November 1921	22, 23
13,13B,13	7/8 November 1921	12/13 August 1941	22, 23, 24, 25, 28, 31, 37, 38, 41, 43, 47, 49, 50, 138
45	7/8 November 1921	25/26 November 1921	22, 23
11,11D,11	13/14 November 1921		22, 23, 24, 25, 28, 29, 31, 37, 41, 47, 50, 52, 53, 59, 63, 67, 71, 74, 79, 81, 91, 100, 101, 110, 121, 122, 124, 129, 131, 138, 141
88A,188,189	17/18 April 1922	3/4 July 1934	22, 23, 24, 25, 28, 29, 30, 31, 35, 37, 38, 138
91A	30 Nov/1 Dec 1924	23/24 February 1925	24
601,299(Leyton)	15/16 November 1927	12/13 May 1941	27, 28, 35, 37, 38, 41, 43, 47, 49, 50, 52, 138
39D,619,290,N90	17/18 July 1928		28, 29, 34, 35, 36, 37, 38, 41, 42, 44, 46, 47, 53, 58, 59, 67, 70, 77, 79, 81, 86, 90, 91, 94, 98, 101, 112, 116, 120, 121, 122, 129, 131, 138, 141
614,297,N97	17/18 July 1928		28, 29, 31, 35, 36, 37, 38, 41, 42, 44, 47, 50, 53, 59, 63, 67, 70, 77, 79, 81, 82, 86, 90, 91, 96, 100, 101, 115, 117, 121, 122, 129, 131, 138, 141
615,292(Aldwych)	17/18 July 1928	30/31 December 1940	29, 31, 37, 41, 43, 46, 47, 49, 50, 52, 138
616,293	17/18 July 1928	12/13 May 1941	29, 31, 37, 41, 43, 46, 47, 49, 50, 52, 138
617,298,N98	17/18 July 1928		28, 29, 32, 35, 36, 37, 38, 41, 42, 43, 44, 46, 47, 49, 52, 53, 55, 59, 67, 69, 71, 77, 78, 79, 81, 82, 83, 91, 94, 100, 101, 111, 112, 115, 117, 122, 123, 131, 136, 137, 138, 141
184,17,289,N89	22/23 August 1933		34, 35, 36, 37, 38, 41, 42, 43, 44, 46, 47, 48, 49, 50, 53, 59, 63, 67, 79, 81, 90, 91, 100, 116, 121, 122, 131, 137, 138, 141
611,295,N95	22/23 August 1933		34, 35, 36, 37, 41, 42, 43, 44, 47, 53, 58, 59, 67, 71, 77, 79, 81, 82, 83, 91, 93, 94, 101, 111, 112, 115, 117, 122, 123, 124, 131, 141, 142
613,296,N96	22/23 August 1933		34, 35, 36, 37, 41, 42, 44, 47, 50, 53, 59, 79, 81, 83, 86, 91, 94, 96, 100, 112, 117, 120, 122, 129, 131, 141

AY,Y2	10/11 January 1934	1/2 September 1939	36, 37, 41, 42, 47, 52
Y	21/22 February 1934	11/12 June 1934	36, 136
617F	16/17 June 1934	29/30 September 1934	36, 37, 41, 137
24	By July 1934	30/31 December 1939	39, 41, 43, 46
25C,25	By July 1934	8/9 December 1936	39, 41, 43
159C,159	By July 1934	20/21 November 1939	39, 41, 43, 46
12B,12	By August 1934	18/19 November 1940	39, 41, 42, 46, 49, 50
614A	7/8 August 1934	1/2 October 1934	38, 41
6	3/4 October 1934	17/18 November 1940	41, 42, 46, 49, 50
121	By December 1934	14/15 October 1939	42, 46
38	5/6 December 1934	By 19/20 April 1943	42, 43, 45, 46, 50
29(Charing Cross SNJs),N29	11/12 December 1940		49, 50, 52, 53, 55, 59, 66, 67, 74, 77, 78, 79, 90, 91, 96, 110, 121, 122, 131, 141
Inter-Station Route	20/21 December 1943		51, 52, 53, 58, 59, 60, 67, 69, 70, 74, 78, 79, 81, 83, 84, 91, 100, 101, 117, 120, 122, 129, 131, 135, 137, 138, 141
168,N68	30 Sept/1 Oct 1950		62, 67, 69, 71, 73, 74, 77, 78, 79, 81, 84, 86, 90, 91, 94, 97, 98, 100, 101, 106, 110, 115, 116, 121, 122, 123, 129, 131, 137, 140, 141
288,N88	1/2 October 1950		62, 67, 73, 77, 79, 81, 86, 90, 91, 94, 100, 101, 106, 116, 121, 122, 123, 129, 131, 137, 140, 141
57A,181,N81	6/7 January 1951	22/23 October 1983	64, 67, 70, 71, 74, 78, 79, 81, 86, 90, 91, 94, 97, 98, 99, 106, 115, 116, 117, 122, 123, 141
287,N87	7/8 January 1951		27, 63, 64, 67, 71, 78, 79, 81, 84, 86, 91, 93, 94, 106, 116, 122, 123, 129, 131, 141
109	7/8 April 1951	12/13 April 1984	64, 67, 74, 79, 81, 84, 91, 106, 107, 110, 111, 116 122, 123, 124, 129, 131, 141
185	6/7 October 1951	12/13 April 1984	64, 67, 71, 74, 78, 79, 81, 86, 91, 95, 99, 110, 115, 121, 122, 124, 131, 141
286,N86	7/8 October 1951		64, 65, 67, 78, 79, 81, 84, 90, 91, 94, 96, 106, 116, 120, 122, 123, 129, 131, 141
285,N85	6/7 January 1952		65, 67, 69, 78, 79, 81, 84, 90, 91, 94, 106, 116, 120, 122, 123, 131, 141
292(Archway),N92	6/7 April 1952		65, 66, 67, 69, 74, 78, 79, 81, 90, 91, 94, 98, 117, 122, 123, 129, 131, 137, 141
177	5/6 July 1952	7/8 April 1984	66, 67, 74, 78, 79, 81, 84, 90, 91, 94, 106, 110, 115, 116, 122, 124, 129, 131, 141
182,N82	5/6 July 1952		66, 67, 69, 74, 78, 79, 81, 86, 91, 99, 110, 115, 116, 122, 129, 131, 141
284,N84	10/11 November 1959	12/13 April 1984	71, 72, 74, 76, 77, 78, 79, 82, 91, 94, 96, 100, 101, 121, 122, 123, 124, 129, 131, 141, 142
299(Chingford),N99	26/27 April 1960		72, 74, 76, 78, 79, 83, 86, 90, 91, 94, 106, 111, 115, 117, 122, 123, 131, 138, 141, 142
220	19/20 July 1960		73, 74, 79, 91, 94, 110, 123, 124, 131, 141
N93	31 Jan/1 Feb 1961		76, 77, 78, 79, 84, 86, 91, 94, 95, 98, 100, 101, 117, 120, 122, 123, 129, 131, 141
N83	18/19 July 1961		77, 78, 79, 84, 91, 95, 96, 100, 101, 115, 116, 121, 122, 123, 131, 138, 141
149	22/23 July 1961	17/18 January 1970	77, 78, 79, 81, 90, 141
221	7/8 November 1961		77, 78, 79, 91, 95, 101, 110, 116, 122, 124, 131, 141
279	24/25 January 1970	20/21 September 1980	90, 91, 110, 116
N80	24/25 June 1983		122, 129, 131

Key: * Routes 94 and 94A were suspended after operation on 14/15 July 1916 until resumption of service on 17/18 August 1920.